EFFECTIVE STRENGTH TRAINING

Analysis and Technique for Upper-Body, Lower-Body, and Trunk Exercises

Douglas Brooks, MS

Human Kinetics

Library of Congress Cataloging-in-Publication Data

Brooks, Douglas, 1957-
  Effective strength training : analysis and technique for upper body, lower body, and trunk exercises / Douglas Brooks.
    p. cm.
  Originally published : Mammoth Lakes, Calif. : Moves International, 2001.
  Includes bibliographical references (p.).
  ISBN 0-7360-4181-8
    1. Weight training. 2. Bodybuilding. 3. Exercise. I. Title.

GV546 .B775 2001
613.7'13--dc21

2001024629

ISBN: 0-7360-4181-8

Essential Strength Training was previously published by Moves International Fitness. Starting in 2001, this book is available exclusively from Human Kinetics Publishers, Inc.

Disclaimer: No manual or book can replace the services of a trained physician, physical therapist, exercise physiologist, or other qualified health or exercise professional. Any application of the information set forth in the following pages is at the reader's discretion and sole risk.

Editor: Candice Copeland Brooks; **Page Designer:** Wally Hofmann, New Times Publishing; **Production:** Nicholas Fiore, New Times Publishing; **Cover Designer:** Conan Palmer, New Times Publishing; **Photographer:** Michael Cooke; **Illustrator:** Kim Gilmor; **Printer:** United Graphics

Printed in the United States of America   10 9 8 7 6 5 4 3 2 1

Human Kinetics
Web site: www.humankinetics.com

United States: Human Kinetics, P.O. Box 5076, Champaign, IL 61825-5076
800-747-4457
e-mail: humank@hkusa.com

Canada: Human Kinetics, 475 Devonshire Road Unit 100, Windsor, ON N8Y 2L5
800-465-7301 (in Canada only)
e-mail: orders@hkcanada.com

Europe: Human Kinetics, Units C2/C3 Wira Business Park, West Park Ring Road,
Leeds LS16 6EB, United Kingdom
+44 (0) 113 278 1708
e-mail: hk@hkeurope.com

Australia: Human Kinetics, 57A Price Avenue, Lower Mitcham, South Australia 5062
08 8277 1555
e-mail: liahka@senet.com.au

New Zealand: Human Kinetics, P.O. Box 105-231, Auckland Central
09-523-3462
e-mail: hkp@ihug.co.nz

To Candice, not only for your business skills and expertise in the fitness professional field, but for being the most incredible wife, mother, companion and friend that I could have ever wished to enter into my life.

Adam and Dylan... for your patience and unconditional love, silly looks and laughs as I chased you out of my office, renewed with your energy. I love you "bad" boys!

To Jesus for blessing me with strength and endurance:
Isaiah 40:31: "...but those who hope in the LORD will renew their strength. They will soar on wings like eagles; they will run and not grow weary, they will walk and not be faint."

--DSB

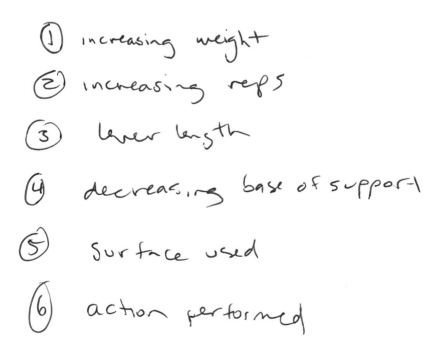

① increasing weight

② increasing reps

③ lever length

④ decreasing base of support

⑤ surface used

⑥ action performed

CONTENTS

PART I: A PRIMER ON RESISTANCE TRAINING

PART II: EXERCISE MECHANICS: HOW TO PERFORM RESISTANCE TRAINING EXERCISES CORRECTLY... AND WHY!

Part III: Resistance Training Program Design

PREFACE

GOING BEYOND TRADITION

Many resistance-training exercises that are performed in gyms and personal training facilities across the world could be characterized as traditional, common or basic to any program, but not necessarily correct. Often, little thought has been given to the lifting mechanics involved and what the risk to effectiveness ratio might be. An exercise that is very effective at developing strength, can simultaneously put joints, soft tissue and the body's musculature at great risk for injury. It is time to start questioning common exercises and put them to the test of objective scientific evaluation. Professionals must evaluate any resistance training exercise and weigh in with a final verdict when strengths of a given exercise are compared to weaknesses.

When an exercise is criticized or praised, it is important to explain "why" from a mechanical/biomechanical, kinesiological and anatomical standpoint. Additionally, this rationale must be appropriately aligned with the training goal(s) and needs of the individual being trained. Then, it is important to follow this with solutions in the form of exercise alternatives or modification if called for. Often, a contraindicated label is attached to an exercise without an explanation of "Why?" The situation can be compounded if no resolution is provided for the consumer or fitness professional in the form of different exercise options or necessary modifications to replace the "old" approach.

On the other hand, many people who teach or participate in strength training justify using an exercise that has come under criticism because the exercise in question "hasn't yet caused injury," or simply base use on the fact the exercise has "been used forever, by everybody." Both positions represent very weak arguments and are not in the best interest of someone you are training.

To bring my point home, consider the following logic. Many people have stated, for example, "I wouldn't use this exercise if I had bad knees or a bad back." So, what they are saying is that they'll keep using the exercise until they do indeed have bad knees or until they injure their back, at which point they might consider modifying or jettisoning the exercise. It sounds ludicrous, but rationale that reflects this type of thinking abounds. It would seem that if an exercise is not a great idea for people with *injured* knees, backs or shoulders, then there exists a high probability that the exercise being questioned is probably not a great exercise for people with apparently *healthy* knees, backs and shoulders.

If the science is there to support the assertion that the exercise falls short of safe biomechanical standards, a more prudent and receptive approach might be to acknowledge the underlying weaknesses and potential problems of a given exercise and take corrective action.

Dogma and myth is passed on at least partially because of denial and a failure to take an honest look at or remain open to the facts. The timeless reality—that it takes effort and focus to change—also plays a role. It's easy to stay in the rut of mediocrity and sameness. One has to believe in what is being taught, especially if it represents a concept that goes against the flow of traditionalism. Commitment to a methodology comes from clarity and certainty that are backed by the facts.

Effective Strength Training provides accurate information to help you form a basis from which you can design and progress successful resistance training programs. Finally, this text gives you a solid scientific foundation and confidence from which to choose how you, or those individuals you teach or help heal, will perform strength training exercises.

ACKNOWLEDGMENTS

MANY THANKS TO...

... John Norton, the International Weightlifting Association (IWA) and the many physical and occupational therapists and other fitness professionals who have believed in this effort, guided me and encouraged me to publish this book.

... My fitness professional peers who have motivated me to question and challenge tradition, and who have taught me so much over the years. You have helped me realize that personal training — as is true for any health or wellness profession — is an art form based on science. Yet, it is how we interpret all of the information presented to us, and then design the program, that sets us apart.

... Snowcreek Athletic Club and owner Tom Dempsey for our photo shoot location. A big thank you to SAC general manager Tom Nishikawa for lending his model-good-looks to the book and giving us access to everything we needed at the club on "photo shoot day."

... All of the models that ranged from fitness experts to clients and fitness enthusiasts. These include: Candice Copeland Brooks, Kathy Dolan, Jeromy and Patty Acton, John and Fran Kelly, West Brazelton and Tom Nishikawa.

... Michael Cooke Photography for expediting the seemingly impossible task of capturing hundreds of images accurately, within a tight time-frame!

... New Times Publishing Editor Wally Hofmann for his personal interest and hands on approach with the overall layout. You're the best! Also, thanks to Kim Gilmor for her expert illustrations, Nick Fiore for his attention to production detail, Conan Palmer for the cover and Patty Cole of New Times for orchestrating the "event."

Finally, a special acknowledgment of God's great grace that covers me. I still have my friends, my wife and two happy children at the completion of this text!

A Primer On Resistance Training

RESISTANCE TRAINING MISINFORMATION AND MYTHS

Myths and misinformation abound in an area of physical training commonly referred to as "strength training" or "weightlifting." Inaccurate information about resistance training has resulted in many people never experiencing this important component of fitness. Resistance training exercise is increasingly being supported by scientific research as the most important activity, bar none, that can enhance personal health and body shape or physique (Brooks, 1997; Wilmore and Costill, 1994; Plowman and Smith, 1997).

Quick Index:

Chapter 3, Benefits of strength training

RESISTANCE TRAINING: WHAT'S IN A NAME?

What's the difference between "Resistance Training," "Strength Training," "Weight Lifting," "Weight Training," "Lifting Weights" and "Pumping Iron?" There really is none. It's no wonder there is so much confusion. Choose your favorite term and stick with it. (Or, I joke with my clients, if you want to impress your friends, use all of them.)

Whenever you work against resistance, for example, lifting a dumbbell or hand-held weight a number of times, exercising in a machine and selecting a number of weight plates, or pulling on rubber tubing, these types of activities characterize training that has the potential to improve strength. The term resistance training is an umbrella term used to cover *all* types of strength or weight training. I refer to the terms *resistance training* and *strength training* most of the time, but regardless, there is no need to be confused by this array of terminology that represents resistance training.

Taking Resistance Training To Higher Ground

Having said what I've said, a philosophy that surrounds the term resistance training can be taken to a higher level that places it on the top shelf of important terminology. Resistance training is definitely the comprehensive term that represents all that is related to developing strength. A deeper philosophy emerges when the term "resistance training" is carefully analyzed. There is more to these two words than meets the eye!

Let's look at the "resistance" and the "training" which comprise the term resistance training. *Resistance* can represent a continuum of load or intensity that ranges from light to heavy. During resistance training exercises we are opposed by it or work against this force. *Training* indicates education, science based knowledge and fact, as well as a systematic process.

Key Point

Resistance training teaches people to move beyond pushing, pulling, pressing, squatting, lifting weights or otherwise mindlessly struggling with something that is heavy or hard to move.

Resistance training instruction shows a person how to engage their whole being—mind and physical self—by first understanding movement, and then engaging the body in a systematic and planned approach that pays close attention to body position and exercise set-up. Furthermore, resistance training requires stabilization throughout the movement as the participant focuses on exerting force via muscular contraction and moving the body in a safe, integrated and coordinated manner. These statements represent the art form and hidden meaning behind this broad and all-inclusive term branded as resistance training.

This type of characterization certainly sounds philosophical, and it is. But, this idealism has its foundation in reality, and this definition guides the approach master trainers use with their clients and patients. A "whole" approach to resistance training sure beats the alternative of allowing the client you're training to evolve into an exercise robot who mindlessly goes through a series of movements where the solitary goal is to push, pull, grunt and struggle against heavy weight.

A complete approach to resistance training involves ten steps outlined in the Any Exercise Drill. "The Drill" not only helps you to evaluate the effectiveness and risk of any given exercise, but also obligates you to:

1) Set a goal.
2) Understand the desired joint action, movement and sustained motion through the exercise that must be maintained.
3) Focus on proper body alignment.
4) Place resistance in opposition to the movement.
5) Use sufficient load or intensity.
6) Understand the different roles muscles play as stabilizers and contributors to movement and desired motion. All of this information is used to maximize exercise benefit while simultaneously minimizing any risk inherent to the performance of each exercise.

Key Point

Resistance training focuses on what the body and mind are doing together, not just the load or force being opposed. This culmination of optimal exercise execution and training result is what I call "resistance training."

Quick Index:

Chapter 4, The "Any Exercise Drill"

TWELVE COMMON RESISTANCE TRAINING MYTHS

Everyone has some idea of what they *think* happens when weights are lifted. But, are these impressions accurate? Following are twelve common resistance training questions my clients frequently ask — and the facts explained in the way that I would communicate to them.

Key Point

Myth-conceptions about strength training are abundant. They're as bad as weeds that spread through your yard and won't go away.

1. Will I get big, bulky muscles, if I strength train?

Maybe, and maybe not! Around puberty, near the ages of 12 to 14, boys and girls are at similar strength levels. Males gain a strength advantage when they enter puberty because their bodies start to crank up production of the predominantly male dominant hormone called testosterone. Men have levels that are 10-30 times higher than women, and it makes it easier for them to build more muscle (Plowman and Smith, 1997; McArdle et al., 1996). Most women don't generally possess high levels of this male predominant hormone and that is part of the reason that you see fewer women who do in fact, build big muscles.

But, this is only one component that determines the size of muscles. Illegal drugs and genetics are the other two important factors. Many of the oversized men and women on the "Pump-You-Up" shows are taking drugs or other illegal products that allow them to develop physiques that to say the least, do not represent the norm. This type of physique development is not natural, safe, ethical or normal!

Your predominant muscle fiber type (fast twitch versus slow twitch), how much muscle you have (men generally have more, not "better" muscle), along with body shape or type are determined by your mom and dad. So, the age-old adage, "Choose your parents well!" actually contains truth that goes beyond tongue-in-cheek wit. In other words, personal genetics greatly influence the results you'll see from any type of strength training program. For example, if you have a small, wiry body you'll see some significant strength improvements if you follow a proper program, but you'll probably never be bulging with muscles. (Refer to myth # 5, What happens to my muscles when I get stronger?)

2. Is it easier for some people to build muscle and get stronger?

Yes. Some people are genetically gifted with regard to developing strength and muscle. Two people (same gender and similar body types) could participate in the exact same program and end up with completely different results. Sometimes it doesn't seem quite fair when two people invest the same effort and time, and one seems to get better results. But, that is what I refer to as the "reality factor." Scientists call it "individual response." You might call it "unfair." No two people will respond in exactly the same way to a given program.

Here's a positive way of looking at it. Don't compare yourself to others. Look at the starting point and note how far you have come in terms of personal fitness improvement. Improvement can be quite significant—sometimes up to 100 percent or more—when compared to a personal starting point.

Key Point

Keep training focused on personal improvements rather than on comparison with others.

Since the outer bounds of personal fitness are genetically determined (You ultimately have no influence even though you would like to look like a svelte model or strong athlete, or become a world champion.), there is a lot of truth to the statement, "Champion athletes are born." Fortunately, health, fitness and personal improvement have little to do with being "the best" or having the perfect body.

3. Do some machines or weight equipment develop "long-lean muscles?"

No! This claim is so far from truth it's hard to figure where it came from. Genetics (there it is again, you can blame it on mom and dad), how much resistance you work against and how often you train are the biggest contributors to how muscles will develop.

Quick Index:

Myth #12, Discussion of the "best" types of resistance training equipment

4. How long before I feel stronger and see changes?

Men and women of all ages (even 70, 80 and 90 years young!) can increase their strength by more than 50 percent just 2 months after beginning a strength training program! If you keep training you can double or even triple your strength!

Many people who start lifting "feel" immediate changes in terms of balance, coordination and strength. Technically speaking, initial strength improvements or adaptations that happen in the first 4-6 weeks of your strength program happen because you get more skillful. This means you learn how to lift better. During these first few weeks, changes occur in the ability of your nervous system to more effectively recruit muscle fiber that was inactive or "sleeping" before you started "pumping weight." Progressive resistance training can serve as a wake up call for the 50 percent of the muscle that was previously inactive prior to starting a strength program.

Quick Index:

Chapter 11, Reps, sets, loads and determining the right intensity of effort

Physical changes in the muscle start after about 6 weeks. This is called hypertrophy, which means an increased size in muscle. Most people believe big muscles are strong muscles. To a certain degree that is true. But, remember that you can get strong (i.e., muscle recruitment via a more efficient nervous system) without seeing your muscle size change. And, "big" muscles don't necessarily translate well to every day tasks that involve coordination and balance. Don't measure muscle strength by size alone!

5. What happens to my muscles when I get stronger?

As already mentioned, most (about 75 to 80 percent) of the strength gains you'll get come from your nerves being able to rally dormant muscle fibers to contract and move the body. The other 20 to 25 percent or so comes from your muscles getting bigger (hypertrophy). The role that your nerves play explains why some people keep getting stronger without getting bigger muscles.

What about bulking up? Quite honestly, most people have difficulty putting large amounts of muscle on their bodies. Certain body types are more likely to develop muscle than others. For example, if you're thin (everyone has been calling you "String-Bean" for years) there's a good chance you won't develop big muscles even though you'll get stronger and more "defined." If you've been nicknamed "Refrigerator" for more years than you'd like to remember, you're a good candidate for the sport of body-building, but don't forget cardiovascular training and developing a strong, healthy heart.

Finally, *nothing* positive will happen to your muscles if you don't use enough weight or resistance in the form of machines, dumbbells, elastic tubing or body weight. (More on this in chapter 11.) On the other hand, if you slack off and don't weight train, your muscles will shrink. This is called atrophy. You've heard it before, "Use it or lose it!"

6. How do I get muscle definition?

Again, choosing your parents well may be the most important step toward getting "defined" or "cut!" This statement tells you that genetics, what you were sentenced to at birth based on genetic inheritance, may be the most important factor. However, the two steps you can take to influence muscle definition are to:

1) Lose fat
2) Strength train

Oh yes, and forget spot reducing, or repeatedly exercising a particular body part with mind-numbing numbers of reps, in hopes of selectively reducing body fat from a specific area of the body. It doesn't work! (See myth # 8.)

7. Do my muscles turn to fat if I stop strength training?

No, no, no, no! Under a microscope fat looks like a thin-walled honeycomb, and muscle like a bundle of straws. The point: They are *different* from one another.

This misconception, muscle turning to fat, may have started because many highly trained athletes have become fat after their sport careers ended. Logical deduction says: "He/she used to have big muscles and no fat; now he/she quit training and the muscle turned to mush." Here's the real picture: The athlete quit training, the muscles shrunk (atrophied from disuse) and the "jock" still continued to slop down the grits, bacon, steaks and beer, or at least took in too many calories. And here's the result: All those extra calories are stored as fat, and the ex-athlete keeps getting fatter because he/she won't eat moderately and exercise regularly, and the muscles won't grow because they're not being challenged by strength training!

8. Does strength training spot-reduce problem areas of my body?

Spot reduction is *not* possible. You can NOT selectively reduce fat from an area of the body by repeatedly exercising it. So, strength training, or for that matter any exercise, has nothing to do with spot reducing. You lose fat when you burn off more calories than you take in. This can be accomplished by exercising (cardiovascular and strength training is the best approach) and moderate calorie reduction if appropriate. Even though you may pump your TV remote or vigorously chomp on gum, this does not reduce fat on flapping arms or double chins. Spot reducing, which always sounds too good to be true, is simply wishful thinking that can lead to futile and ineffective exercise pursuits.

9. Should I get in shape before I start lifting weights?

This is one of the biggest *myth*-conceptions of all and deters many people who should be lifting weights. Just to make sure this registers, the answer is, "No!" People who are extremely over-fat or clinically obese often begin a strength training program *before* aerobic training! Why? Increased strength may help protect joints from injury and improve aerobic activity that requires lower body strength. Low level cardiovascular returns can also be gained. Lifting weights is non-impact and increased muscle gained from lifting can help you burn more calories, lose weight and increase metabolism. Besides, it's fun, interesting and keeps you motivated, especially when compared with *only* doing endless miles on a treadmill!

10. Do I have to spend hours strength training to get results?

It's not a requirement that you sentence yourself to 4 to 6 hours in the gym laboring over weights, divorce your spouse and forget about your kids to receive benefits from strength training. Here's the *minimal* commitment: Strength train 2 times per week for about 20 minutes per workout. "That's it?" Yes, and no strings attached. Now, I've just retired your last reason for not strength training—that being not enough time!

Quick Index:

Chapters 10-13, Resistance training program design

11. Should a woman's strength program differ from a man's?

It is NOT true that a woman's strength training program should differ from that of a man's, based on a pure physiological perspective. While I acknowledge that women have special concerns, many books titled in such a manner infer that women need to train differently. Sorry. Not true! Additionally, upon review of several weight training books for women, you'll find the approach is quite similar to how you would train the male counter-part, and vice-versa.

No physiologist has ever been able to differentiate a female or male muscle fiber under a microscope. There are, simply, muscle fibers and a right way to perform exercises, regardless of gender. Correct technique should not change from gender to gender! When women are placed on the same strength programs men are using they make the same, if not greater, gains in muscle strength and endurance (Freedson, 2000).

Key Point

Men and women are different, but quite possibly, a more accurate principle to follow is that we are all different. Period.

Certainly, women have special concerns that need to be considered that include past societal and cultural influences, hormonal and menstrual impacts and structural issues such as the Q-angle formed by the width of the hip and the line it forms with the knee. However, with regard to muscle, the quality of a woman's muscle fiber compares to that of a man's, though she may have less (quantity) and may not have as big an influence from the muscle building hormone testosterone. These influences aside, men and women should not train differently. It might be interesting to note that *The Recommended Quantity and Quality of Exercise for Developing and Maintaining Cardiorespiratory and Muscular Fitness, and Flexibility in Healthy Adults* (ACSM, 1998) does not specify guidelines based on gender. As more and more women are encouraged to engage in strength training a more accurate teaser to pique interest might be titled, "A Comprehensive Look At Why and How Women Should Train For Strength." After reading the essay, you would note that you could insert "men" in the title to replace "women," and still have a completely accurate article that was helpful to both sexes.

12. Is there a best type of resistance training equipment?

There is no magical or "best" type of resistance training equipment. If you can progress the training by having the ability to adjust the load to heavier and lighter intensities, you will get superb training result. Excellent resistance training equipment is stamped with these two qualities:

1. You can easily adjust the load you are working against and can adjust the load to be heavier or lighter in small- or micro-increments, such as 1 to 3 pounds. Sometimes equipment that can only be adjusted in 5 to 10 pound increments is too much. *See fig. 1*

2. Well designed resistance training equipment will not impede correct exercise mechanics, is designed to work with the body, and allows the user to determine the path of movement.

Fig. 1, Dumbbell with micro-magnets being attached

RESISTANCE TRAINING EQUIPMENT

Many experts believe that intensity of effort is the key training variable for optimizing resistance training results. Here is the point. You can still get results while using poor technique if you work against enough resistance, using any type of equipment. On the other hand, you can utilize perfect technique and state of the art equipment, and if the load is not sufficient to cause training adaptations to take place, the end training result will not be optimized. The idea is to combine the best of these worlds. Use equipment that allows "user defined" range-of-motion, versus a predetermined, one size movement pattern that fits no one. In other words, choose equipment that allows you to work *with* the body—which limits orthopedic risk—and choose equipment where load can be quickly and easily changed.

Quick Index:

Chapter 11, Discussion of reps, sets and loads

Key Point

Contrary to what you may hear, no one type of resistance training equipment can be classified as superior when physical conditioning benefits are compared.

Fig. 2, Dumbbells, barbell and plates

Fig. 3, Multi-station machine

Don't believe it when you read, or someone tells you, that "weight machines" or "multi-station gyms" are the safest. Safest, compared to what? It is true you can't drop a weight on the floor, or your toe, when using these units. But, what good is this safety feature if you end up wrecking your shoulder because an exercise motion is incorrectly designed and you have no way to correct or modify the movement. What if you get into or out of a machine incorrectly, and strain a muscle or other soft tissue? Like most pieces of exercise equipment, machines aren't bad if they're used properly and designed correctly. Any piece of equipment can be either safe or dangerous depending on how it is used and its appropriateness to your body and program.

There is a wide variety of strength exercise equipment available for you to effectively train the entire body. There is overlap from category to category. They include:

Free-weights. Dumbbells, barbells and hand-held weights can be used to create a myriad of exercise options that are biomechanically correct. *See fig. 2*

Multi-station weight machine. This type of unit has its pros and cons and is generally a pulley/cable system that is routed to selectorized plates or weight stacks. Some movements are limited by what the cable connects to, for example, a straight bar or chest flye attachment, but to its credit, generally the machine can be used without a spotter. *See fig. 3*

Fig. 4, Pulley/cable system with composite load

Fig. 5, Tubing attached to door frame

Pulley/cable systems. As mentioned, multi-station gyms are often cable/pulley systems that use weight stacks for resistance and the cable(s) connects to various exercise devices. Bowflex® is an example of a pulley-cable system that uses composite resistance rods to produce progressive resistance (rather than weight stacks) and the use of cables attached to hand grips allows you to lift correctly with unlimited exercise design capability. However, the principles of each type of equipment—the use of cable/pulley systems—as applied to creating effective strength gains, remains similar. *See fig. 4*

Elastic resistance cable or tubing. Elastic resistance can be classified as a "cable system" and can be directed through pulleys or used without pulleys. It can be attached to the wall or a door frame and provides unlimited and versatile exercise options. This "stuff" really works if you get pieces of tubing that are strong enough to effectively resist the exercise movement! *See fig. 5*

Training without equipment. Calisthenics and using your own body weight have limitations with regard to progressive overload and working out at the right level of resistance. Generally, the exercise is either too hard or too easy, and if the load is just right, it won't be too long before it becomes too easy. Take push-ups, dips or chin-ups as examples. Some people can't do any, others a

Fig. 6, Dip performed on edge of bench

"straining-few," and a small number can crank out reps until the "cows come home." *See fig. 6*

Body weight can provide enough resistance for some exercises, while in some situations it's too light. Don't count on this type of exercise to indefinitely progress strength. Calisthenics and/or body weight is not an issue of "good" or "bad." Simply, realize their limitations. You can use these types of exercises to maintain some level of strength, and a quick set of push-ups never hurt anyone. To determine their effectiveness, ask this question: Can I fatigue the muscles I'm using in 6 to 20 reps? If you can't, you're not optimizing strength results or the use of your time!

Choose resistance training equipment which offers you the option to increase resistance as a client gets stronger. Free weights, multi-station weight machines, pulley/cable systems, and elastic resistance cables and tubing are good examples of equipment that can provide progressive overload. This type of equipment allows you to increase weight once you can perform more repetitions than your recommended range.

Quick Index:

Chapter 11, Recommended repetition ranges

EQUIPMENT ESSENTIALS: THE FINAL WORD

Don't believe all the "gym stories" that attest to a particular piece of equipment's overstated magnificence, effectiveness and "magical qualities." You've got to use the right equipment (defined by your goal and how the body works), like using it, use it correctly, and modify that which is poorly designed, or choose not to use it!

Technically, and from a physiological standpoint, how the body adapts to overload to which it is not accustomed, does not change. Neither does the body's musculature differentiate from one piece of equipment to the next. Muscle only understands effective training and correct overload, regardless of equipment choice.

 Key Point

Muscles only understand overload and correct mechanics. They can not differentiate the type of equipment being used.

What's the best equipment? You can answer that by asking another question: "Can the equipment I'm using deliver?" In other words, principles of overload do not change. If the equipment allows your client to exercise harder than she is used to, and she enjoys doing it on a regular basis, she'll get results. High-priced equipment won't do the work for your client, or necessarily give better results or make exercise safer or more correct when compared to less expensive equipment. Obviously, it is you, following the right training guidelines and using correct exercise technique that optimizes result.

Quick Index:

Chapters 10-13, Resistance training program design

NAMING A RESISTANCE TRAINING EXERCISE: SAY WHAT YOU MEAN!

It seems that there is little logic or thought process involved when it comes to naming strength exercises, or for that matter, resistance training equipment. Often, the choice is based on who first "invented" the movement or equipment (i.e., Scott bench arm curl), what "it" looks like or what the exercise appears to be doing (i.e., pullover, crunch or curl), or where "it" or the variation was invented (i.e., Nebraska squat).

Continuing this thinking, when and why did the terms "preacher curl" or "French curl" originate? Logical deduction would say that the first person to perform the preacher curl was indeed a preacher, or maybe it represents a reverent position of prayer. Was the French curl first performed in France or by a French citizen? Additionally, many exercises have many names. A lateral dumbbell raise can be referred to as a shoulder raise or flye, or medial deltoid flye or raise, and the French curl can be referenced as a triceps curl, triceps extension, or more accurately be described as a supine dumbbell triceps press or supine elbow extension.

You get the idea. Exercises with names like "French curl," "preacher curl," or "military press," give you little insight about the exercise. An exercise coined as a triceps kickback may give you faulty information because its name indicates that the exercise should be performed quickly and/or ballistically. Is that what the person naming the exercise really had in mind? On the other hand, give an exercise a name like "seated dumbbell press overhead," "supine dumbbell chest press," or "kneeling triceps press back," and not only is a starting position revealed, but the desired physical movement or motion is apparent, and in the case of a "press back," this type of terminology indicates the press is done with control.

Though subtle, and it may be argued that what is being discussed is more a case of semantics, naming exercises should be given more attention. Appropriately named resistance training exercises will benefit not only your clients, but will provide a common reference from which professionals and lay people alike can be assured they're talking about the same exercise. For consistency and educational purposes a more technical and useful descriptive approach is used in naming exercises in this text.

Key Point

Within a resistance training exercise name, information may be plentiful or be completely lacking. For example, an "Arnold" exercise doesn't tell me a whole lot!

What Variables Should Be Considered When Naming Exercises?

Generally, it's a good idea to name or refer to a resistance training exercise based on one or more informative variables:

- Body or start position such as supine, seated, sidelying, or prone
- Joint action such as flexion or extension
- Motion or movement being performed such as press, curl, row, pull-down, squat or lunge
- Prime or main muscle group or groups being targeted such as latissimus or deltoids, or major body part being focused on such as chest or back
- Type of equipment or resistance being used such as dumbbell, cable, barbell or machine
- Type of movement speed desired such as kneeling triceps "press" back versus "kickback"

Calling an exercise "what it is" helps to instruct a client as to what motion is going to be performed, what the start or body position will be, what equipment is being used and/or how the exercise should be executed. With instructive intent in mind, a huge wealth of knowledge and information can reside in a resistance training exercise name.

FINITE OR INFINITE NUMBER OF EXERCISE VARIATIONS?

When it comes to defining correct mechanics many professionals are overwhelmed when it comes to discerning correct, safe or "the best" exercise technique. This uncertainty can loom large because of the existence of what seems like an infinite number of exercise variations that appear to be very different from one another.

Classifying Movement

The key to determining whether —

- the given exercise is correct as stands,
- the movement needs modification,
- the exercise shouldn't be used for the existing goal or particular client,
- the risks associated with the exercise outweigh any potential physical benefits
                              — is to logically *classify* gross physical movement.

For example, a number of strength training exercises can be identified as pressing or pushing or pulling movements. These types of motions can be matched to the area of the body, or the muscle groups and joint actions they target. When all of the movements or motions of the body are accounted for it is possible to place every exercise variant within each classification or grouping.

Once this finite aspect of exercise options and body motions is understood, and once it is believed that accuracy is independent of body position or type of equipment being used, the mystery and overwhelming nature of sound exercise mechanics disappears.

Key Point

Recognition of the simplistic nature of movement analysis and the evident overlap of similar movement truths, as applied to joint actions, motions or movement patterns, helps dispel the myth of what seems to be the existence of infinite exercise variations.

The necessity of seeing this "big picture" of similarity between many strength exercise movement patterns is critical if resistance training analysis is to be mastered and the information gathered is going to be useful for application to every day training situations.

Quick Index:

Chapter 4, The "Any Exercise Drill"
Chapters 5-9, How to perform resistance exercises correctly

Grouping Resistance Training Exercises

An accurate categorization or classification of resistance training exercises can help to remove some of the mystery surrounding what seems like an infinite number of exercise variations. There are a finite number of "exercise movements" or categories, of which many exercise variations fit within.

For example, chest press movements can include push-ups, supine dumbbell or barbell presses, machine presses, standing or seated steel cable presses, elastic resistance presses from supine, standing and seated positions, as well as flat, incline and decline chest press variations. Within this category of chest press movements—the hands are moved or pressed away from the chest or shoulders—it is obvious there are numerous other possible variations. This is also true for all other exercises that are grouped because of their sameness with relationship to joint actions/muscle group involvement or similar exercise motion. What is important to note is that every exercise variation mentioned under, for example, this umbrella category of chest press movements utilize the same joint actions or motion, and muscle group involvement.

Key Point

It is easy to see how one category, such as chest presses, accounts for a large number of seemingly different variations, when in fact, the biomechanics, as well as teaching instructions will largely apply to most variants within the category.

The point that is being illuminated is that chest press variations are (as is true for other categories that target different body parts and muscle groups) not that different from one another when it comes to joint mechanics, muscles used, exercise set-up/stabilization and exercise performance. In other words, a template of correct execution and procedure can be painted for an exercise category or motion that identifies the strengths and weakness of each variation in the category independent of the equipment being used. Each variation within an exercise category does not require a return to the "How do I perform this exercise?" drawing board.

DETERMINING OPTIMAL RESISTANCE TRAINING EXERCISE PERFORMANCE

A variety of factors, that include the type of equipment being used and path or range-of-motion available, will greatly influence optimal exercise execution. Equipment availability should rarely represent a major limiting factor with regard to correct exercise performance. However, a piece of equipment that proves to be unyielding in terms of necessary modifications you would like to make to enhance the safety and effectiveness of the movement, can be omitted from the repertoire. Or, if the exercise motion is deemed unacceptable from a risk versus effectiveness standpoint, equipment that allows the user to change the range-of-motion and correct the exercise execution would be acceptable.

Key Point

A little creativity, coupled with intelligent strategy and understanding, and a confidence in knowing when to modify or choose not to use a specific piece of equipment will help you avoid poor equipment choices. Do not use traditional approaches to exercise performance that fall short of biomechanical excellence.

A perspective that allows equipment or traditional teaching approaches by themselves to dictate exercise performance and precede fore-knowledge that is based on sound anatomical, orthopedic and biomechanical perspective, should not be adopted. In other words, equipment design or gym-dogma must not determine the course of action.

You must know what you would like to accomplish and how you would like to see the movement performed, first and foremost. Once your plan of attack is known and you understand what works best with the body and have considered known orthopedic concerns or risks, it is appropriate to look at what equipment is available to accomplish the correct resistance training exercise technique that has already been established in your mind. Equipment by itself, or tradition for the sake-of-tradition should never dictate exercise biomechanics. Always ask, "Does the equipment or teaching approach I'm using allow me to attain desired and established biomechanical standards?" To reach this position, you have got to know "the drill!"

Quick Index:

Chapter 4, The "Any Exercise Drill"

In future chapters, it will be shown that, for example, the base mechanics of any chest press movement should adhere to pre-established proper mechanics, regardless of body position or equipment being used. For example, don't use a machine with a predetermined range-of-motion unless the unyielding movement pattern meets biomechanical standards that are acceptable to you. Be careful not to blindly follow cueing or teaching techniques that are not grounded in science.

Key Point

When designing or evaluating resistance training exercises the idea is to understand what you want to accomplish with the body — *before* choosing or considering any exercise equipment.

What seems like an endless array of exercise variations really boils down to understanding how to perform a common exercise motion correctly. Exercise variations off of the base movement pattern, such as the chest press, are placed into the same base-movement category. Mechanics and proper execution should not vary when body position or equipment is selected or changed. Instead, the performance, independent of these and other variables, must still be commanded by fore-knowledge and mechanical accuracy that is supported by scientific facts.

Quick Index:

Chapter 4, "Any Exercise Drill"
Chapters 6-8, Optimal exercise execution

THE MUSCULOSKELETAL SYSTEM AND MUSCULAR FORCE PRODUCTION

*K*inesiology is defined as the science of human movement. Improvements in muscular strength and physical development by using correct kinesiological/biomechanical principles—supported by science and practical applications of exercise physiology—result in improved physical performance and health at all levels. An understanding of the musculoskeletal system, types of resistance, and muscular force production is essential for fitness and health professionals who are involved in the maintenance, development or rehabilitation of the muscular/skeletal system.

FOUNDATION FOR STRUCTURAL KINESIOLOGY

It is not necessary to have an in-depth knowledge of the 600-plus muscles and 200-plus bones found in the body to adequately teach others how to strengthen the body. While a mastery of micro-anatomy is not necessary, it is important to have a working knowledge of the skeletal system and an understanding of fewer than 100 of the largest and most important muscles, called the prime movers. In most gross motor movement situations, exercises that involve the primary movers also challenge other smaller contributing muscles. Muscles attach to and move bones. The interface between bones allows or limits movement based on their different sizes and shapes, especially at the joints.

Skeletal System

Approximately two hundred six bones make up the skeletal system. *See fig. A* for an anterior and posterior view of the skeletal system. This bony lever-system provides a means by which movement can occur via the muscles by contributing anchoring spots for muscles to attach to bones. Additionally, the axial skeleton—which consists of the head, neck and trunk—represents the main support column of the body. The appendicular skeleton—bones of the hands, arms, pelvis, legs and feet—provide support and protection for other systems and organs of the body, and generally are "moved" during strength training exercise.

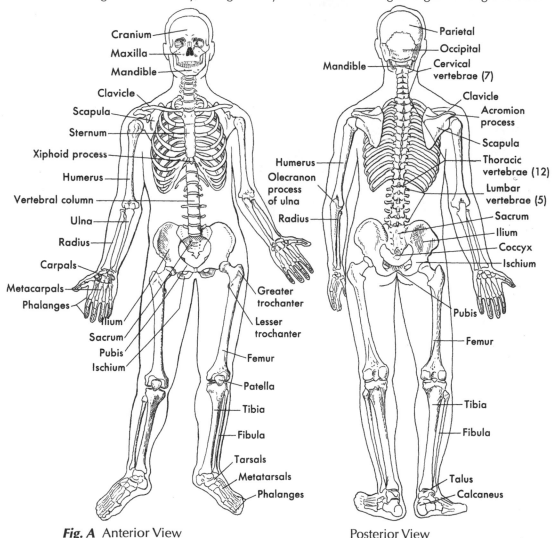

Fig. A Anterior View   Posterior View

Muscular System

The total superficial muscular system of the body is shown here. *See fig. B.* Any figure is limited since many muscles are not surface muscles, but this figure will help you get an overview of the entire superficial muscular structure.

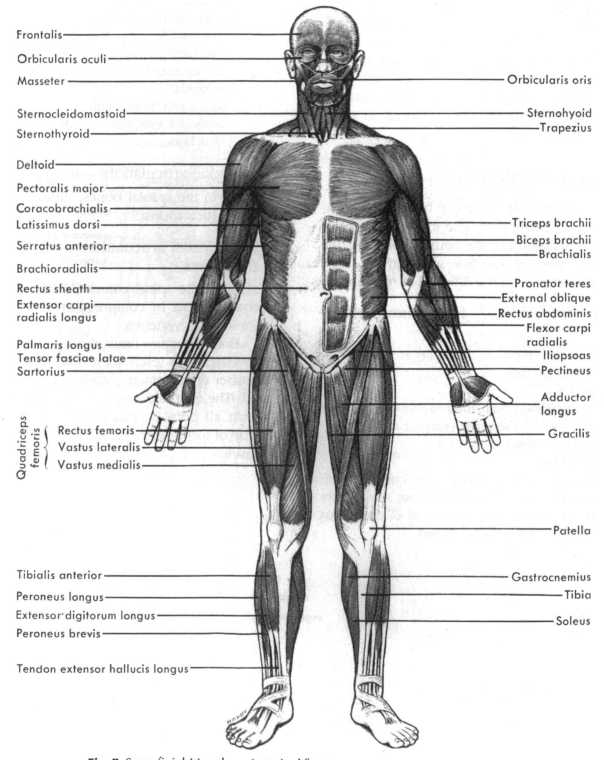

Frontalis

Orbicularis oculi

Masseter

Sternocleidomastoid

Sternothyroid

Deltoid

Pectoralis major

Coracobrachialis

Latissimus dorsi

Serratus anterior

Brachioradialis

Rectus sheath

Extensor carpi radialis longus

Palmaris longus

Tensor fasciae latae

Sartorius

Quadriceps femoris { Rectus femoris
Vastus lateralis
Vastus medialis

Tibialis anterior

Peroneus longus

Extensor digitorum longus

Peroneus brevis

Tendon extensor hallucis longus

Orbicularis oris

Sternohyoid

Trapezius

Triceps brachii

Biceps brachii

Brachialis

Pronator teres

External oblique

Rectus abdominis

Flexor carpi radialis

Iliopsoas

Pectineus

Adductor longus

Gracilis

Patella

Gastrocnemius

Tibia

Soleus

Fig. B Superficial Muscles - Anterior View

28

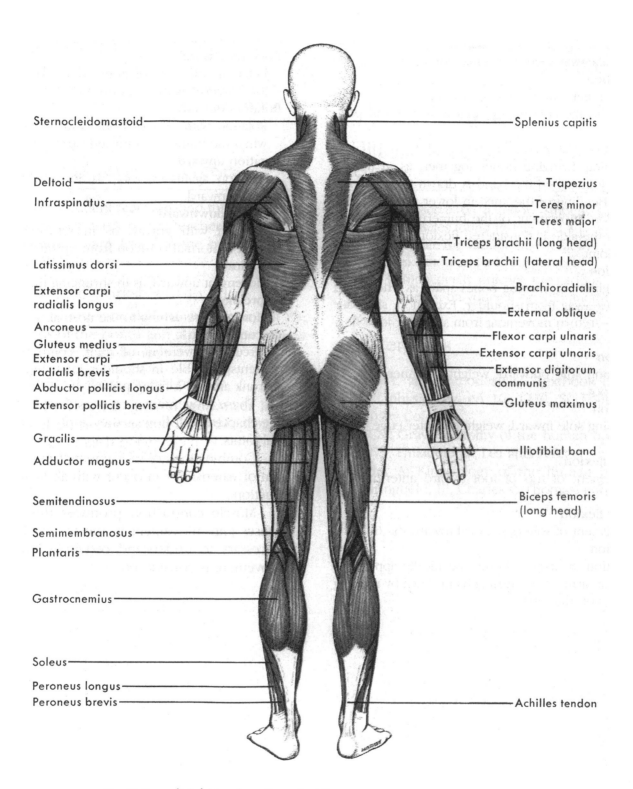

Sternocleidomastoid

Deltoid
Infraspinatus

Latissimus dorsi

Extensor carpi
radialis longus

Anconeus
Gluteus medius
Extensor carpi
radialis brevis
Abductor pollicis longus
Extensor pollicis brevis

Gracilis

Adductor magnus

Semitendinosus

Semimembranosus
Plantaris

Gastrocnemius

Soleus
Peroneus longus
Peroneus brevis

Splenius capitis

Trapezius
Teres minor
Teres major
Triceps brachii (long head)
Triceps brachii (lateral head)
Brachioradialis
External oblique
Flexor carpi ulnaris
Extensor carpi ulnaris
Extensor digitorum
communis

Gluteus maximus

Iliotibial band

Biceps femoris
(long head)

Achilles tendon

Fig. B Superficial Muscles - Posterior View

PLANES OF MOTION

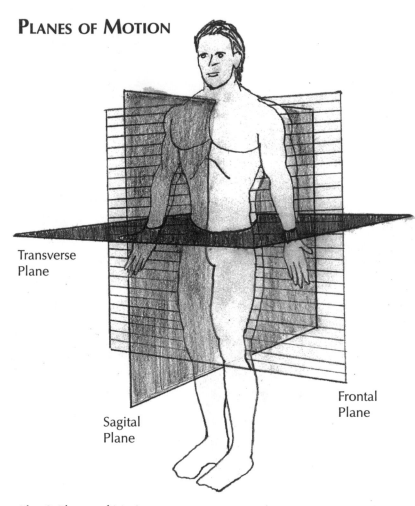

Transverse Plane

Sagital Plane

Frontal Plane

Fig. C, Planes of Motion

Because movement is so dynamic and varied—even a simple task like picking up a child is complicated to analyze—it is important to have a "common language" so that professionals can discuss movement and understand one another. As is true for skeletal and muscle terminology, and joint motions, it is also important to have a working knowledge of the anatomical planes of motion that apply to human movement. *See fig. C*

Sagital or Median Plane. The sagital plane divides the body into right and left halves as it passes front-to-back. Motions like hip or shoulder flexion, running and stepping occur in the sagital plane. The sagital plane is often mistakenly referred to as a "frontal" plane.

Frontal or Coronal Plane. The frontal plane divides the body into front and back halves as it passes side-to-side. Motions like hip or shoulder abduction, and inline skating occur in the frontal plane.

Transverse or Horizontal Plane. The transverse plane divides the body into top and bottom halves as it passes perpendicular or horizontal to the long axis (spinal column) of the body.

JOINT MOVEMENT

Joint motion is often termed joint action, but more accurate references use the terms joint movement or joint motion. Some joints allow a wide range of movements, whereas others limit available motion. Overall movement is largely dependent on joint structure.

Abduction

Movement away from the midline of the body or axis of the trunk characterizes abduction. Examples include raising the arms from the side to a horizontal position *(See fig. 7a)*, lifting the leg to the side *(See fig. 7b)* and moving the scapulae away from the spinal column. *See fig. 7c*

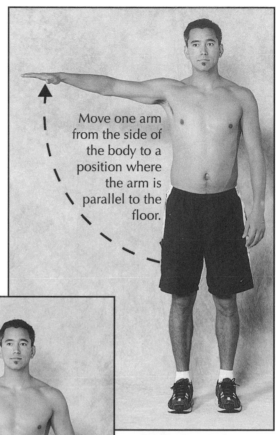

Move one arm from the side of the body to a position where the arm is parallel to the floor.

Fig. 7a, Shoulder Abduction

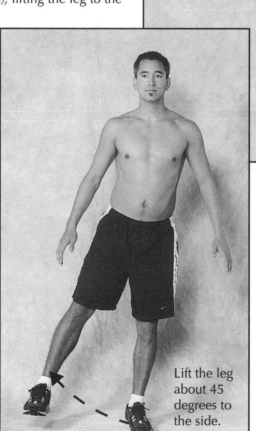

Lift the leg about 45 degrees to the side.

Fig. 7b, Hip Abduction

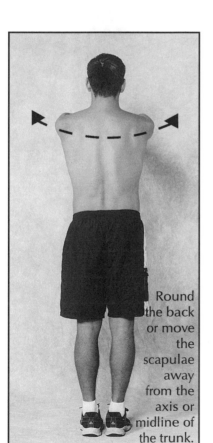

Round the back or move the scapulae away from the axis or midline of the trunk.

Fig. 7c, Scapular Abduction or Protraction

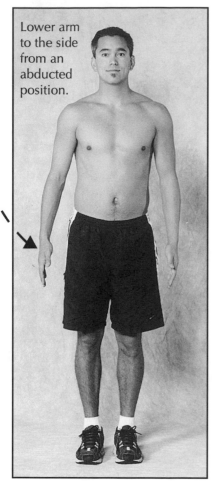

Lower arm to the side from an abducted position.

Fig. 8a, Shoulder Adduction

Adduction

Movement toward the axis or midline of the trunk characterizes adduction. Examples include lowering the arms to the sides of the body from a horizontal position *(See fig. 8a),* returning the leg from a side lifted position so that the legs are together *(See fig. 8b),* and pulling the shoulder blades together toward the axis of the trunk. *See fig. 8c*

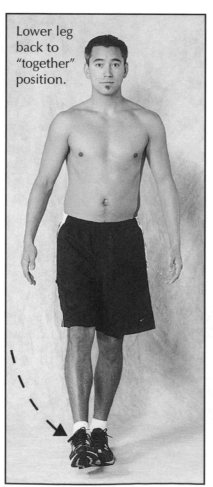

Lower leg back to "together" position.

Fig. 8b, Hip Adduction

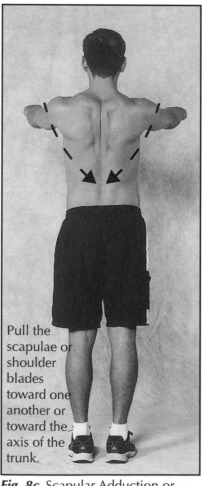

Pull the scapulae or shoulder blades toward one another or toward the axis of the trunk.

Fig. 8c, Scapular Adduction or Retraction

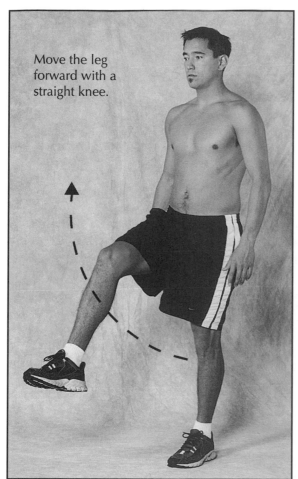

Move the leg forward with a straight knee.

Fig. 9a, Hip Flexion

Flexion

Flexion is characterized by bending and bringing bones together or toward one another. Flexing the knee or drawing the heel toward the buttocks, flexing the elbow or drawing the hand toward the shoulder, flexing the hip by moving the leg forward or drawing the knee up *(See fig. 9a),* and flexing the trunk or rounding the lumbar spine *(See fig. 9b)* are good examples. An exception to this rule is represented by shoulder flexion *(See fig. 9c),* where the arm is raised in front of the body.

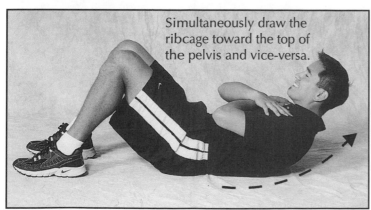

Simultaneously draw the ribcage toward the top of the pelvis and vice-versa.

Fig. 9b, Trunk Flexion

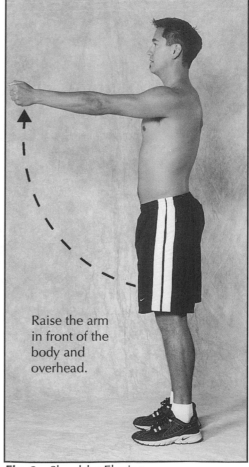

Raise the arm in front of the body and overhead.

Fig. 9c, Shoulder Flexion

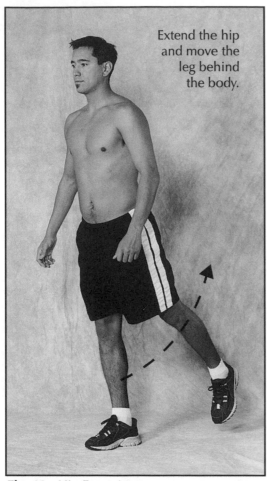

Extend the hip and move the leg behind the body.

Fig. 10a, Hip Extension

Extension

Extension is characterized by straightening and moving bones apart or away from one another. Extending or straightening the knee, moving the hand away from the shoulder or extending the elbow, extending the leg behind the body *(See fig. 10a)* and arching or extending the trunk *(See fig. 10b)* are good examples. An exception to this rule is represented by shoulder extension *(See fig. 10c),* where the arm is returned from shoulder joint flexion.

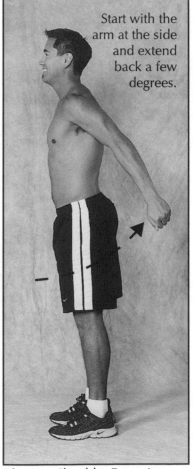

Start with the arm at the side and extend back a few degrees.

Fig. 10c, Shoulder Extension

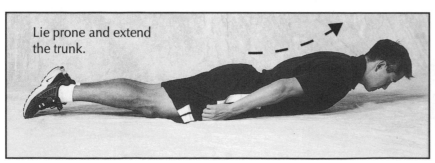

Lie prone and extend the trunk.

Fig. 10b, Trunk Extension

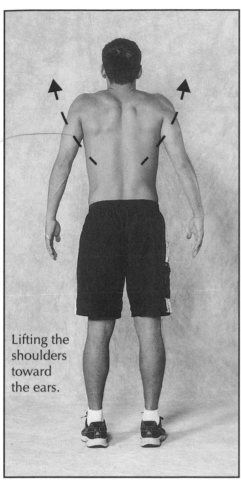

Lifting the
shoulders
toward
the ears.

Fig. 11a, Scapular Elevation

Scapular Elevation

Movement upward, as in shrugging the shoulders or lifting the shoulders toward the ears characterizes scapular elevation. *See fig. 11a*

Scapular Depression

Movement that returns the shoulders to a neutral position from an elevated position, or continues into active scapular depression or movement down away from the ears, characterizes scapular depression. *See fig. 11b*

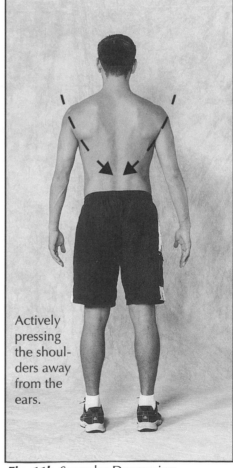

Actively
pressing
the shoul-
ders away
from the
ears.

Fig. 11b, Scapular Depression

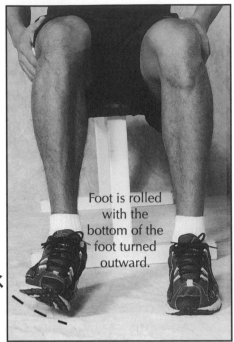

Foot is rolled with the bottom of the foot turned outward.

Fig. 12a, Ankle Abduction or Eversion

Ankle Abduction or Eversion (often called pronation)

Ankle abduction or eversion is characterized by movement of the bottom of the foot outward. In a weight bearing posture, the weight of the body is on the inner edge of the foot. *See fig. 12a*

Ankle Adduction or Inversion

(often called supination)

Ankle adduction or inversion is characterized by movement of the bottom of the foot inward. In a weight bearing posture, the weight of the body is on the outer edge of the foot. *See fig. 12b*

Foot is rolled with the bottom of the foot turned inward.

Fig. 12b, Ankle Adduction or Inversion

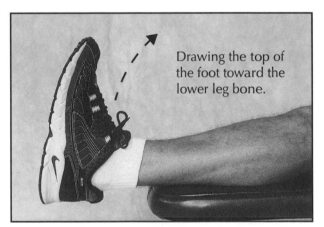

Drawing the top of the foot toward the lower leg bone.

Fig. 13a, Ankle Flexion or Dorsi Flexion

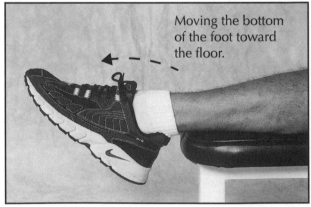

Moving the bottom of the foot toward the floor.

Fig. 13b, Ankle Extension or Plantar Flexion

Ankle Flexion (Dorsi Flexion)

Movement of the top of the foot upward, toward the shin or anterior tibia bone, characterizes ankle flexion or dorsi flexion. *See fig. 13a*

Ankle Extension (Plantar Flexion)

Movement of the bottom of the foot downward toward the floor characterizes ankle extension or plantar flexion. *See fig. 13b*

The hand is turned palm up, as is exemplified when turning the knob on a door to open it.

Fig. 14a, Elbow Supination

The hand is turned palm down.

Fig. 14b, Elbow Pronation

Supination

Rotation along or on the axis of a bone characterizes supination. This motion is specifically applied to the elbow or forearms, as in turning the hand palm-up, by rotating the radius on the ulna. *See fig. 14a*

Pronation

Rotation along or on the axis of a bone characterizes pronation. This motion is specifically applied to the elbow or forearms, as in turning the hand palm-down, by rotating the radius on the ulna. *See fig. 14b*

Fig. 15a, Shoulder Horizontal Flexion

Horizontal Flexion (or adduction)

Movement of the humerus or femur from a side-horizontal to front-horizontal position characterizes horizontal flexion or adduction. *See fig. 15a*

Horizontal Extension (or abduction)

Movement of the humerus or femur from the front horizontal to the side-horizontal position characterizes horizontal extension or abduction. *See fig. 15b*

Drawing the humerus from a side-horizontal position toward the midline of the body.

Moving the humerus from the midline of the body toward a side-horizontal position.

Fig. 15b, Shoulder Horizontal Extension

Fig. 16a, Hip Internal Rotation

Rotation Inward (or internal rotation)

Rotation of a bone toward the midline of the body characterizes rotation inward or internal rotation. Examples include when the humerus, or femur, is turned inward. *See fig. 16a*

Rotation Outward (or external rotation)

Rotation of a bone away from the midline of the body characterizes rotation outward or external rotation. Examples include when the humerus, or femur, is turned outward. *See fig. 16b*

Fig. 16b, Hip External Rotation

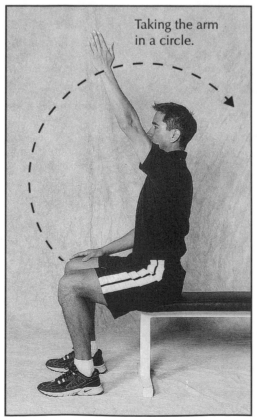

Fig. 17, Shoulder Circumduction

Circumduction

Circumduction is characterized by circular motion of a joint. It combines movements that are possible at the shoulder joint, hip joint and trunk. Movement occurs around a "fixed" point or region of the joint. *See fig. 17*

RESISTANCE, MUSCULAR FORCE PRODUCTION AND MOVEMENT

Muscles move the body by pulling. They contract toward the middle of their "muscle belly" and pull the more moveable attachment (usually the insertion) of the muscle toward its more stable attachment (usually the origin). This results in movement. It should be noted that typical origin and insertion orientation can be reversed by stabilizing the body in such a manner that the origin is pulled toward the insertion. A classic example is reverse trunk flexion as shown in chapter 6. Fiber direction—the direction fibers run from attachment point to attachment point—along with skeletal limitations and stabilization choices—largely determines how the body should and will move.

Participation in resistance training exercise requires a resistance, load or force to work against, or to be placed in opposition to the movement pattern. You can use a variety of equipment to create resistance. Common examples include dumbbells, barbells, elastic resistance, selectorized plate machines and pulley/cable systems, to name a few.

Quick Index:

Chapter 1, The "best" resistance training equipment

TYPES OF RESISTANCE AND FORCE PRODUCTION

To follow is a synopsis on the current thinking and definitions for the most common types of resistance and muscle force production.

Isometric (Static) Force Production

Isometric training represents force production and a type of resistance. With *isometric* or static force development, an increase in muscle tension does occur though there is no significant displacement or movement at the joint. (Technically, as is true for eccentric movement, a "contraction" does not occur since no *shortening* of the muscle occurs during the isometric hold or eccentric movement. It is more accurate to describe isometric or eccentric action as muscular force production.) During isometric force production, the muscle does not generate enough force to move the object that is resisting it. For example, when pressing against an immovable object such as a wall, or when using free weights or a machine that is loaded beyond your client's maximal concentric strength, isometric force production occurs. Typically, a static force production occurs when a weak muscle works against a stronger muscle, or a movement is attempted against a load that is too heavy to be accomplished with a concentric contraction. For example, try to flex your right elbow and resist this movement by pressing down with your opposite hand. The stronger triceps can effectively resist the weaker biceps of the right arm. This type of training appears to strengthen the muscle at the point where isometric force production takes place.

Concentric Force Production

Concentric muscle contraction (also referred to as positive resistance training, or the positive phase) causes *shortening* of the muscle during force production. This can occur when you lift weight or pull, push or press against another form of resistance. Dynamic constant, progressive and variable resistance exercises generally require concentric contractions as part of the movement (refer to the definitions that follow).

Eccentric Force Production

Eccentric muscle training (also referred to as negative resistance training, or the negative phase) results in a *lengthening* of the muscle, while the muscle simultaneously produces force in an attempt to counter the resistance imposed upon the muscle. This type of force production is common to activities in daily life. For example, walking down a hill or section of steps requires the quadriceps and hip extensor muscles to perform eccentric contractions to decelerate the movement. Resistance that is lowered (i.e., biceps curl) during strength exercises requires eccentric force production. Dynamic constant, progressive and variable resistance exercises generally require eccentric force production as part of the movement (refer to the definitions that follow). Eccentric force production is required whenever a muscle lengthens and produces force, while simultaneously controlling any type of motion.

Eccentric muscle force contraction can generate up to 30% more force than a concentric contraction (Wilmore and Costill, 1994). Eccentric training is effective in moving clients off strength training plateaus, but this type of force production is associated with delayed onset muscle soreness (DOMS). Do not overemphasize loaded eccentric movement with new trainees or deconditioned clients.

> Quick Index:
>
> *Chapter 12, High-intensity strength training techniques*

Dynamic Constant Resistance

A typical example of *dynamic constant resistance* is lifting a dumbbell. The resistance used—the dumbbell—is "constant" throughout the entire movement. However, the force generated by the muscle is "dynamic" and changing through a given range of motion. These force changes are represented by a *strength curve* that varies for each muscle as the position of the joint changes.

Dynamic constant resistance is often incorrectly labeled "*isotonic.*" Iso means "same" and tonic refers to "tension." The term isotonic implies that the same tension is generated by the musculature through a given exercise range of motion. As is well documented, the same tension is *not* exerted through an entire range of motion due to leverage variations that change with mechanical advantage, or disadvantage, of the involved joint. Therefore, the term dynamic constant best describes this type of resistance.

Dynamic Variable Resistance

A more sophisticated approach to using variable resistance—when compared to Dynamic Progressive (refer to the definition that follows)—involves equipment that changes the amount of resistance being lifted through a lever arm, cam or pulley arrangement, and which attempts to match the strength/force curve of the muscle through the entire range of motion. The "dynamic" aspect of this type of resistance relates to the muscle's capacity to generate different forces throughout the ROM.

The resistance is made "variable,"—not necessarily in a progressive manner—in an attempt to match the increases and decreases of the strength curve exhibited by the muscle. In theory, this matching of force production capability by the muscle with a variable load would result in the muscle being required to exert maximal effort throughout the entire ROM. Ideally, there would be no part of the ROM that would be "too easy" or "too hard."

Unfortunately, due to the unique variations in each person's limb length, muscle attachment points and body size, it is impossible to envision one mechanical arrangement of lever arms, pulleys or cams that could accommodate each and every strength curve. This is not "good" or "bad," but a point of which you should be aware. Even without a perfect match of load to strength—as is evident by training with fixed loads such as dumbbells—if the load presented is new, strength training results will occur.

Dynamic Progressive Resistance

Examples of *dynamic progressive resistance* include elastic tubing, springs and composite rods that bend. These types of resistance provide more resistance when they are stretched or bent. The resistance afforded through the range-of-motion is progressive, meaning the more the device is stretched or bent, more resistance is presented. Dynamic simply refers to the varied force curve, or the varying amount of force a muscle can produce along a range-of-motion continuum. This type of variable resistance is cost effective and easy to transport, yet can provide progressive resistance without requiring, for example, the poundage associated with dumbbells and weight plates.

Isokinetic Resistance

Isokinetic training involves either a concentric or eccentric production of force where limb-movement velocity is held constant. Isokinetic equipment offers no preset resistance, but the velocity is fixed. Any force applied against this type of machinery results in an equal reaction force supplied by the machine. This means that the speed is constant but not necessarily the resistance. Theoretically, this makes it possible for the muscle(s) to exert a continual, maximal force production throughout a given motion, at a constant speed of movement.

Proponents of this type of training, which requires fairly expensive equipment, *feel* that movement speeds that mimic athletic performance can be challenged more effectively, and they *believe* that the ability to exert maximal force throughout a full ROM leads to optimal strength increases. But, this question needs to be asked: "Optimal strength increases for what?" The requirement for maximal force exertion through an entire ROM is absent from most daily activities and athletic performances. Also, studies indicate that there is no clear superiority of isokinetic training over other types of training (Fleck and Kraemer, 1997). A skilled trainer might be able to apply this type of "accommodating" resistance using hands-on spotting techniques.

UNDERSTANDING HUMAN MOVEMENT

To understand movement of the human body, it is helpful to envision muscle attachment points and fiber direction, as well as have a command of what common joint motions are available to each specific joint in the body. Having this information at your disposal allows you to work with, instead of against, the body. This knowledge will help you to better evaluate the effectiveness and risk of resistance training exercises.

Quick Index:

Chapter 4, Exercise analysis
Chapter 9, Understanding controversy that surrounds resistive training exercise

3

BENEFITS OF RESISTANCE TRAINING

Strength training not only develops muscular strength, muscular endurance and improves performance, but it can also help muscles recover from daily physical stresses of life and change how people look. Additionally, physical fitness declines with age. However, many of the detrimental changes in physiological function are due to decreased physical activity that often accompanies aging and resultant muscle loss. Negative, age-related changes in physiological function that are associated with a gradual decline in muscle mass can be minimized because strength training increases and/or preserves muscle.

Key Point

The so-called "inevitable decline" in personal health as we age results largely from muscle loss and can be prevented to a large degree with a regular strength training program. Strength training only twice per week can avoid a cascade of negative health consequences.

FIVE IMPORTANT REASONS TO STRENGTH TRAIN

I give a packet to my clients and patients with handouts explaining each component of fitness. The following reasons to strength train are written in "client" language:

1. Lose Fat And Control Your Weight

One advantage resistance training offers, is a leaner body. Maintaining or increasing muscle mass preserves your ability to burn greater numbers of calories. Your body is operating at a higher metabolic rate and it's easier to maintain or lose weight.

Strength training may be the most important exercise you can do for losing fat and maintaining weight, because it can increase your metabolism. Don't throw away your running and walking shoes just yet. Even though biking, running and dance aerobics do not develop muscle to any great extent, aerobic training is still important for cardiorespiratory health and weight control. But, one of the biggest reasons people gain weight is because they lose muscle.

Metabolism refers to the number of calories you're burning whether sleeping, watching TV or exercising vigorously. Metabolism slows with age, but the bulk of the decrease has nothing to do with getting older. It seems to be caused mostly by physical inactivity. You can lose 1% of your muscle annually if you don't exercise, which means from the age of 30-75 you can lose 45% of your muscle! If you only do cardiovascular workouts like running, walking and biking, you will lose muscle over time! The key to avoiding muscle loss is to strength train!

Key Point

Increase muscle and you'll burn more calories naturally—24-hours per day—even at rest! This will help you *lose* fat and *maintain* weight-loss.

You burn calories during and after lifting. Strength training increases your metabolism (the rate at which you burn calories) at rest because it causes an increase in lean muscle tissue. Muscle tissue is very "metabolically active." Muscle is like PacMan®; it gobbles up lots of calories to maintain itself, unlike fat, which requires almost no calories to exist. Muscle makes you a calorie "waster," which means you burn more calories that won't be stored as fat. Bottom line: increasing or maintaining muscle will help you burn more calories and keep the fat off!

2. Improve Your Personal Appearance

We all like to be pleased with what we see in the mirror. Regardless of how you *think* you look, self-acceptance is important.

Strength training does some good things for your image that cardiovascular training can't. It shapes, strengthens, builds and develops muscle. This has a direct impact on how you look. For example, your padded shoulders are now the result of muscles being developed, a caved in chest now looks strong, full and expanded, and your sleeveless dress shows off tone where "flappies of fat" used to hang from the back of your arms. Though you can't spot-*reduce* (selectively cause fat to disappear from a particular body part), you can spot-*tone*.

Key Point

Strong muscles help to maintain an erect posture and could eliminate many orthopedic problems associated with the back, hips and knees. Resistance training can do more to reshape your body than any other type of training.

3. Get Stronger And Reduce Your Risk Of Injury

Strong muscles will make you less likely to get hurt. With strong muscles come strong ligaments (they support your joints) and strong tendons (they connect muscles to bone). What this means is that you have margin for error. For example, if you stumble or lose your balance there's a good chance you can right yourself without falling or hurting yourself, or straining a muscle.

Key Point

Resistance training provides good "armor" for the body during cardiovascular workouts. Strong and resilient muscles, bones, tendons, ligaments and cartilage protect the joints from potential injury in all kinds of daily and recreational activity.

4. Keep Strong, Healthy Bones

Millions of the world's population have osteoporosis, which is a disease that cripples by weakening bones. Bone loss can lead to fractures in the hip, back and wrist. Fracture complications can result in complete inactivity and an astonishing decrease in personal well-being. Don't think you have to fall to break a weak bone. A quick turn of the head can break a vertebrae or catching your balance after a slip can fracture a hip that is weakened by osteoporosis. Strong bones are solid and dense, like a strong slab of oak. Diseased bones look like porous sponge and easily break when stressed.

You might ask, "Isn't osteoporosis a disease of the frail and elderly?" Osteoporosis *can* contribute to making a *healthy*, older person frail, weak and sick. But, it is a disease of the young, too. It starts early in life and is a killer because you don't know you have it until it's difficult to reverse the damage. The key to preventing osteoporosis is to maintain the bone you have. Good nutrition and exercise are the keys, starting in the teen years. Even if you're well beyond this youthful age, you can still build some bone back by strength training and participating in weight-bearing cardiovascular exercise like walking. Proper intake of calcium and vitamin D are also important.

Strong muscles mean strong bones. When you contract your muscles by lifting weights, the point at which the muscles attach to the bone are positively stressed. These attachment points actually pull on the bone when the muscle contracts. This is what keeps your bones strong, along with adequate nutrition. Complete inactivity is a "killer" that contributes to weak and unhealthy bones.

Key Point

Bones and muscle deteriorate with age and especially inactivity. The best way to strengthen the bones is to stimulate the muscles that pull on them, eat a healthy diet and to participate in weight-bearing or low-impact activity.

5. Stay Healthy
Strength training can lower your blood pressure if it's high and reduce your risk for diabetes and some types of cancer. It can also lower your risk for heart disease by increasing "good" cholesterol and decreasing "bad" cholesterol.

HEALTH BENEFITS ASSOCIATED WITH RESISTANCE TRAINING

This is information from another "resistance training benefits" handout that I give to clients and patients – written in language that they can understand.

- **Fat Loss, Weight Control and Weight Maintenance.** Losing scale weight is the wrong goal. You can lose the wrong kind of weight (muscle and bone) and still be fat. Focus on dropping fat and gaining muscle.
- **Increased Metabolism.** If you have a lot of muscle your metabolism is higher and you burn more calories since muscle is metabolically active (think of PacMan® gobbling up calories).
- **Increased Calorie Burning During Resistance Training.** Any activity, including strength training, burns calories during the activity and contributes to fitness.
- **Increased Calorie Burning After Exercise.** Vigorous strength training significantly elevates calorie burning (metabolic rate) anywhere from 30- to 60-minutes or longer after you've finished.
- **Reductions in Resting Blood Pressure.** If you have high blood pressure or borderline high blood pressure, generally it's acceptable to use moderate loads and 15-20 repetitions. Diet (decrease alcohol and salt) and exercise can lower blood pressure. Check with a doctor to get a specific recommendation.

• **Decreased Risk for Diabetes.** Diabetes ultimately results from an inability to control blood sugar levels. Insulin that is secreted from your pancreas normally controls blood sugar levels. Muscle tissue is programmed to respond to insulin and as ordered by this hormone, to take sugar out of the blood into the muscle. As people get fatter, older and inactive the muscle tissue they have left doesn't obey insulin command orders. Solution: lift weights, build muscle and lose fat! Resistance training increases muscle mass and increases insulin action or decreases insulin resistance. Both cardiovascular and metabolic benefits can be gained by engaging in a resistance training program.

• **Positive Changes in Blood Lipid Profiles.** HDL cholesterol (the "good guy") is raised primarily by exercise (cardiovascular and strength training) and losing fat. Of course, diet (moderate, healthy eating) is important to lower harmful LDL (the "bad guy" cholesterol) and tryglycerides (fat).

• **Decreased Risk for Osteoporosis and Increased Bone Mineral Content.** You can avoid weaker, less dense and more brittle bone by strength training and using weight bearing (i.e., walking and running) exercise. You'll be at less risk for fracture resulting from inactivity if you maintain weight-bearing aerobic exercise and strength training throughout your life.

• **Improved Structural and Functional Integrity of Tendons, Ligaments and Joints.** Stronger muscles increase the thickness and strength of tendons (connect muscles to bones) and ligaments (provide integrity to joints by connecting bone-to-bone). Stronger muscles let you exert more force, perform better, and with less chance of injury to the muscles, tendons, ligaments and joints.

• **Personal Physical Independence.** Many people lose their "freedom" because they've lost the strength to be mobile.

• **Enhanced Physical Activity Experiences.** Strong individuals perform better and physical activity feels good to their bodies.

• **Improved Posture.** Strength and flexibility are the keys to correct body alignment. You'll look and feel better, guaranteed!

• **Improved Physical Image.** Strength training will change how you look. If you don't believe this, take a look at a runner who only trains the cardiovascular system.

• **Improved Self-Esteem.** You'll feel strong, look strong and think that you're strong. In fact, you *will* be strong!

THE IMPORTANCE OF RESISTANCE TRAINING

The message is loud and clear. Strength training keeps muscles stronger, preserves physical independence, limits the likelihood of several chronic diseases such as diabetes and osteoporosis, and helps keep aging bodies physiologically younger than chronological age says they should be.

Recent research (Evans, 1991; ACE, 1998; ACSM, 1998; Pollock et al., 1998; Mazzeo et al., 1998 and others) suggests that the single most important step to not just retard, but to reverse the aging process, is strength training. It is a myth that the older adult or elderly lose their ability to respond to a strength training stimulus. Early studies seemed to support this view, but erroneous study design—too little resistance was used—doomed the expected "strength response" to failure. It was not that the older adult would not respond to strength stimuli as some studies indicated, simply, they were not presented one! Strength levels have tripled in well controlled and designed strength studies using older adults and other studies have shown strength improvements as high as 200 percent (Evans, 1991; Mazzeo, 1998). However, the older adult, as is true for any age, must work sufficiently intense to optimize the strength training response and to see significant strength training gains.

Quick Index:

Chapter 11, The right mix of reps, sets, and load

The rewards of resistance training are indeed plentiful. Many young and older adults comment that they get a "kick" out of their new body. Their abdomens firm up — something walking never did for them. Their arms and legs are strong and toned. They stand up straight, lift heavy "things," work with renewed energy and play vigorously.

Key Point

Being independent, in of itself, may be one of the best reasons for everyone, at any age, to begin strength training.

Exercise Mechanics: How To Perform Resistance Training Exercises Correctly... And Why!

4

THE "10-STEP ANY EXERCISE DRILL" - EXERCISE ANALYSIS MADE EASY

Unbiased and effective resistance training exercise analysis and application requires an open mind, as well as accurate anatomical, biomechanical and orthopedic information. Once this information is considered and matched accordingly to the exercise goal or goals, you have an excellent foundation from which to design resistance training exercise programs. Combine this with a professional desire to create the safest, most effective resistance training exercises for clients and patients, and you've got the essence of what can be accomplished when you use the step-by-step process I call "The Drill."

To attain optimal resistance training exercise design, you must consider the goals of the individual being trained, their unique anatomy and injury history, benefits as related to health, performance and/or rehabilitation outcome, and finally, you have to weigh any risks versus possible benefit or gain.

Most exercise variations are permutations (sometimes mutations!) from a select group of correct, basic and finite joint motions available to the body. The "10-Step Any Exercise Drill" can help you learn how to apply biomechanical commonalties and truths to similar motions (such as the barbell squat and seated leg press, or supine dumbbell chest press and seated machine chest press), and can quickly help you assess the worth of an exercise in terms of how successful it is at developing strength in a safe, effective manner.

Quick Index:

Chapter 1, How to group resistance training exercises by common motions
Chapters 5-8, Exercise technique for the trunk, lower and upper body
Chapter 9, Understanding controversial resistance training exercise

WITH THE RIGHT APPROACH, YOU CAN MAKE THE BEST RESISTANCE EXERCISE CHOICES

Consumer fitness magazines and popular strength training books are filled with numerous strength training exercise variations. You can select from an enormous variety of exercises and equipment, and you'll hear all types of conflicting advice when it comes to exercise technique. In the "weight room" it's possible to observe a number of interesting, and sometimes astounding to say the least, performances of so called strength exercises. With such an array of choices, how do you know which is the "best" resistance-training exercise?

The "best" resistance training exercises should be chosen more for their "correctness" than for their novelty. They should maximize effectiveness, safety, proper biomechanics, muscle function and client compliance.

But how do you make those "best" choices? As you are well aware, you can select from an amazing variety of exercises, advice and equipment. In addition, each client poses a unique challenge, with an individual combination of abilities, interests, history and health circumstances. Many trainers voice frustration when confronted with the challenge of evaluating a new or traditional exercise, because they're unsure of how to go about determining its safety, effectiveness and overall correctness.

Rarely should the *type* of resistance-training equipment represent a limiting factor in creating proper strength training biomechanics. For example, if the equipment in question does not allow the correct mechanics to take place and cannot be modified, choose not to use the equipment and accomplish the training goal using other equipment. Beyond this piece of advice and the previous philosophical spin, you've got to know "The Drill!"

Key Point

Whether you are using sophisticated and high-priced machinery, free-weights, water as a resistance medium, elastic resistance or body weight—the process for developing resistance-training exercise biomechanics stays the same.

The "Any Exercise Drill" helps you develop a consistent, comprehensive methodology from which to base your exercise choices. The objectives of this "big picture" approach to resistance training are to establish:

1. An evaluative or objective process for determining the effectiveness and safety of strength training exercises
2. A creative process for modifying existing exercises that have weaknesses and developing new resistance training exercises

This systematic and unbiased approach is especially useful when you have identified participants' goals. Training procedures, progressions, exercise selection, exercise creation and the clients' personal histories should walk hand-in-hand with individual exercise goals.

By following the steps of the "Any Exercise Drill" and answering the 10 questions the drill prompts, you will be well on your way to confidence and clarity as it relates to your resistance training exercise design and selection. Most important, the exercise execution you choose to implement will withstand the test of careful scrutiny, rather than existing "because it's been around forever," or existing simply for the sake-of-variety.

"THE ANY EXERCISE DRILL" — 10 STEPS TO CREATING AND SELECTING EFFECTIVE RESISTANCE TRAINING EXERCISES

This drill, which consists of 10 key questions and a statement (Bonus Step 11: Find A Creative Solution), will help you evaluate the effectiveness of any *given* resistance training exercise and enable you to develop new exercises. This drill will also help you weigh exercise effectiveness against safety concerns. Step 11 has been added to remind the trainer that a creative solution must be found to accomplish the training goal when an exercise is deemed unacceptable.

1. What is the goal?
The goal of the exercise is usually to challenge a particular body part, muscle or group of muscles, or to enhance spinal or knee joint integrity. For example, if your goal is to target the chest, it is important to identify a number of effective exercises for this body part using different body positions and equipment. If you want to increase the integrity of the knee joint, it's important to use exercises that strengthen the knee, but don't simultaneously contribute to instability. Terms like functional or closed chain exercise—in other words, terms that imply "usable strength" that has carryover to daily life and sport application—will further clarify and customize the planning process. Once a client's goal is defined, the next three questions pinpoint correct movement mechanics related to the targeted area of the body.

2. What is the joint motion(s)?
There are a finite number of *intended* joint motions or actions in the body. Generally, if the motion is unintended or abnormal, it works against the body and can lead to injury. Joint

motion is largely determined by the anatomical structure of the joint and muscle attachment points. Mastery and understanding of the key joint actions that are related to gross motor movement are important in order to see through the *seemingly* infinite number of movements available to the body.

> ## Quick Index:
> ### Chapter 2, Important joint motions or movements

3. What muscles are being used to create movement at the joint(s)?

Once the joint motion(s) has been identified and you've chosen an exercise movement(s) that is appropriate, you can identify the muscle(s) involved in the movement. As is true for joint actions, it is imperative that you have a solid understanding of the function of the muscles that contribute to large, or gross, motor movements of the body. Understanding muscle function is most easily accomplished by visualizing attachment points of key muscles. Muscles contract along the lines of their fiber direction. For example, the fibers of the chest or pectoralis major run predominantly from the sternum to the upper part of the arm or humerus. Since muscles contract toward the belly of the fiber, the least stable attachment (the insertion) will be pulled toward the more stable attachment (the origin). As the chest fibers contract, the arms will be pulled horizontally across and in front of the body toward the midline. By "seeing" attachment points and knowing joint actions, it's easy to understand what movements can and should occur at the joints. Additionally, Step 8 requires you to place resistance in direct opposition to the movement. In other words, for the above example, to perfectly align resistance in a way that opposes the pull of the arms toward the center or middle of the body, the force must be placed in opposition to this desired movement pattern. Information like this will assist in having resistance properly aligned or directed to oppose the targeted muscles.

4. What is the proper path of motion?

Specific joint motions(s) and muscles that contribute to a proper path of motion must be identified in relation to anatomical considerations, muscle attachments or fiber direction, body position, the type of equipment being used and the goal of the exercise. For example, if the goal of a lateral shoulder raise is to challenge shoulder abduction and the middle deltoid, a specific body position and path of motion of the arms must be maintained. During a chest press or flye, horizontal adduction or flexion at the shoulder represents pulling the arm across the body toward its center and is the strongest movement of the pectoralis major muscle. If the goal of the exercise is to fully challenge the pectoralis muscle, this position must be maintained throughout the movement. In other words, the elbow must not be dropped (i.e., external shoulder rotation) or raised (i.e., internal shoulder rotation). The desired plane of motion should be kept constant. Do not alter or compromise correct path of movement because of limitations imposed by external factors such as machine design. Remember, mechanics are mechanics, are mechanics!

> ## Key Point
>
> Neither the type of equipment nor the position of the body during an exercise should alter correct mechanics.

Quick Index:

Chapters 6-9, Correct mechanics for trunk, upper and lower body exercises, as well as controversial resistance training exercises

5. What is the proper range of motion (ROM) at the joint?

Range of motion at the joint can be estimated by learning the average, or so-called "normal," range of motion at each joint of the body. Information like this is provided in various anatomical textbooks. However, each of your clients has unique and various factors that influence ROM. Factors that influence ROM are flexibility, strength, anatomical irregularities and current or previous injury. Though classic textbook ROM characterization may provide a good estimate of general movement capabilities at each joint, the best starting point with your clients is to determine their active range of motion (AROM).

Quick index:

Chapter 2, Joint actions and common degrees of motion at various joints

6. What is the active range of motion (AROM) at the joint?

Flexibility, or range of motion about a joint or joints is generally limited by the strength of the agonist muscle(s) at the joint, lack of flexibility in the antagonistic muscles (specifically the muscle fascia) and natural or other anatomical limitations such as injury.

Proper range of motion at a joint or joints is probably best—and most safely—determined by the participant's AROM. To determine a client's AROM for a specific joint, have her perform the desired movement pattern with no resistance. Subsequently, the client should work the resistance training exercise within this AROM.

Key Point

Proper range of motion at a joint or joints is probably most accurately identified and safely determined by assessing your client's active range of motion for any given movement.

7. Is the overload effective in terms of the amount of resistance?

Effective overload for the majority of your clients means working to the point of muscle fatigue, or to the point where the client is thinking, "This is about the last repetition I can do with good form." Muscle fatigue should be attained for most of your clients, in about 6 to 20 repetitions, or in about 30 to 120 seconds. Occasionally you may choose to use an exercise or piece of equipment that does not produce muscle fatigue within this repetition framework, if the exercise or equipment is focusing on functional strength, balance or stabilization.

8. Is the direction of force or resistance in perfect opposition to the movement pattern?

Is the body properly positioned in relation to the equipment and to the direction of resistance the equipment creates? The body must be correctly positioned to ensure that the resistance created by the equipment opposes, as closely as possible, the client's movement pattern.

Fig. 18a, The direction of force provided by elastic resistance is directly opposite and in line with its attachment point.

For example, because of gravity, the direction of force created by free weights is always straight down. The resistance from selectorized plates is normally routed through a system of pulleys and cables, and the force of elastic resistance is directly opposite and in line with its attachment point. *See fig. 18a*

The direction of force provided by free weights and gravity is, for example, the reason that a standing chest press using dumbbells is *not* effective. *See fig. 18b*

Each type of equipment will present limitations regarding body position and direction of force. Because of this, the trainer must understand how the body works and how forces must be aligned in opposition to the movement pattern, in order to effectively train all muscle groups.

Fig 18b, The direction of force is perpendicular to the movement pattern, rather than opposing the movement.

Key Point

Regardless of the type of equipment you're using, always position the body so the direction of resistance opposes the movement pattern.

Proper positioning assures a higher level of efficiency (i.e., load on the muscle) and a greater margin of safety. Exercise set-up and stabilization requires participation and integration of the whole body. Obviously, the client's attentiveness and understanding of this process is a big part of whether this important aspect of resistance training execution is successful, or not.

9. Has the necessary stabilization been established in the body prior to the movement and sustained throughout the duration of the movement?

You might want to put a little asterisk next to Step 9. Quite possibly, one could argue that the most important initial physical step in any resistance training exercise is stabilization. Being aware of, and maintaining and/or returning to neutral lumbar and cervical posture is critical for effective, safe and functional movement. (Notable exceptions to this general rule of "neutral" include traditional trunk flexion and extension exercises, where it is essential to move in and out of neutral lumbar spine to flex, laterally flex and extend the trunk, and some sport-specific resistance training movements that are dynamic.) Stabilization may also occur in other areas of the body, such as the upper back (scapular stabilization), shoulders, hips and knees. Stabilization and general body awareness are important for maintaining desired alignment and starting positions throughout the performance of the exercise.

Quick Index:

Chapter 5, Understanding the trunk and neutral posture

Stabilization generally refers to a position that the client assumes before starting the exercise—called the exercise set-up or starting position—and maintains during the exercise. Stabilization is an essential component for correct exercise execution. Effective stabilization occurs when the participant maintains the starting set-up position with no variance, until she has completed the exercise or set of repetitions. Stabilization occurs from within the exerciser, and should not be dependent on a machine or trainer.

Effective cues that encourage maintenance of the set-up position include, "Keep your set-up," "Maintain your starting position," and "Where you start is where you stay." Your client needs to mentally and physically lock in on this crucial starting point and sustain it during exercise execution.

10. Do the risks of the exercise outweigh its potential effectiveness?

What about orthopedic concerns? An exercise may be effective in challenging a particular body part or group of muscles and in creating excellent strength gains. However, when you consider known orthopedic risks such as unsupported forward flexion, loaded and fully flexed knees, shoulder impingement and uncontrolled movement speed, the risks may outweigh any potential benefits for some exercises. An exercise can be very effective at developing strength in a particular muscle or muscle group, but if the risk of joint damage or other soft tissue injury is high, this weakness must be considered and then corrected or minimized, as is appropriate to the training goal.

Key Point

When you factor in risks associated with an exercise, and they outweigh the potential benefit offered by the exercise, exercise design needs to change.

11. Bonus Step: Find A Creative Solution!

Everyone gets frustrated with policy, doctrine or law that takes away fun or options. After the 10-step evaluation, if the trainer determines that the exercise is unacceptable, solutions must be found to remedy the situation. I try never to condemn or imply an exercise is weak without having at least one replacement solution or modification in place. One fitness professional voiced his frustration to me regarding copious opinions and biomechanical mandates that he felt left him with few exercise choices by saying, "If you help us understand why an exercise motion is weak, don't stop there. Give us a fix by helping fitness professionals see the light in the form of alternate exercise selection and/or modifications!" I couldn't have said it better!

The Any Exercise Drill

1. What is the goal?
2. What is the joint motion(s)?
3. What muscles are being used to create movement at the joint(s)?
4. What is the proper path of motion?
5. What is a normal range of motion at the joint?
6. What is the active range of motion at the joint?
7. Is the overload effective in terms of the amount of resistance?
8. Is the direction of force or resistance in direct opposition (or as close as possible) to the movement pattern?
9. Has the necessary stabilization occurred in the body prior to the movement and has it been maintained during the movement?
10. Do the risks of the exercise outweigh its potential effectiveness?
11. Bonus Step: Find a creative solution if the exercise is labeled as unacceptable.

ILLUSTRATING THE DRILL

An analysis of the unsupported bent-over row offers a good example of practical application, and of how to use the Any Exercise Drill as an evaluative tool. Let's look at how this exercise stacks up against the drill:

1. The goal of this exercise could be to target the elbow flexors, back of the shoulders and upper-back musculature.
2. The joint motions include elbow flexion, horizontal shoulder abduction or extension, and scapular adduction or retraction. The movement of the arms backward is often referred to as a "high elbow row."

3. The major muscles involved in this movement are the biceps brachii, posterior deltoid, latissimus dorsi (to a lesser degree), and the middle trapezius and rhomboid muscles as stabilizers.

4. The path of motion is horizontal abduction. The plane of this motion is maintained throughout the exercise by avoiding internal or external rotation of the shoulder.

5. Combine steps 5 and 6.

6. Determine the client's AROM by having them move through the path of motion without any resistance.

7. Establish proper load or resistance based on the client's training goals and current level of strength fitness. Dumbbells could be chosen that would produce fatigue within a desired repetition framework.

8. From this bent over position, the direction of the resistance—due to the dumbbells and gravity's effect — directly opposes the movement.

9. The body is in a position of 90 degrees flexion at the hip, with the torso parallel to the floor. The hip is flexed, not the trunk. Neutral posture is maintained in the spine and is represented by neither the cervical or lumbar curvatures being excessively arched or flat. This set-up, or stabilized position, should be maintained throughout the exercise.

Fig. 19, Unsupported bent over row with dumbbells

Thus far, this exercise has passed most of the "Any Exercise Drill" criteria.

10. However, regardless of the many "positives" of this exercise, when you get to this step, consider the orthopedic concerns (risk versus effectiveness), and the unsupported bent-over row falls apart. The risk of injury and cumulative stress to the spine can be high, particularly if the lumbar spine flexes, rather than neutral posture being maintained, if the knees are locked or hyperextended, and if the cervical spine is extended. *See fig.19*

In addition, even if neutral posture is maintained in the trunk, this posture (unsupported forward hip flexion) is passively supported by ligaments and fascia in the low-back and spinal region to some degree. The stabilizing muscles of the spine are not in a good position to exert force in this position because muscle activity of the spinal extensors decreases rapidly as the torso flexes forward and/or if the spine flexes. The resultant effect is that the vertebral column can only resist the force of the weight being lifted through ligament and fascial support.

Adding resistance—the stronger you are the more potential risk—in this position increases the stress. In conclusion, done "correctly" with neutral spinal posture intact, there is still potential shearing force on the discs positioned between the vertebrae of the spine, as well as unnecessary lateral forces placed against stabilizing spinal ligaments and associated fascial structures. This results in the stabilizing effects of the ligaments and fascia associated with the vertebral joints of the spine being compromised.

While the effectiveness for the exercise is high in its ability to overload the targeted musculature, for most clients any potential advantage is far outweighed by the high risk of potential injury or cumulative stress (i.e., micro trauma) to the spine.

FINDING A CREATIVE SOLUTION

As long as you have a solid foundation in kinesiology and movement mechanics, and now that you have the help of the "Any Exercise Drill," you can have fun (success!) and enjoy unlimited creative freedom in exercise selection and modification. If an exercise is not recommended or its relative risk is high, you can find a solution — and that is your challenge. A client should be able to safely and effectively challenge the same muscles and joint actions by putting the body in a different or supported position and/or by using a different piece of exercise equipment.

Quick Index:

Chapter 2, Working knowledge of basic anatomy and kinesiology
Chapter 9, Refer to the section titled "Trunk Flexion" for additional discussion and analysis.

For example, instead of doing an unsupported bent-over row, the client could simply lie face down on a flat bench with a dumbbell in each hand (*See fig. 20a*). The prone position safely supports the spine and challenges the same movement. Alternatively, the client could adopt a standing or seated position in an appropriately designed machine (*See fig. 20b*). Cables or elastic resistance attached to a wall or step

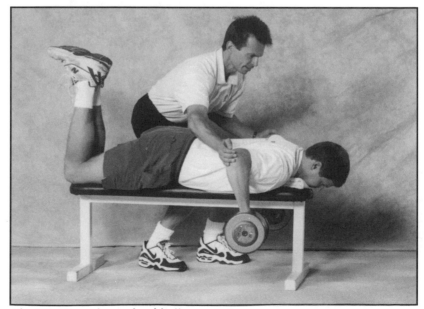

Fig. 20a, Face down dumbbell row

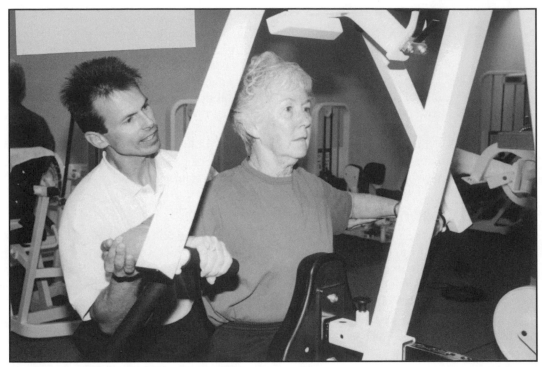

Fig. 20b, Seated Cybex high elbow pull-back

platform in front of the client could provide resistance in opposition to the movement, as could a machine. From a kneeling position on a bench, a unilateral or one arm dumbbell high elbow row could accomplish the same goal *(See fig. 20c)*.

So, there you have it! By using the drill you can create safe, effective exercise solutions that replace less than optimal exercises by thoroughly analyzing exercise charac-teristics and wisely choosing a creative solution or in fact, several!

Fig. 20c, Kneeling one arm dumbbell high elbow row

Key Point

"The Drill" was designed to minimize risk, while simultaneously maximizing compliance and result!

SEVEN PRINCIPLES TO INCORPORATE IN ALL RESISTANCE EXERCISES

These 7 principles evolve from the Any Exercise Drill. Execution of an excellent resistance training exercise should reflect all seven principles.

1. Attempt to emphasize movements that are natural to the body. Joint motion and muscle function, as related to muscle fiber direction and attachment points, will provide the leading "clues" to natural movement.

2. Increase the joints' active range of motion (AROM) if not contraindicated by injury or other medical limitation. Though ROM is sometimes overemphasized—more is not always better—generally the maintenance of intended, functional and desired ROM is good.

3. Maximize motor unit recruitment and efficient muscle contraction by using all joint motions appropriate to the movement, full AROM and proper overload (intensity). Intensity is the key to training results, followed closely by correct mechanics and controlled movement speed. But, all three work in tandem to create optimal resistance training exercise.

4. Create resistance that is, as closely as possible, in direct opposition to the path of movement. Align the resistance to the body or the body to the resistance.

5. Decrease the likelihood of injury by taking into account known orthopedic principles and orthopedic concerns/history of the client. An exercise is not fully analyzed until any inherent risks are corrected, or weighed against possible gains.

6. Include an awareness and execution of stabilizing forces in every resistance training exercise. Keep the set-up positioning, moving only the body parts necessary to perform the intended movement.

7. Balance resistance training exercise program design with exercise choices that include traditional lifting (i.e., isolated movement exercises) and functional (closed chain and balance training activity) approaches to training.

Quick Index:

Chapter 9, Functional, isolated, closed and open chain exercise

Not only does using the "Any Exercise Drill" allow you to quickly and accurately analyze *any* exercise and determine if it is appropriate for your client, but "The Drill" also gives you a process to remedy any resistance training exercise with mechanics that are less than optimal.

Key Point

Individuals who learn to train properly get better results, stick with their program and get injured less often. Trainers who take the time to rise to the level of master trainers, have clients who stick with them over the years and see outstanding results.

5 UNDERSTANDING THE TRUNK

Whether someone is an active parent, elite-amateur athlete, weekend warrior, or a professional athlete, the same questions arise. A sampling includes:

- How can I get faster and quicker?
- How can I improve my balance?
- What do I need to do to get stronger?
- How can I develop power?
- How can I learn to change directions quickly?
- What do I have to do to keep from injuring myself?
- How can I improve my level of skill?
- My back bothers me, what can I do?

Those who ask questions like these are often surprised at my response. The place to start with regard to improvement in these performance and health related areas is not necessarily the arms, shoulders, chest, upper back, hips, upper or lower legs. Instead, I will probably suggest starting with a progressive program of trunk flexibility and strength conditioning.

The region of the body that houses the abdominal and back muscles is commonly referred to as the "the core," "low torso" or as the "center of power." Though many people are preoccupied (obsessed!) with this area of the body, ironically, it is often under-trained or incorrectly trained.

THE TRUNK "POWER CENTER"

The core of the body is a major connecting link in the body's musculoskeletal chain. The trunk is the center of power, or the "command center" for skilled performance in a literal and physical sense.

If you view the body as a chain, it is only as strong as its weakest link. Let's say a client has very strong legs and arms, but an undeveloped low torso or trunk. Force cannot efficiently be transferred between the two body parts if the midsection-linkage lacks the strength to stabilize the low torso during movement. In other words, the body needs a strong base or foundation from which to direct effort so that energy that is created for movement ends up being a part of that movement, rather than wasted. Misdirected energy is not harmless; it can lead to poor performance and injury.

Key Point

If the core is weak, force development or movement potential of the muscles is dissipated, or absorbed, rather than being directed into the intended movement.

The midsection or "connecting-links" of the body need to be solid and strong, and the musculature needs to be able to stabilize spinal and pelvic positioning, as well as contract dynamically. This is in contrast to a core that is deconditioned and represents something more like a blob of jelly (i.e., weak in structure), which in effect would stop the transfer of force and impede efficient, safe movement.

Adequately conditioned abdominal and back musculature represents the key "coupling" link of the body that connects movements between the upper and lower body. The strength and importance of the body's core—its power or command center—is reflected by modern conditioning programs that emphasize core training as a primary objective, though not to the exclusion of other important aspects of fitness.

This power center of the body — the trunk — is the literal and physical bridge that allows for dynamic, powerful, coordinated, skillful and integrated responses of the whole body. Core training extends well beyond vanity and into the domains of improved fitness, maintaining health or enhanced athletic performance.

MOVING TOWARD A HEALTHY TRUNK

If I were to offer a lecture named, "100 Ways To Bust Your Gut," a large number of people would be in attendance. A workshop titled, "How To Create A Healthy Trunk," lacks the sizzle, pop and sensationalism to draw huge crowds. In fact, some people might be confused and believe the lecture was for veterinarians who specialized in care for the "snout" of an elephant.

The issue being brought up here is that many people don't know why they should be training their midsection, though if surveyed, the average consumer would tell you they want to look better and get rid of the fat on their abdominal region. (Of course, spot reduction is not possible.) Few would offer a sophisticated reply that would include a desire to prevent the occurrence or recurrence of back pain, a hope that their posture would improve or that they would be able to pursue recreational sports, or play with their kids more vigorously without injuring themselves.

A balanced approach to ab and back training looks at strengthening both the abdominal and back muscles and stretching key postural muscles. In addition, the musculature should be exercised with a variety of approaches that include isolated training as well as functional or stability training. The trunk, as a functioning unit in daily life and sport, operates as an integrated, interdependent unit. The goal is to determine a balanced and diverse approach for targeting this critical area of the body so that it is optimally developed.

Most current training theories emphasize optimal stimulation by training the trunk as a whole versus an isolated part. These methodologies include:

1. Trunk exercises that emphasize pelvic stabilization and functional movement. The primary function of abdominal and back muscles is NOT to create movement at the spine. Stabilization and maintenance of spinal neutral and related pelvic positioning are their key functions. However, abdominal and low back stabilization, pelvic stabilization and functional training should not be utilized to the exclusion of traditional, "mover-type" abdominal or back extensor exercise.

2. Trunk exercises that work through a controlled range-of-motion in a variety of planes. Disc nutrition and the sponge-like process of imbibition (See Movement and Imbibition in the Spine, this chapter) are largely dependent on the alternating compression and release of the intervertebral discs. This fact alone supports the continued use of traditional approaches that are utilized for abdominal and low back training such as mover-type or isolated abdominal and back work, as well as stabilization training.

3. Trunk exercises that favor ambidextrous movement. In other words, you don't want to have a "favorite," "good" or "dominant" side. When performing sport skills like a tennis forehand or golf swing, or while carrying luggage, it is worthy to adopt a habit of practicing the stroke, or carrying the luggage, on both sides of the body.

4. Trunk exercises that use "non-traditional" exercise equipment to develop strength and flexibility. A round, air filled ball, generically termed a "stability ball" represents a good example of this type of equipment. The stability ball's effectiveness is backed by years of use in the physical therapy and rehabilitation fields, and gives you a way to train the trunk in a way that emphasizes stabilization and balance, when compared to what traditional approaches to core training have to offer. Remember, that this is not a case of "good" or "better" versus "bad" or "less-appropriate," but one of different training methods that can be used to more completely train the trunk.

5. Trunk exercises that emphasize balance. The complex region of the low torso works synergistically as a unit. The trunk should never be viewed in the context of abs versus back training, or vanity versus function, or seen solely as low back health or sport performance focused. Present a balanced and well-thought out plan of attack and your

client will benefit in all of these important areas. To fill in the holes, consider complementing the client's current program by training what you are not currently training (i.e., functional versus traditional training), and don't make the mistake of permanently choosing one method over another or to the exclusion of another.

Key Point

To determine whether you should be performing functional/stabilizing exercises for the trunk, or doing traditional ab and back work, the best idea might be to emphasize what you are currently NOT doing in your program.

STEPS TO ACHIEVE A HEALTHY TRUNK

A combination of strength, flexibility and stability is the key to a healthy trunk. Many experts believe that the following four steps could prevent a great deal of the back pain that is so prevalent in our population, much of which is associated with poor posture and incorrect movement patterns.

1. Increase flexibility of the hip flexors.

As a result of daily habits that encourage a seated position and rounded (spinal flexion) low back posture, it is arguable that the low back area is rarely tight and generally overstretched, though this is not always true. On the other hand, tight hip flexors (rectus femoris, iliacus and psoas) are rampant in our largely sedentary society. Lack of flexibility in the hip flexors can result from seated postures, rhythmic activities (such as walking, running and cycling) that utilize a repetitive, short range of movement, as well as a lack of commitment to regular stretching. This short-arc training, plus repetitious daily movement patterns and habits, leads to adaptive shortening and possible hyperlordosis or spinal misalignment because of tight hip flexors. An anterior pelvic tilt (arched back) can be created by inflexible rectus femoris and iliacus muscles, since their attachment points to the pelvis are on the anterior portion (just below the iliac crest anatomical landmark) of the pelvis (hip bone). Additionally, a tight psoas, based on its anatomical attachments

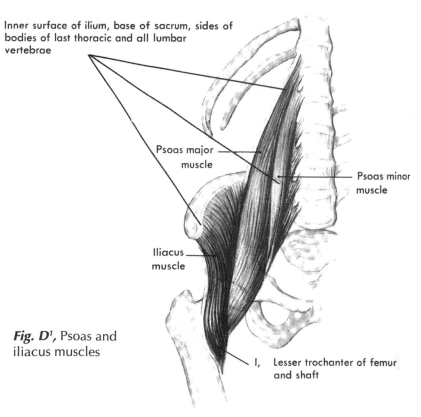

Inner surface of ilium, base of sacrum, sides of bodies of last thoracic and all lumbar vertebrae

Psoas major muscle

Psoas minor muscle

Iliacus muscle

I, Lesser trochanter of femur and shaft

Fig. D¹, Psoas and iliacus muscles

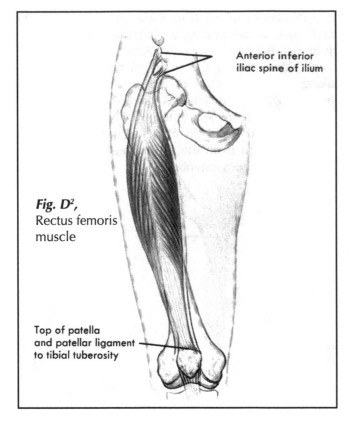

Fig. D²,
Rectus femoris muscle

Anterior inferior iliac spine of ilium

Top of patella and patellar ligament to tibial tuberosity

at the medial and upper aspect of the femur (insertion) and sides of the lumbar vertebrae, can cause compression and shearing forces on the spine and intervertebral discs. *See fig. D¹ (previous page) & D²*

2. Increase flexibility of the hamstrings.

Tight hamstrings, which attach below the posterior side of the knee joint, and originate at the ischial tuberosities (i.e., the "sit-bones") can cause the pelvic bowl to rotate posteriorly toward a flat back position. This motion is called a posterior pelvic tilt. If both the hip flexors and hamstrings are tight, the pelvis can be relatively immobile. Not only are you unable to dance — move your pelvis freely — but this "permanent" misalignment and associated lack of movement is stressful to the soft tissues of the spine.

3. Increase strength of the rectus abdominis, internal and external obliques and spinal extensor muscles.

Each of these muscle groups plays an important part in trunk health. Is one muscle group more important to challenge than the others? Let's break down the function(s) of each muscle group and decide.

Rectus abdominis. The rectus abdominis muscle, especially the fibers or motor units in the lower region, are important to help counter the pull of the hip flexors during exercise. The hip flexors can exert a pull on the pelvis which can result in the pelvis rotating anteriorly, which in turn causes the back to be "forced" into hyper-lordosis, or an extremely arched and misaligned spine. The lower region and its associated motor units are important in controlling or limiting excessive lordosis.

The rectus abdominis controls the positioning of the pelvic bowl or pelvis. With adequate strength in this muscle, as well as adequate flexibility in the hip flexors and hamstrings, and a knowledge of how to position the pelvis, it is possible to maintain a neutral lumbar spinal position or return to this position when desired.

Spinal extensors. The spinal extensors help maintain an upright and stable spinal column. The erector spinae and multifidus muscles function mainly to provide posterior stability for the vertebral column. They also oppose the force of gravity to help maintain an erect posture and control the degree of forward flexion.

Oblique muscles. Arguably, the key abdominal muscles for low back health are the obliques since they insert on the fascia of the erector spinae, in the lumbosacral area of the low back. Strong oblique muscles reinforce the erector spinae fascia and pull it laterally. In theory, this would place less strain on the spine and enhance its stability (Plowman, 1992).

The combined forces of the rectus abdominis, obliques and erector spinae assist in the maintenance of the upright posture, as well as providing for the ongoing integrity of the spine. Obviously, all three muscle groups are important to challenge; one is not more important when compared to another.

4. Maintain awareness of neutral posture throughout the day and during exercise.

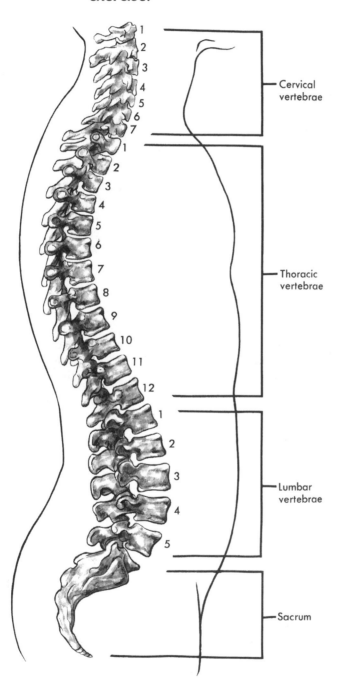

Cervical vertebrae

Thoracic vertebrae

Lumbar vertebrae

Sacrum

Fig. E, Vertebral column exhibiting the normal curvatures inherent to a healthy and properly aligned spine

Neutral posture, can simply be defined as avoiding the extremes of sustained spinal flexion (rounded spine) or extension (arched spine), or positioning the spinal column and pelvis in a manner that reflects a mid-position between the extremes of these two joint actions. A total approach to abdominal and back strengthening, and back wellness, teaches the concept of neutral posture, which follows in the next section. Avoiding the extremes of sustained flexion and extension should be taught for both the cervical (neck) and low back (lumbar) areas of the spine.

Key Point

A complete trunk conditioning program not only strengthens and stretches key muscles of the spine, but teaches the concept of neutral posture. Neutral posture helps to conserve the integrity of spinal discs, ligaments and joints. Awareness of neural posture encourages a return to, or maintenance of, spinal alignment during daily tasks or sport movement.

NEUTRAL SPINAL POSTURE

Neutral spinal posture can, in a simplified manner, be defined as an absence of tension in the neck (cervical spine) or low back (lumbar spine). The strongest position of the spine and the position least likely to contribute to increased risk of injury or chronic degenerative spinal disease is represented by neutral posture. Neutral spinal posture refers to the

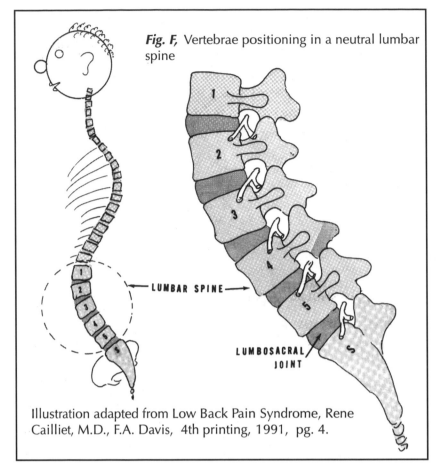

Fig. F, Vertebrae positioning in a neutral lumbar spine

LUMBAR SPINE

LUMBOSACRAL JOINT

Illustration adapted from Low Back Pain Syndrome, Rene Cailliet, M.D., F.A. Davis, 4th printing, 1991, pg. 4.

maintenance of normal spinal curves that are inherent to a healthy, strong and properly aligned spine. *See fig. E*

Neutral spinal posture involves maintaining good alignment of the body. When performing any exercise, sport movement or daily task — whether seated, prone, supine or sidelying — proper alignment in the cervical, thoracic and lumbar regions should be considered. Decisions need to be made with regard to whether or not neutral spinal posture should be maintained (i.e., during a dynamic sporting activity or when performing trunk stability exercises), or if intentionally, the exerciser should choose to "go out" of neutral (i.e., performing trunk flexion which is typically referred to as a trunk curl or crunch).

It is critical to physical movement and back-health to have mastered the skill of freely and intentionally moving from and returning to neutral spinal posture, as well as maintaining spinal neutral throughout an exercise or movement when appropriate.

Neutral spinal posture is best illustrated by the maintenance of the cervical, thoracic and lumbar curves. (*See fig. F*) It is important to observe the natural spinal curves and that the vertebrae are not stacked vertically upon one another. Yet, you can see through the preservation of the desired or normal curvatures of the spine, that this positioning protects the integrity of the spinal ligaments, joints and intervertebral discs. When the spine is neutral, the weight of the spine, gravity and other forces are equally distributed across the weight bearing surface of the discs and spinal joints, and are less likely to stress the functional units (the dynamic joints and supportive soft tissue structures) of the spine. Neutral posture minimizes compressive, sheer and rotary torque forces.

NEUTRAL POSTURE OF THE LUMBAR SPINE

There is not a widely accepted definition of "neutral lumbar posture" in reference to what is healthy, or "acceptable" versus "unacceptable." It would be inappropriate to categorize this posture reference as such because there are a wide range of pelvic/spinal positions that avoid the extremes of spinal flexion and extension that could be termed, or in fact represent, healthy or functional "neutral." Additionally, because a client possessed a "perfect" representation of anatomical neutral, does not mean the person would never experience back pain or be at no-risk for spinal degeneration or injury.

However, since the majority of clients will fall into line with statistical likelihood, it still makes good sense from an anatomical/injury perspective to understand and strive for an improved neutral posture. Neutral posture can be described as a mid-position between the two extremes of maximum anterior tilt (arched back) and maximum posterior tilt (flat back). In addition, it is critical to remember that every client has a given posture that is "normal" for her. The key is to identify the amount, if any, of normal lumbar spinal curvature. This identification procedure gives you a starting point for exercises, and an awareness of the position your client should return to after each repetition of an exercise, sustain through an exercise, or attempt to maintain throughout the day. The trainer should be able to determine a reference point for an "individual neutral" that is based on the client's current level of trunk strength, flexibility and ability to position the pelvis and spine. It is from this personal starting point that a client can choose to sustain, move away from neutral and/or return to this starting posture or neutral reference point. Neutral posture can change as strength and flexibility of key spinal muscles increase, or as the flexibility of key postural muscles (i.e., hamstrings and hip flexors) is improved, and as the client becomes more skillful in her ability to sense and attain neutral positioning.

IDENTIFYING NEUTRAL LUMBAR POSTURE

In order to work with each individual's unique physical traits, it is helpful to teach the client how to identify her unique neutral or natural lumbar spinal position.

The Wall Method

One of the easiest ways to identify "neutral" posture in the lumbar region is to stand with the heels close to or touching a wall. The protrusion of the buttocks and shoulder blades (scapulae) should lightly touch the wall. Attempt to slide one hand, palm facing the wall, between the small of the back and the wall surface (*See fig. 21a*). Many clients who have self-administered this evaluation find there is no space. Some find that two or three fingers may fit in nicely. Others, with significant lordosis, report that they can "drive a truck" through the existing space!

Regardless of curvature, as measured by how the hand or fingers fit into the lumbar space, this becomes the client's reference point for returning to "her" neutral. It should be noted that external observance by a fitness professional should be just that, an observance. Diagnostic tools provided by a medical professional should be suggested if excessive curvature or lack of curvature give cause for concern. There is no "perfect" amount of curvature, nor is it within the scope-of-practice of most personal trainers to try and attempt to ascertain whether a specific spinal curvature is desired, or represents an unhealthy situation.

The Rock 'n Roll Method

Another method that can be used to identify neutral posture is to slowly rotate the pelvis into an anterior tilt (arching the low back) and then slowly rotate the pelvis

Fig. 21a, Wall Method for Determining Neutral Lumbar Posture

into a posterior tilt (flattening the low back). Find a neutral point that represents a position between the two extremes. *(See fig. 21b & 21c)* This method can effectively be used by placing the client in a hands and knees position on the floor, a standing position with a slight bend in the knees against a wall, or by positioning the client in a seated position on a stability ball.

NEUTRAL POSTURE OF THE PELVIS

For many clients and patients the idea of lumbar and pelvic neutral can be clarified by characterizing the pelvic bowl as a bucket full of water. Neutral pelvic position is represented by a full bucket of water that keeps its content intact. An anterior pelvic tilt (arched back) is represented by water spilling over the front edge of the pelvis or front brim of the bucket. A posterior

Fig. 21b and c, Rock 'n Roll Method for Determining Neutral Lumbar Posture

pelvic tilt (flat back or spinal flexion) would be represented by water being splashed over the back edge of the pelvis or bucket.

NEUTRAL POSTURE OF THE CERVICAL SPINE

The major area of focus and concern during activity tends to be the lumbar spine. However, of equal concern is the cervical spine (neck). Neutral position of the cervical spine occurs when the head is comfortably balanced and the natural existing curvature of the cervical spine is maintained. There should be a minimum of muscle activity and stress in the neck. Generally, the head is neither forward nor back, or tilted to either side of the body, and the chin is level or parallel to the ground.

If you have questions or concerns about your client's spinal curvature, consult with a licensed and appropriately trained health care professional. If indicated, there are strengthening and stretching exercises that may help a person with poor back or neck posture attain a more neutral and healthy position of the spine. In some extreme cases, the proper care may be temporarily out of your domain. Generally, if this is the case, you will become part of a team approach that meets the physical and medical needs of the client.

TRUNK FLEXION AND EXTENSION

Early anatomy books illustrate that both excessive arching and/or rounding of the back result in disproportionate and unequal stress on the discs located between the vertebrae. Over time such stress could result in herniated discs, and resultant swelling, nerve root irritation or impingement, and/or degeneration of the vertebrae. Sustaining a misalignment like this during dynamic movement or throughout the day (sitting with a rounded back), may cause irreparable and cumulative damage that can lead to pain, injury and a loss of mobility in the low back region.

Vertebral or spinal flexion is characterized by compression to the anterior aspect of the disc. Spinal flexion occurs when performing traditional ab and back "curls" where the rib is drawn toward the pelvis, or vice-versa, or when a client sits with a rounded low back at her desk. Posterior ligaments, the muscle sheath, and other soft tissue limit excessive flexion. (*See fig. G*) Spinal extension is restricted by mechanical impact of the facet joints and by the anterior longitudinal ligament. (*See fig. H*)

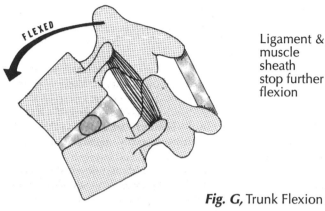

Ligament & muscle sheath stop further flexion

Fig. G, Trunk Flexion

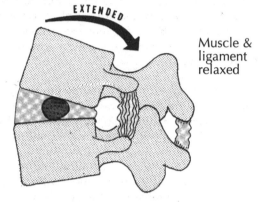

Muscle & ligament relaxed

Fig. H, Trunk Extension

Illustrations adapted from Low Back Pain Syndrome, Rene Cailliet, M.D., F.A. Davis, 4th printing, 1991, pg. 90.

When neutral alignment of the lumbar spine is maintained, the forces on the discs between the vertebrae are greatly reduced, as well as stretch forces to stabilizing spinal ligaments. Neutral posture more evenly spreads compression, sheer or torque forces over the load bearing surfaces of the intervertebral discs. This helps avoid a concentration of high stress forces in small areas of the discs.

NEUTRAL POSTURE APPLICATION

In an extensive review, Plowman (1992) highlights the importance of neutral spinal posture in the lumbar region. Greater posterior tilt (toward flat back position) increases low back muscle and ligament tension and, as a result, compression on the spine. It is reasonable to conclude that a sustained flat back position inherits many of the same risks that a sustained and excessively arched back does. Specifically, the ligaments, muscles, fascia and discs that make up the spinal column are put at risk for chronic, degenerative processes to occur.

To command a client to flatten her low back (excessive posterior pelvic tilt or trunk flexion) is not a protective position, nor does it represent the strongest, least stressful, most stable position of the spine. Consider this fact, and the implications, if a client is encouraged to sustain a flat back during exercises commonly referred to as crunches or ab curls. Instead, the participant should return to neutral, or allow the slight curvature of the spine that represents starting neutral lumbar posture to recur between each repetition, or at least after several. There is no need to sustain a flexed spinal position for an entire set of repetitions. Besides limiting range-of-motion by 10-degrees, it imparts unnecessary stress to the spine.

Additionally, encouraging a client to flatten her low back during a bench press or incline press overhead may be putting that client at risk for back stress. Better instruction and direction would be to tell the client to position the spine in neutral.

An excessively arched back (anterior pelvic tilt) is the mirror image of the extremely flexed or flattened low back. For years fitness professionals have knowingly encouraged clients and group exercise participants to avoid an arched lower back, or forced hyperextension of the spine. (Note: Moving into active hyperextension of the lumbar spine is often desirable, if the range of motion is not excessive or performed in a ballistic manner.) But unwittingly, it seems that over the years, in an attempt to avoid arching the low back, an over-correction of sorts has resulted. A flat back position that is instituted in hopes of lessening the occurrence of forced hyperextension has gone too far, and while avoiding spinal stress associated with ballistic hyperextension, has created the mirror image stress on the opposite side of the spine and disc. The solution of course is not over-correction, but a directive that employs the clients to set-up neutral spinal posture, which avoids the extremes of both excessive spinal flexion and extension.

It must be emphasized that the back was meant to flatten as well as arch, and was meant to laterally flex and rotate. Keep in mind that your client cannot perform effective, full range mover (or isolation) type abdominal or back work without flexing or extending the spine.

Key Point

Whether your client is sitting at a desk, driving her car, riding a stationary bike or walking, she should ideally strive to preserve neutral spinal posture throughout the entire day.

Flexion and extension are well tolerated by the spine and its associated soft tissues, including the spinal discs. In fact, this type of movement is necessary, for example, to achieve disc nutrition. Dynamic movement would not be possible if the spine did not tolerate this type of movement. However, excessive and uncontrolled (ballistic) movement of the spine, as well as rotation that is combined with a poorly aligned spine, can be detrimental. Remember that the devastating nature of back pain is not associated with a "lightening strike." Instead, a habit we might characterize as seemingly innocuous, such as sustaining poor seated posture over long periods of time, is a leading contributor to low back pain and discomfort.

POSTURE AND LOW BACK PAIN

Back pain is among the most common medical complaints, second only to the common cold (Shiple, Treating Low-Back Pain, Physician and Sportsmedicine, Vol. 25, No. 8, August, 1997). An estimated 80 percent of the population suffers at least one episode in their lifetime, and in as many as 50 percent of cases, the problem will recur within the following 3 years (Shiple, 1997). In many cases the pain will be self-limiting and disappear as mysteriously as it appeared. However, experiencing recurring back pain is not only unfortunate, but can deal devastating blows to physical well-being and independence, as well as financial outlook and emotional status. It's wise to avoid the back-pain-nightmare-scenario.

What Causes Back Pain?

The "big event" that is often associated with a back "going out," or being injured, usually has little to do with being the underlying reason the individual now has a back problem. The incident that seems to have caused the trauma to the back — slipping and catching one's balance, changing a tire, reaching for a child or working out — is rarely the real culprit. Any number of events can trigger an event that finally uses up the "safety margin" and pushes that area of the body — the back in this example — over the brink. In reality, the recent activity that is often reported with the onset of back strain or pain and is thought to have caused the aggravation has little to do with what really placed the spine in a position to be vulnerable to injury. Usually, years of "small" abuses to the body in the form of poor posture, failure to maintain adequate strength and flexibility in key postural muscles, and utilization of poor movement/exercise mechanics signals an invitation to back trouble. It is this scenario that commonly represents the "cause" of back pain syndrome.

Key Point

Back pain and injury usually result from an accumulation of trauma over time. Doing little things wrong over long periods of time can lead to the straw that literally "breaks" the back.

It would certainly be far more exciting after "blowing out your back" to explain in great detail and with much enthusiasm how you had gotten "big air" off a cliff while skiing and had trouble landing the jump. Your admiring audience might shake their heads in disbelief and awe, knowing "that kind of injury comes with the risk of performing such a feat." They leave, still considering you to be the hero they have always ascertained you were. Or, consider the alternative, which more closely defines how and why most backs are injured. "So, how did your back 'go out'?" "Oh, I sat with poor posture for years, never stretched and allowed my "power center" to become weak as a blob of jelly!" With a definite lack of awe, your audience, heads shaking in disbelief, sadly leaves the room.

TRUNK SPINAL ANATOMY

The spine, pelvis, sternum and ribs represent the skeletal foundation of the body's trunk. The vertebral column is a complex structure with many supporting ligaments, vertebrae, joints, intervertebral discs, fascia and musculature playing supporting roles in maintaining posture, allowing for dynamic movement, and protecting the spinal cord.

Quick Index:

Intervertebral Discs

Cartilaginous intervertebral discs are located between the vertebrae and are ringed with a tough, fibrous outer material called the annulus fibrosus and are filled with a thick, soft jelly-like material called the nucleus pulposus. When talking to my clients, I compare discs to being somewhat like a donut filled with jelly. In part, a healthy trunk is dependent on keeping the jelly from oozing out of the donut's casing (i.e., a ruptured disc). A ruptured disc can initiate a cascade of events that are detrimental to the low back and include chronic degenerative back disease and inflammation or impingement of nerves, all of which can lead a person into the frightening arena termed "back pain syndrome."

In the following illustration, "disc man" or the nucleus gel within the disc creates an outward pressure that demonstrates the relationship between the outer fibrous covering (annulus fibrosus) and inner jelly-like material (nucleus pulposus). (*See fig. I*) This internal pressure or equilibrium exists in an intact and healthy disc. The nucleus pulposus or thick gel creates an intrinsic pressure that keeps the disc from falling in on itself and helps to prevent vertebrae degeneration and related back pain from a spinal column that is literally, collapsing if back health is less than optimal.

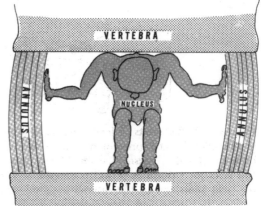

Fig. I, "Disc Man" demonstrates how the nucleus gel creates an outward pressure on the disc. (Illustration adapted from Low Back Pain Syndrome, Rene Cailliet, M.D., F.A. Davis, 4th printing, 1991, pg. 9)

MOVEMENT AND IMBIBITION (DISC NUTRITION) IN THE SPINE

Intervertebral discs can be compressed, which results in movement such as flexion, extension, lateral flexion and rotation of the spine. Additionally, the disc's ability to compress not only accounts for spinal movement, but also positions the disc to intercede and act as the spine's "shock absorber."

Disc Nutrition. Compression of the discs also allows for disc nutrition to occur through a process called "imbibition." In early human development discs are nourished by a direct blood supply. Upon maturation the epiphysis of the vertebral endplate closes. The blood vessels that once fed the discs disappear and the intervertebral disc becomes ischemic due to the reduced blood flow. From this point on, disc nutrition is accomplished by osmosis and imbibition (Cailliet, 1991). Imbibition, which is a key factor in disc nutrition, does not occur to a great extent unless an alternating compression and relaxation of the disc occurs. The sponge-like imbibition, which is represented by the physical compression and release of the disc during spinal movement (i.e., spinal flexion, extension and lateral flexion), ensures the entry of nutrient loaded fluid into the liquid nucleus of the disc.

Disc Health. Another image I paint for my clients that is simple, but helps the client understand the importance of disc health, is having the client think of the disc as the image of a fully hydrated grape. I have them envision biting into the grape, hearing the crunch and feeling the rush of juices into their mouths. A raisin represents an unhealthy disc, which is the dehydrated sibling of the grape. It is dark in color, wrinkled, small in size and offers little liquid when consumed. It is from this starting point or "working analogy" that the client and I begin a discussion as to the importance of disc and spinal health. We talk about neutral posture and its impact on the spine and reemphasize trunk exercise from a healthy back perspective. So whether you go with the donut filled with jelly analogy, a hydrated grape or the more technical characterization of annulus fibrosus or nucleus pulpolsus, it is apparent to the client that the health of the disc and spine are dependent on good posture and sound exercise mechanics.

THE ABDOMINAL MUSCULATURE

When I lead a discussion on ab and back training I usually start with an overview of trunk anatomy (discs, ligaments, and the mechanics of spinal flexion, extension and rotation) and then turn my discussion to the rectus abdominis. There is more confusion, inaccuracies and myths associated with the rectus abdominis and in general, the abdominal area, than with almost any other region of the body.

The Rectus Abdominis

The insertion of the rectus abdominis (rectus means straight) runs from the cartilage of the fifth, sixth, seventh ribs and the xiphoid process, and originates from the base of the pelvis at the crest of the pubis (*See fig. J*). Based on muscle attachment and fiber direction, it is obvious that the rectus abdominis is capable of flexing and laterally flexing the spine or trunk (Thompson, 1989).

Simply, the ribs can be pulled toward the top of the pelvis (i.e., abdominal curl or trunk flexion) and the pelvis can be pulled toward the bottom of the ribs (i.e., reverse abdominal curl, posterior pelvic tilt or trunk

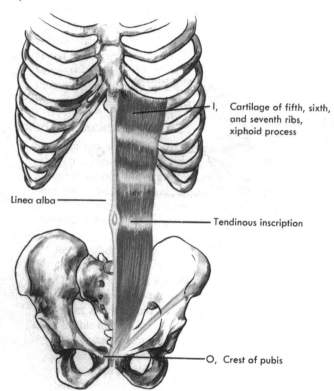

I, Cartilage of fifth, sixth, and seventh ribs, xiphoid process

Linea alba

Tendinous inscription

O, Crest of pubis

Fig. J, Rectus Abdominis Muscle

flexion). The lumbar spine is capable of about 45 degrees of trunk flexion. Five lumbar vertebrae allow for approximately 9 degrees of movement between each vertebrae, which accounts for available motion at the spine (Cailliet, 1991). The rib-to-pelvis curl or crunch accounts for about 30 to 35 degrees of movement, while the pelvis-to-rib reverse curl accounts for the other 9 or 10 degrees. Both movements are small and precise, and both are termed trunk flexion. When the movements are combined, around 45 degrees of trunk flexion is attainable.

Quick Index:

Chapter 6, Examples of these and other trunk exercises

Tendinous Inscriptions

The rectus abdominis muscle is literally, divided into sections by a vertical tendinous inscription called the linea alba, and by horizontal tendinous inscriptions. These inscriptions are very apparent in the abdominal area of a person who is sufficiently lean, and often appear to divide the musculature into a resemblance that is commonly referred to as "6-packs," "speed bumps" or "wash-board abs." The process of attaining this look is commonly called getting "cut," "sliced" or "ripped." It should be noted that the depth and width of the tendinous inscriptions are genetically determined. No amount of "specialized" ab training or performing endless repetitions can deepen or increase their width. This predetermined genetic factor — width and depth of the tendinous descriptions — explains why some people who are very lean do not exhibit marked "separation" between the abdominal sections, and never will. How do you get washboard abs? Lose subcutaneous body fat by expending more calories than you take in, hope the fat is used from the abdominal area, and choose your parents well.

Upper And Lower Abdominal Emphasis

Is there an upper and lower abdominal muscle? To remain technically correct you have to answer "No." But, you also have to be able to explain why some abdominal exercises (i.e., traditional curl or crunch) are felt in the upper region of this one long muscle, the rectus abdominis, and why others (the reverse curl, crunch or hip lift) are felt more in the lower region. A clearer answer might be, "Yes, it is possible to emphasize the upper or lower region of the rectus abdominis." This represents a more professional and accurate character-ization of the muscle, versus calling it upper and lower abs.

To emphatically tell someone there is no such "thing" as an upper and lower abdominal muscle, and to leave it at that, does not lead to understanding. An interesting characteristic of the rectus abdominis muscle is that it is stimulated or activated by nerves (motor neuron) like any other muscle, via what is termed segmental nerve innervation. Various "sections" (i.e., as divided by the tendinous inscriptions) receive separate nerve innervation that activate the motor units (groups of muscle fibers) in various regions of the rectus abdominis muscle. What segmental innervation reveals is that different parts or regions of the rectus abdominis can be more or less active dependent on the exercise being performed, the position of the exerciser and the load being worked against. Note the word choice. I did not say that the upper ab can be activated, while the lower is dormant, and vice-versa. What I did say, was that the entire rectus abdominis muscle is active for a given abdominal exer-cise, but the upper or lower regions, for example, can be more or less active, depending on a number of factors.

Key Point

The upper, middle and lower sections of the rectus abdominis do not turn on and off like a light switch. Envision their activation more like the effect a dimmer switch would have on a light bulb. Depending on the movement, body position and load, different regions of the rectus abdominis will shine (activate) more or less brightly. Low level illumination (muscle activation) is always present in the entire muscle (the light bulb).

Application

Segmental nerve innervation explains why someone "feels" a basic ab curl in the upper region of the rectus abdominis and "feels" a reverse curl in the lower region of the rectus abdominis. You can't tell someone it's one long muscle, there's no such thing as an upper and lower ab and insist that they don't feel something they do indeed feel! Segmental nerve innervation helps the client understand what they are feeling, and why. When someone wants to target the lower region because they believe they can spot reduce the area and they want an exercise they can "feel" targeting that area, you can explain that although it is possible to "spot tone" or strengthen any specific area of the body, it is impossible to "spot reduce." Furthermore, you can tell them "why" they should really want to work the lower region of the rectus abdominis, or for that matter the trunk.

Why Train The Abdominal Muscles?

Understanding these abdominal facts can lead to a more accurate and effective approach to training the abdominal region. As mentioned, numerous requests are made for "lower ab" exercises because the exerciser wants to feel the exercise where the fat is deposited in the hopes of spot reducing this area of the body that often represents a "fat collection zone." In reality, fat is lost in a predetermined order that cannot be impacted by training, and is largely dependent on genetics and creating a negative calorie balance. While spot reduction is not possible, and the motivation to lose fat from a specific area of the body is off base, it is important to isolate the muscles in the lower abdominal region with exercise. This musculature is critical to counter the pull of the hip flexors and for positioning the pelvis — via a partial posterior pelvic tilt — into neutral position.

Key Point

The lower abdominal region is important for controlling the degree of arch or excessive lumbar lordosis.

It would be blissful if the average person on the street was excited to train the abdominal muscles for the reasons of reducing her chances of low back pain and improving her posture. A reality check suggests otherwise and indicates that the average person's motivation to train the midsection exists for superficial reasons – how they look! Many consumers are driven by misconceptions that include spot reduction or targeting fat deposit areas. There is a rich opportunity to get clients back on track with regard to how and why they must continue to train the abdominal and back musculature. The end result of looking better will be realized if the trunk is trained with an intent to:

1. Prevent or reduce lower back pain.
2. Gain an understanding of neutral lumbar posture.
3. Use a variety of exercises to strike a balance between training the abdominal muscles as "movers" that target the upper and lower regions of the rectus abdominis, as well as training the abdominal muscles as stabilizers.

Quick Index:

6

TRUNK EXERCISES

A variety of movements and types of training must be used to ensure total development of the trunk region. Core movements should be trained in isolation (mover-type activity that includes spinal flexion, extension, lateral flexion and rotation), as well as using functional exercises that require the trunk muscles to synchronize their activation. Functional or stabilization training of the abdominal region represents synergistic movement that demands an integrated, interdependent response of the trunk — muscles working together to stabilize spinal position.

BALANCED APPROACH TO CORE CONDITIONING

Functional training of the abdominal and back muscles involves training them in a manner in which they are required to work on a daily basis. The key function of the abdominal and back musculature is not to create movement at the spine, but to exert isometric or stabilizing muscular force production in order to maintain spinal and pelvic position. (Note: These comments are not intended to infer that mover-type or isolation trunk exercises are poor choices. The intention is to recognize that stabilization training is different than active-isolation exercise which utilizes movement at the spine, and that both should be used to optimally develop and challenge the trunk.)

> ### Quick Index:
> *Chapter 5, Understanding the trunk and neutral spinal posture*

TRUNK STABILIZATION EXERCISES

PRONE OPPOSITE ARM AND LEG RAISE

Body Parts Targeted: Lower back (stabilization); front of the shoulder; posterior hip
Joint Motion(s): Shoulder flexion; hip extension
Primary Muscles Strengthened: Spinal extensors (stabilizers); anterior and medial deltoid; gluteus maximus and hamstrings
Setup and Alignment: Lie prone on the floor or a mat. Extend one or both arms overhead. Keep the legs straight and about hip width apart. Rest the forehead on a folded towel, an arm, or turn the head to one side. *See fig. 22a*
Performing the Exercise: With control, raise one arm and the opposite leg. Keep the head in contact with the pad, arm or towel, and press the hips firmly into the ground by slightly contracting the abdominals. Maintain neutral lumbar spinal position throughout the

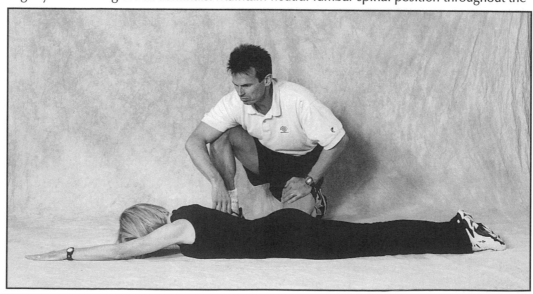

Fig. 22a

exercise. Continue to raise the arm and leg, and focus on reaching out, rather than up. Pause at the top of the contraction, and then slowly lower back down to the starting position. Repeat this exercise by alternating sides after each repetition, or by performing multiple repetitions on each side. See *fig. 22b*

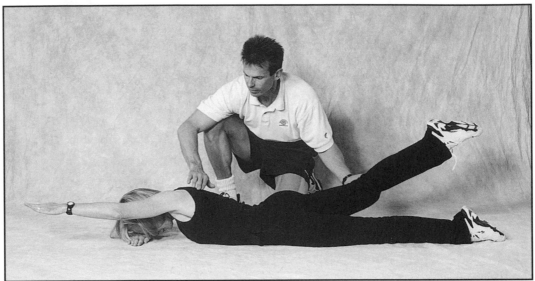

Fig. 22b

Comments: The prone opposite arm and leg raise provides an excellent way to strengthen the spinal extensors (i.e., erector spinae) as stabilizers, without creating movement at the spine. The muscular challenge of this exercise is the isometric contraction of the spinal extensors as stabilizers, and not the muscles that flex the shoulder and extend the hip. Training the spinal extensors as stabilizers has great carry over to daily activity and sport.

Safety Considerations: Do not allow the chest, hips or head to lift. Keep the hips and shoulders square to the floor. Avoid rotating, twisting or rolling the body. Maintain neutral lumbar posture by concentrating on lengthening the body, rather than extending the spine, and by keeping tension in the abdominal muscles.

Exercise Variations: This exercise is referred to by many names and can be performed with a variety of equipment and in different body positions. The opposite arm and leg raise can be performed with the trunk elevated on a pad or adjustable step platform, which allows the arms and legs to start in a lower position, thereby increasing range-of-motion. Moving to a hands and knee position or utilizing a stability ball can accomplish the same purpose and make the activity more challenging by adding the component of balance.

STABILITY BALL OPPOSITE ARM AND LEG RAISE

Body Parts Targeted: Lower back (stabilization); front of the shoulder; posterior hip
Joint Motion(s): Shoulder flexion; hip extension
Primary Muscles Strengthened: Spinal extensors (stabilizers); anterior and medial deltoid; gluteus maximus; hamstrings
Setup and Alignment: Begin in a prone position with the ball supporting your trunk. Both your hands and feet are in contact with the floor. The shoulders should be aligned over the wrists, and the feet placed about hip width apart. Center the ball under the pelvis, with the lumbar and cervical spine in neutral posture. *See fig. 23a*

Performing the Exercise: Slowly and simultaneously, raise one arm and the opposite leg to about hip and shoulder height. Maintain neutral lumbar spinal posture by slightly contracting the abdominal muscles. Avoid lifting the head in order to preserve a neutral cervical spine. Focus on lengthening the arm and leg away from the core of the body, rather than emphasizing height. Do not rotate your hips or shoulders. Pause at the top of the contraction, and then slowly lower down to the starting position. Repeat this exercise by alternating sides after each repetition, or by performing multiple repetitions on each side. *See fig. 23b*

Comments: With the use of a stability ball, the opposite arm and leg raise becomes a significant balance challenge for any level of fitness. When performed on the floor, this exercise can eventually lose its ability to challenge and overload as a client progresses. The ball adds a whole new dimension for less conditioned and highly fit clients. Training the trunk, shoulder girdle and hip areas as stabilizers can have a great carry over to daily activity and sport.

Safety Considerations: Avoid hyperextending the cervical spine by keeping the head still and positioned in neutral during the movement. Perform the exercise slowly and with control. Adjust the width of the legs and arms slightly to facilitate balance, but do not compromise correct alignment.

Fig. 23a

Fig. 23b

STABILITY BALL SIMULTANEOUS LEG AND ARM RAISE

Body Parts Targeted: Lower back (stabilization); front of the shoulders; posterior hip
Joint Motion(s): Shoulder flexion; hip extension
Primary Muscles Strengthened: Spinal extensors (stabilizers); anterior and medial deltoids; gluteus maximus; hamstrings

Setup and Alignment: Begin in a prone position with the ball supporting your trunk. Both your hands and feet are in contact with the floor. The shoulders should be aligned over the wrists, and the feet placed about hip width apart. Center the ball under the pelvis, with the lumbar and cervical spine in neutral posture. Then, slowly raise both legs until they are at about hip height. *See fig. 24a*

Performing the Exercise: Slowly lift your torso, raising both arms until they are parallel to the floor. Maintain neutral spinal posture. Hold and balance in this "Superman" position for as long as you are able. With control, slowly lower to the starting position. The emphasis of this exercise is balance and stabilization, so progressive duration in the position is more desirable than multiple repetitions. *See fig. 24b*

Comments: Sometimes referred to as the "stability ball wobble," this exercise presents a significant physical challenge (and an element of fun!) for most people, as they attempt to hold the position for a number of seconds.

Safety Considerations: Avoid hyperextending the cervical spine by keeping the head still and positioned in neutral during the movement. Perform the exercise slowly and with control, only moving your hands and feet away from the floor when you feel you can control the movement from start- to end-position.

Exercise Variations: This exercise can be taught on the floor, or with the hips padded and elevated slightly. A good progression is to lift just the upper body off the floor, then just the lower body. When upper and lower body control and alignment can be maintained independently, then the simultaneous movement can be attempted.

Fig. 24a

Fig. 24b

PRONE BENT-ELBOW PLANK

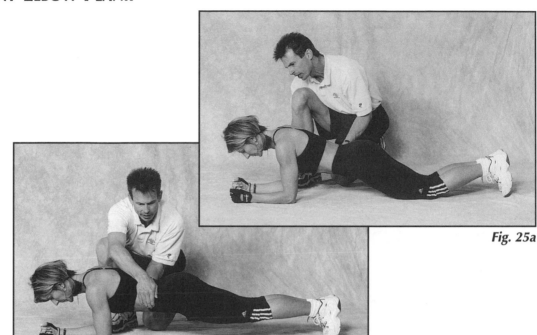

Fig. 25a

Fig. 25b

Body Parts Targeted: Shoulders; abdominals; hips; legs

Joint Motion(s): Stabilization at the shoulders, trunk, hips, knees and ankles (no movement at the joint)

Primary Muscles Strengthened: Posterior and medial deltoids; rectus abdominis, obliques and transversus abdominis; iliopsoas and iliacus; quadriceps (all as stabilizers)

Setup and Alignment: Kneel on "all fours" with your hands and knees about shoulder and hip width apart, and your neck in line with your spine. Lower your elbows to the floor, while maintaining neutral lumbar posture. *See fig. 25a*

Performing the Exercise: Straighten your legs one at a time behind you, until you are balancing on your forearms and the balls of your feet. Contract your abdominals slightly and hold your body in a straight line — as if you were a plank. Continue breathing and hold this position for a number of seconds. If it is too difficult to hold the straight-body plank for more than a few seconds at first, simply bend your knees until they touch the floor and lift the knees again, when ready. *See fig. 25b*

Comments: The plank is a good exercise to get the entire body working as a dynamic, integrated unit. If one part of your body feels weak, this could represent the "weak link" in the chain, and you may need to focus an extra measure of concentration on those muscles, or train them in isolation, to complement stabilization training.

Safety Considerations: Keep your body in a straight line. Don't let your head drop or your lower back sag. Maintain neutral lumbar and cervical spinal posture and keep breathing as you hold the straight-body plank position.

Exercise Variations: You can progress to the straight-body plank by first performing a bent leg variation. Start on your hands and knees, and lower your elbows to the floor, as above. Begin with your hips over your knees. Slowly inch the hands, elbows and hips forward. Eventually, you can progress to a straight-body position with knee support.

STABILITY BALL GLIDING PLANK

Body Parts Targeted: Shoulders; back of the upper arms; trunk

Joint Motion(s): Shoulder flexion and extension; hip flexion and extension

Primary Muscles Strengthened: Primary *movers*: Latissimus dorsi; posterior deltoids; long head of the triceps; pectoralis major. Primary *stabilizers*: Cervical spinal extensors; posterior and medial deltoids; rectus abdominis, obliques and transversus abdominis; iliopsoas, iliacus and rectus femoris; and quadriceps

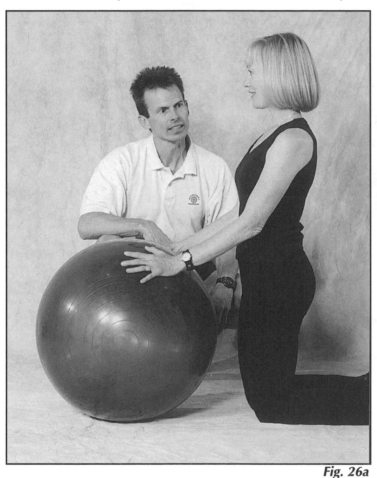

Fig. 26a

Setup and Alignment: Begin in a kneeling position on the floor with your knees placed about hip width apart. Set the ball in front of your thighs with your hands resting on top of the ball about shoulder width apart. *See fig. 26a*

Performing the Exercise: There are three levels of difficulty in this progression.

Level I: Flex your shoulders and hips, pushing the ball away from your body, until the forearms are supported on the ball. Your hips should flex about 90 degrees and stay aligned over your knees. Pause at the end of this movement, contracting the abdominals for stabilization. Then, keeping the elbows as straight as possible, slowly extend the shoulders and roll the ball back into the starting position. *See fig. 26b*

Level II: Flex the shoulders, rolling the ball forward as in Level I. Continue to extend the hips as far as possible, while still maintaining neutral lumbar posture. You should eventually attain a straight line between the knees and shoulders, with no hip flexion. Keeping the body in this straight line, contract the abdominals and extend the shoulders to roll back into the starting position. *See fig. 26c*

Level III: When the straight body position in Level II can be maintained with relative ease, hold the position and extend the knees until you are in a full plank position. Hold this position for any number of seconds and return the knees to the floor with control. Keeping the hips extended, slowly extend the shoulders and roll the ball back into the starting position. Maintain neutral lumbar and cervical spinal posture throughout the movement. *See fig. 26d*

Comments: These exercises should be progressed slowly, as the strength and stabilization in the abdominals, shoulder joint and shoulder girdle adapt to each level. Once you are able to execute the gliding plank movement at any level, add stabilization challenge by holding at the peak of the movement for a few breaths, then return to the starting position.

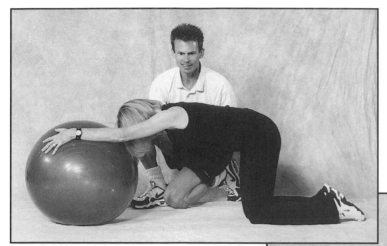

Safety Considerations: Stay within a range-of-motion where you are able to maintain neutral spinal position and proper shoulder alignment.

Exercise Variations: Similar variations of this stability ball exercise can be performed with different pieces of equipment. Examples of equipment that imitate this movement include the Torso Track®, Ab Mouse®, Ab Dolly®, and Wonder Wheel®.

Fig. 26b

Fig. 26c

Fig. 26d

PRONE STRAIGHT-ELBOW PLANK

Body Parts Targeted: Arms; shoulders; chest; legs; trunk

Joint Motion(s): Stabilization at the shoulders, arms, chest and trunk (no movement at the joints)

Primary Muscles Strengthened: Rectus abdominis, obliques and transversus abdominis; posterior and medial deltoids; triceps; iliopsoas and iliacus; quadriceps (all as stabilizers)

Setup and Alignment:

Position yourself on "all fours," with the hips aligned over the knees, and the hands directly under the shoulders. This "box" position should be maintained with neutral spinal posture in both the lumbar and cervical regions. *See fig. 27a*

Performing the Exercise:

There are two levels of difficulty in this progression.

Level I: From the box position, slowly walk your hands forward, letting the hips extend, until a straight line is formed between the knees and shoulders. Hold this position for any number of seconds and return to the box position. *See fig. 27b*

Level II: From the Level I position, tuck your toes under and extend your knees. You should have a straight body position from your heels through the top of your head. Hold this full plank position for any number of seconds, lower to your knees and return to the box position. *See fig. 27c*

Comments:
The goal of this exercise is not to challenge the arm, shoulder and chest muscles as "movers" by lowering the body and pressing it away from the floor. The focus is trunk, upper and lower body stabilization. The challenge of maintaining lumbar neutral becomes increasingly difficult as the body is lengthened at the hip toward a straight body position (Level II).

Safety Considerations:
If neutral posture of the lumbar and cervical spine cannot be sustained for the desired duration, the exercise is too difficult. Be careful not to exceed the endurance capabilities of the upper body, as it is possible that the arms could collapse and cause an unprotected fall — unless spotted at the shoulder and hip — on the face.

Exercise Variations:
The "Prone Bent Elbow Plank" is an easier variation of this exercise, while the "Stability Ball Prone Plank" will add more balance challenge.

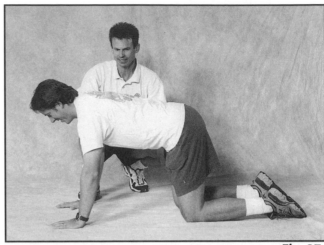

Fig. 27a

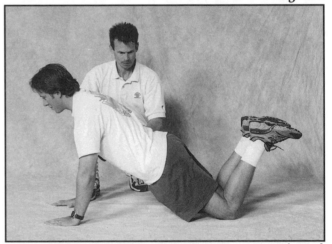

Fig. 27b

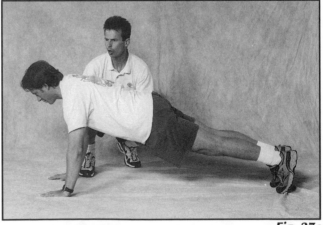

Fig. 27c

STABILITY BALL PRONE PLANK

Body Parts Targeted:
Arms; shoulders; chest; legs; trunk

Joint Motion(s):
Stabilization at the shoulder, arm, chest and trunk (no movement at the joints)

Primary Muscles Strengthened: Rectus abdominis, obliques and transversus abdominis; posterior and medial deltoids; triceps; iliopsoas and iliacus; quadriceps (all as stabilizers)

Setup and Alignment:
Begin in a prone position with the ball supporting your thighs. Keep your shoulders aligned over your wrists and maintain neutral posture of the lumbar and cervical spine. *See fig. 28a*

Fig. 28a

Performing the Exercise: From the set-up position, walk forward until the ball is under your lower legs or ankles. Keep your shoulders aligned over your wrists and maintain neutral posture of the lumbar and cervical spine. Hold this position for any number of seconds, then walk the hands back into the starting position. *See fig. 28b*

Fig. 28b

Comments: The goal of this exercise is not to challenge the arm, shoulder and chest muscles as "movers" by lowering the body and pressing it away from the floor. The focus is trunk, upper and lower body stabilization. As the ball moves down the legs toward the feet, the stability and balance challenge becomes greater.

Safety Considerations: If lumbar neutral posture cannot be sustained for the desired duration, the exercise is too difficult. If you are fatiguing, or feel you could lose control, decrease the intensity of the position by "walking" the ball back toward the hips. Be careful not to exceed the endurance capabilities of the upper body, as it is possible that the arms could collapse, causing an unprotected fall — unless spotted at the shoulder and hip — on the face.

Exercise Variations: Push-ups can be performed while maintaining spinal neutral for added upper body and trunk stability challenge. One leg can be lifted and/or moved outward for additional stability challenges.

SUPINE PLANK

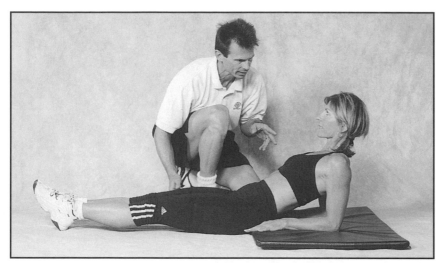

Fig. 29a

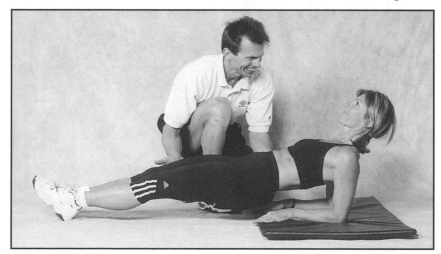

Fig. 29b

Body Parts Targeted: Shoulders; lower back; hips; legs

Joint Motion(s): Hip extension (to attain the plank position); stabilization at the shoulders, trunk, hips, knees and ankles after initial lift (no movement at the joints)

Primary Muscles Strengthened: Primary *movers*: Gluteus maximus; hamstrings (during hip extension to plank position); Primary *stabilizers*: Cervical spinal flexors; posterior and medial deltoids; trapezius and rhomboids; lumbar spinal extensors; gluteus maximus; hamstrings

Setup and Alignment: Begin seated on the floor with your legs extended out in front of you. Walk your hands back until you can rest your elbows on the floor. Your elbows should be directly under your shoulders, and your palms flat on the floor. *See fig. 29a*

Performing the Exercise: Keep your chest lifted slightly by pulling your shoulder blades together (scapular retraction) and lift your hips up and off the floor. The body is balanced between your heels and lower arms. Continue to breathe and hold this plank position for any number of seconds. Progressively increase the duration that you are able to hold the position. *See fig. 29b*

Comments: If it is too difficult initially to lift the hips and hold them up in the plank position, keep the hips on the floor and contract until you just "unweight" the hips slightly. As your strength and endurance increase, continue to lift the body higher toward the fully lifted plank position.

Safety Considerations: Maintain neutral lumbar spinal posture as you hold the plank position. Do not hyperextend the lumbar spine while extending the hips. Retract your scapulae as you hold the position. Keep your neck in line with the rest of your spine at all times (neutral cervical posture). Try not to let the head drop excessively forward or back.

Exercise Variations: For more balance and stabilization challenge, lift one leg up and then abduct it a few degrees to one side. Hold for a few seconds, then change sides.

STABILITY BALL SUPINE DECLINE PLANK

Body Parts Targeted: Hips; legs; trunk

Joint Motion(s): Hip extension (to attain the plank position); stabilization at the shoulder girdle, trunk, hips, legs and ankles after initial lift (no movement at the joints)

Primary Muscles Strengthened: Primary *movers*: Gluteus maximus; hamstrings (during hip extension to plank position); Primary *stabilizers*: Trapezius and rhomboids; lumbar spinal extensors; external obliques; gluteus maximus; hamstrings; ankle flexors and extensors; ankle abductors and adductors

Setup and Alignment: Begin in a supine position on the floor with your legs elevated and heels supported on top of the ball. Rest your hands on the floor near your sides. *See fig. 30a*

Performing the Exercise: Slowly extend your hips, lifting them off the floor until they are fully extended. Continue to breathe and hold this decline plank position for any number of seconds. Progressively increase the duration that you are able to hold the position. *See fig. 30b*

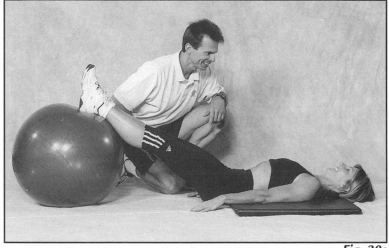

Fig. 30a

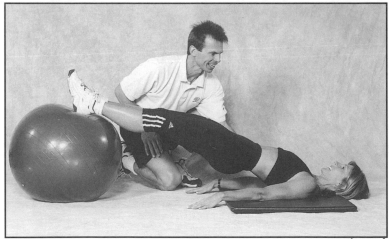

Fig. 30b

Comments: The goal of this exercise is to maintain neutral lumbar spinal posture throughout the exercise, during both the lifting and holding phases. The stability ball adds balance challenge as you attempt to stabilize the ball and keep it from rolling side to side.

Safety Considerations: Your weight should be supported across the shoulder area, not on the back of the head or neck. When learning this exercise, press your arms down against the floor to assist with balance and stabilization. Eventually, progress to a light touch on the floor, or cross the arms over the chest and place your hands on opposite shoulders.

Exercise Variations: After attaining the lifted position and focusing on stabilization, you can choose to target active spinal extension by moving the lumbar spine a few degrees past neutral into hyperextension. Additionally, the decline plank can be performed with any equipment — benches, adjustable step platforms, etc. — that elevate the ankles above hip height. Be certain that the height the feet are elevated (a resistance training bench might be too high for some people) is appropriate, and realize there is less balance challenge when compared to using the stability ball.

STABILITY BALL SUPINE BRIDGE

Body Parts Targeted:
Hips; legs; trunk

Joint Motion(s): Hip extension (to attain the bridge position); stabilization at the shoulder girdle, trunk, hips, legs and ankles after initial lift (no movement at the joints)

Primary Muscles Strengthened: Primary *movers*: gluteus maximus; hamstrings (during hip extension to bridge position); Primary *stabilizers*: Trapezius and rhomboids; lumbar spinal extensors; external obliques; gluteus maximus; hamstrings; ankle flexors and extensors; ankle abductors and adductors

Setup and Alignment:
Begin in a seated position on top of the ball. Keeping the shoulders centered over the ball, slowly walk the feet forward and let the ball roll up the back. Continue "walking" until the ball is supporting the head, neck and shoulders. Stop in this position and adjust the feet until they are hip width apart and aligned directly under the knees. *See fig. 31a*

Fig. 31a

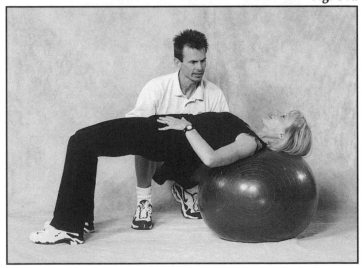

Fig. 31b

Performing the Exercise: Extend the hips, lifting until the trunk and thighs are parallel to the floor. The hands may be placed on the floor to assist with balance, or they maybe placed on the hips or across the chest for more balance challenge. Continue to breathe and hold this bridge position for any number of seconds. Progressively increase the duration that you are able to hold the position. *See fig. 31b*

Comments: The goal of this exercise is to maintain neutral lumbar spinal posture throughout the movement. This exercise places an active stretch on the hip flexors when the bridge position is held.

Safety Considerations: Keep the knees aligned over the heels while walking forward and while holding the bridge position. Be careful not to lean forward during the transition from seated to supine position. If the shoulders are not centered over the ball, there is a danger that the ball could slip out from under the hips and cause a fall. To return to a seated position, flex your trunk slightly and walk your feet backward toward the ball, letting it roll down your back toward your hips, until you are seated upright again.

Exercise Variations: Balance and stabilization can be further challenged in the bridge position by bringing the feet and legs into a narrow stance. Placing the hands on the hips or across the chest, or lifting one leg off the floor will also create balance challenges. This same exercise can also be performed using other equipment. For example, an adjustable step platform or bench can be used to perform the supine bridge. However, it is more difficult to move in and out of the starting position, and there is less stability and balance challenge when compared to the stability ball.

TRUNK EXERCISES

Traditional approaches to training the ab and back muscles have focused on the muscles of the trunk being used in isolation, or as "prime movers." Working the muscles in an isolated or open chain fashion should be differentiated from training the trunk muscles functionally or as stabilizers, though one type of training should not be classified as superior when compared. Instead, they are "different." Trunk flexion, extension, lateral flexion, rotation and circumduction should be challenged with specific, mover-type exercises. Trunk mobility exercises can enhance the general movement capabilities of the pelvis, lumbar spine and hip areas, as well as teach spinal flexion, extension, lateral flexion and circumduction.

ANTERIOR/POSTERIOR PELVIC TILT MOBILITY EXERCISE

Fig. 32a

Body Parts Targeted: Low back and abdominal regions; general mobility and strength for the pelvis, lumbar spine and hip areas

Joint Motion(s): Spinal extension (anterior pelvic tilt); spinal flexion (posterior pelvic tilt)

Primary Muscles Strengthened: Spinal extensors (erector spinae group); rectus abdominis, external obliques

Setup and Alignment: Sit upright on top of the ball with your arms naturally relaxed on your thighs or at the sides of the ball. Set neutral postural alignment in the lumbar and cervical spine, and slightly retract the scapulae. Place your feet flat on the floor, about shoulder width apart, with minimal weight supported by the feet. *See fig. 32a*

Performing the Exercise: Perform an anterior pelvic tilt until your lumbar spine is extended as far as is comfortable. The ball will roll back slightly as you tilt. *See fig. 32b* Hold this position for a few seconds, then slowly return to your starting position, and

Fig. 32b

Fig. 32c

reestablish neutral posture. Then, perform a posterior pelvic tilt until your lumbar spine is flexed as far as is comfortable. The ball will roll forward slightly as you tilt. *See fig. 32c* Hold this position for a few seconds, then slowly return to your starting position and neutral posture. Begin with a small range of motion. Focus on isolating the anterior and posterior tilts, and gradually increase range of motion with control as your flexibility and strength levels allow.

Comments: Mobility exercises should be performed within a range-of-motion (ROM) that is not forced, and should be performed with control. They are designed to increase active ROM as well as strengthen the targeted muscles. Be sure to focus on the targeted muscles and avoid using other muscles to "help." For example, use your abdominal muscles to pull the pelvis under you toward the flexed spine position, rather than your gluteal muscles. A good self-check is to place one hand on the lower region of your abdominal muscles and the other hand on your gluteal muscles. Check to make sure that the gluteals stay relaxed and the abdominals are contracting during the posterior tilt movement.

Safety Considerations: Keep your body balanced and properly aligned in both the starting and ending positions of the tilts. Do not allow the upper body to lean or move forward or backward as the pelvis is tilting. Avoid pushing the head forward or tilting it back. Maintain neutral posture of the cervical spine and thoracic spine throughout this exercise.

Exercise Variations: The following variations will challenge balance and stabilization on most stability ball exercises performed in a seated position:
• Place your feet closer together, with ankles and knees lightly touching
• Place your feet closer together, and lift one foot slightly off the floor

SUPINE TRUNK FLEXION

Body Parts Targeted: Anterior trunk musculature/abdominal area
Joint Motion(s): Trunk flexion
Primary Muscles Strengthened: Rectus abdominis; external obliques
Setup and Alignment: Lie supine on a comfortable surface. Establish neutral lumbar posture or a slight curvature in the low back. Flex the knees to form an angle which approximates 90 degrees. Externally rotate the hips a few degrees to help decrease hip flexor involvement. (It should be noted that the hip flexors can still be used if the feet are held or "fixed," or if too much range-of-motion is attempted.) Arms may be placed at your sides, across the chest or behind your head (press your head back into the hands to avoid pulling on the head). Or, the fists can be placed at the temples, which helps prevent pulling the head or neck out of alignment. Set scapular retraction to reduce the likelihood of protracting the scapula, which can introduce momentum into the movement. *See fig. 33a*

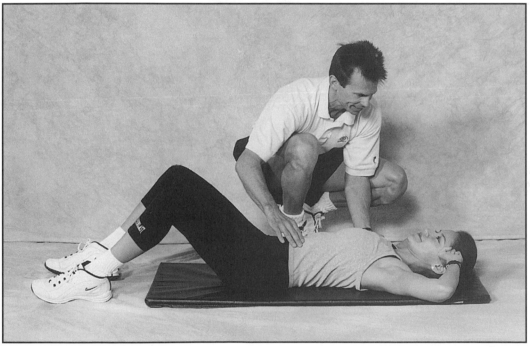

Fig. 33a

Performing the Exercise: Maintain scapular retraction and isometrically contract the abdominals. Then slowly flex the trunk and exhale, pulling the bottom of your ribcage down toward the top of your hip bones. The shoulders and upper back will lift slightly as you contract, while the low back will flatten and press firmly into the padded surface. Keep pulling the ribs toward the pelvis until the abdominals have reached full contraction, or about 30 to 35 degrees of trunk flexion. Return to the start position with control. *See fig. 33b*

Comments: As the hands move from the sides and chest positions, to overhead, the exercise becomes more challenging. At no time is the goal to lift the head and shoulders from the floor, though this may occur. Instead, concentrate on drawing the ribcage down toward the pelvis, shortening the distance from point A (the bottom of the ribcage) to point

B (the top of the pelvis). Movement in the lumbar trunk region occurs between the ribcage and pelvis, and can be monitored with a "self-check" by placing the thumb on the base of the ribs, and the little finger on the top of the same side hip bone. The distance between these two points should become smaller while contracting the abdominal muscles.

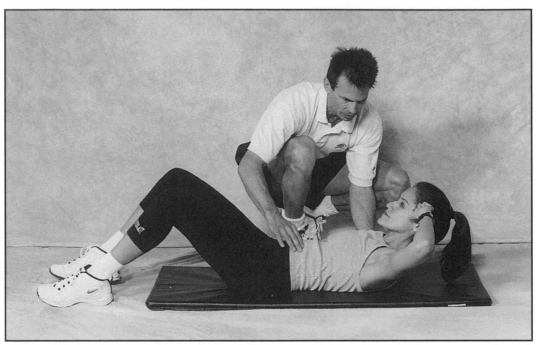

Fig. 33b

Safety Considerations: Do not introduce extra motion of any kind. Trunk strengthening exercises are characterized by relatively small, precise range-of-motion. Shoulder girdle involvement, excessive neck motion, active hip flexion and uncontrolled movement are examples of poor exercise technique which may lead to injury or an end result where the abdominal muscles are not even targeted to any great extent. Work with control, keep tension in the abdominal muscles and maintain proper head/neck alignment throughout the exercise.

Exercise Variations: The simple act of trunk flexion is known by a host of other names and represents dozens of abdominal "crunch" or "curl" variations. These variations encompass simple floor exercises and include the use of sophisticated and pricey equipment. However, the core mechanics, in terms of performing trunk flexion, do not change.

TRUNK FLEXION EXERCISE VARIATIONS

Following are five variations on the basic trunk flexion exercise previously described. The joint motion(s) and primary muscles strengthened are the same. These variations are accomplished with different body positions and equipment.

1. INCLINE TRUNK FLEXION

Setup and Alignment: Lie in an inclined position (head higher than hips) on an adjustable step platform or bench. The surface should be comfortable. Establish neutral lumbar posture or a slight curvature in the low back. Flex the knees to form an angle which approximates 90 degrees. Externally rotate the hips a few degrees to help decrease hip flexor involvement. Arms may be placed at your sides, across the chest, behind your head, or your fists can be placed at the temples. Set scapular retraction to reduce the likelihood of protracting the scapula, which can introduce momentum into the movement. *See fig. 34a*

Performing the Exercise: Maintain scapular retraction and isometrically contract the abdominals. Then slowly flex the trunk and exhale, pulling the bottom of your ribcage down toward the top of your hip bones. The shoulders and upper back will lift slightly as you contract, while the low back will flatten and press firmly into the padded surface. Keep pulling the ribs toward the pelvis until the abdominals have reached full contraction, or about 30 to 35 degrees of trunk flexion. Return to the start position with control. *See fig. 34b*

Comments: Trunk flexion performed on an incline can be termed "gravity assisted"

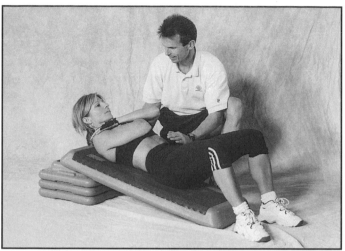

Fig. 34a

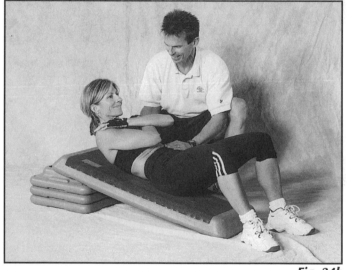

Fig. 34b

and is an easier exercise when compared to flat or decline positions. As the hands move from the sides and chest positions, to behind the head, the exercise becomes more challenging. At no time is the goal to lift the head and shoulders from the inclined surface, though this may occur. Instead, concentrate on drawing the ribcage down toward the pelvis, shortening the distance from point A (the bottom of the ribcage) to point B (the top of the pelvis). Movement in the lumbar trunk region occurs between the ribcage and pelvis, and can be monitored with a "self-check" by placing the thumb on the base of the ribs, and the little finger on the top of the same side hip bone. The distance between these two points should become smaller while contracting the abdominal muscles.

Safety Considerations: Do not introduce extra motion of any kind. Trunk strengthening exercises are characterized by relatively small, precise range-of-motion. Shoulder girdle involvement, excessive neck motion, active hip flexion and uncontrolled movement are examples of poor exercise technique which may lead to injury or an end result where the abdominal muscles are not even targeted to any great extent. Work with control, keep tension in the abdominal muscles and maintain proper head/neck alignment throughout the exercise.

2. DECLINE TRUNK FLEXION

Setup and Alignment: Lie in a declined position (head lower than hips) on an adjustable step platform or bench. The surface should be comfortable. Establish neutral lumbar posture or a slight curvature in the low back. Flex the knees to form an angle which approximates 90 degrees. Feet can be supported or placed on the floor. Externally rotate the hips a few degrees to help decrease hip flexor involvement. Arms may be placed at your sides, across the chest, behind your head, or the fists can be placed at the temples. Set scapular retraction to reduce the likelihood of protracting the scapula, which can introduce momentum into the movement. *See fig. 35a*

Performing the Exercise: Maintain scapular retraction and isometrically contract the abdominals. Then slowly flex the trunk and exhale, pulling the bottom of your ribcage toward the top of your hip bones. The shoulders and upper back will lift slightly as you contract, while the low back will flatten and press firmly into the padded surface. Keep pulling the ribs toward the pelvis until the abdominals have reached full contraction, or about 30 to 35 degrees of trunk flexion. Return to the start position with control. *See fig. 35b*

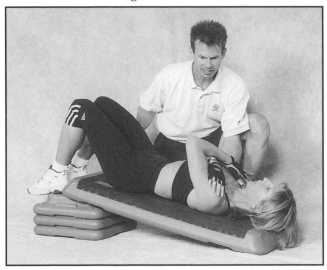

Fig. 35a

Comments: Trunk flexion performed on a decline can be termed "gravity resisted" and is a harder exercise when compared to flat or incline positions. As the hands move from the sides and chest positions, to behind the head, the exercise becomes more challenging. At no time is the goal to lift the head and shoulders from the declined surface, though this may occur. Instead, concentrate on drawing the ribcage down toward the pelvis, shortening the distance from point A (the bottom of the ribcage) to point B (the top of the pelvis). Movement in the lumbar trunk region occurs between the ribcage and pelvis, and can be monitored with a "self-check" by placing the thumb on the base of the ribs, and the little finger on the top of the same side hip bone. The distance between these two points should become smaller while contracting the abdominal muscles.

Safety Considerations: Do not introduce extra motion of any kind. Trunk strengthening exercises are characterized by relatively small, precise range-of-motion. Shoulder girdle involvement, excessive neck motion, active hip flexion and uncontrolled movement are examples of poor exercise technique which may lead to injury or an end result where the abdominal muscles are not even targeted to any great extent. Work with control, keep tension in the abdominal muscles and maintain proper head/neck alignment throughout the exercise.

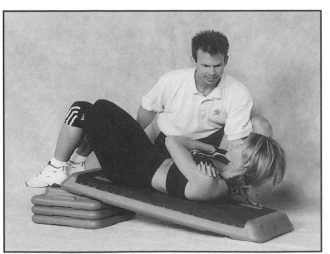

Fig. 35b

3. STABILITY BALL TRUNK FLEXION

Fig. 36a

Fig. 36b

Setup and Alignment: Begin in a supine position with the ball supported under your mid and lower back. Place your hands across the chest, behind your head, or place your fists at your temples. Let your spine extend slightly over the ball. Flex your knees approximately 90 degrees and align them over the ankles. Position the feet about hip width apart, or slightly wider for stability. Set scapular retraction to reduce the likelihood of protracting the scapula, which can introduce momentum into the movement. *See fig. 36a*

Performing the Exercise: Maintain scapular retraction and isometrically contract the abdominals. Then slowly flex the trunk and exhale, pulling the bottom of your ribcage toward the top of your hip bones. The shoulders and upper back will lift slightly as you contract, while the low back will press down into the ball. Keep pulling the ribs toward the pelvis until the abdominals have reached full contraction, or about 30 to 35 degrees of trunk flexion. Return to the start position with control. See *fig. 36b*

Comments: A variety of positions are possible on the ball and can represent gravity neutral, assisted or resisted exercise. How you position the body on the ball determines the resistance. If the head is inclined higher than the hips, the exercise will be easier. Walking your feet back toward the ball, and letting the ball roll down your back toward the lumbar spine, will put your trunk in a position that is more parallel to the floor. Continuing to move the ball down under the hips will decline the head and upper trunk slightly. This progression — moving from incline toward supine or decline — represents easier to more difficult exercise. Performing trunk flexion on a stability ball allows you to start the motion with a slight degree of trunk extension, yet the back is fully supported. This increases the range-of-motion that is resisted and enhances trunk mobility. Since the ball is designed to be an unstable exercise surface, more muscular stabilization is required when compared to a bench or the floor. Controlling this lateral movement puts more demand on the obliques. Moving the feet to narrower positions increases the stability challenge.

Safety Considerations: Avoid excessive hyperextension of the low back by controlling movement in and out of the extended position over the ball. Keep tension on the abdominals throughout the exercise and perform the movements slowly. Keep the neck aligned in neutral throughout the movement.

4. KNEELING TRUNK FLEXION

Setup and Alignment: This exercise is performed on a cable machine. Use a split rope or similar attachment. Kneel on a padded surface with your knees about shoulder width apart. Keep your shoulders and hips over your knees, and set an upright, neutral spinal posture. Hold the split rope or cables with your hands apart and pulled into the chest. Set scapular retraction to reduce the likelihood of protracting the scapula, which can introduce momentum into the movement. *See fig. 37a.*

Performing the Exercise: This exercise is performed like any other trunk flexion exercise. Maintain scapular retraction and isometrically contract the abdominals. Exhale and slowly flex your trunk as you pull the bottom of your ribcage down toward your hips. As you contract the abdominal muscles, the low back will round. Don't allow the hips to move forward, back, up or down, the upper torso to move excessively toward the floor, or the arms to pull down and back. Keep the arms in the set-up position and the head aligned over the shoulders. Contract the abdominals until you have reached a full range-of-motion, or about 30 to 35 degrees of trunk flexion. Return slowly to the starting position, and re-set neutral lumbar posture. *See fig. 37b*

Comments: The technique for this trunk flexion exercise (often called a split strap, rope or cable pull-down crunch) is no different when compared to the supine curl performed on the floor. The scapulae should be retracted, no movement should occur in the shoulders, elbows, hips or knees, and the movement should be isolated so that the ribs are being drawn toward the top of the pelvis.

Safety Considerations: Shoulder extension or hip flexion movement should not occur. Do not introduce extra motion of any kind. Trunk strengthening exercises are characterized by relatively small, precise range-of-motion. Work with control, keep tension in the abdominal muscles and maintain proper head/neck alignment throughout the exercise.

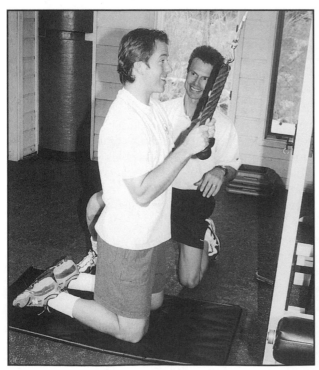

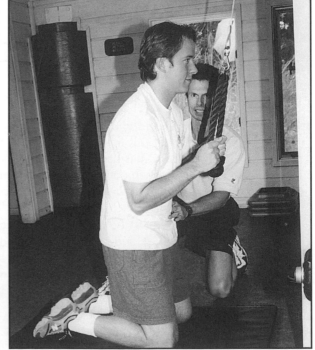

Fig. 37a   *Fig. 37b*

5. MACHINE TRUNK FLEXION

Setup and Alignment: This exercise uses a selectorized plate type machine. Although machines vary, generally you should align the axis of rotation of the body (between the bottom of the rib cage and the top of the hips) with the axis of rotation of the machine by adjusting the seat to the proper height. Place the hands and feet in a position so they do not assist the movement. Keep your head and shoulders over the hips, and sit upright with neutral spinal posture. Set scapular retraction to reduce the likelihood of protracting the scapula and introducing momentum into the movement. *See fig. 38a*

Performing the Exercise: This exercise is performed like any other trunk flexion exercise. Maintain scapular retraction and isometrically contract the abdominals. Exhale and slowly flex your trunk, pulling the bottom of your ribcage down toward your hips. As you contract the abdominal muscles, the low back will round. Keep the arms positioned in the set-up position and the head aligned over the shoulders. Contract the abdominals until you have reached a full range-of-motion, or about 30 to 35 degrees of trunk flexion. Return slowly to the starting position, and re-set neutral lumbar posture. *See fig. 38b*

Comments: An advantage that a machine like this has over other types of abdominal equipment (or lack of equipment), is that the selectorized plate stack allows you to easily progress the load as the client gets stronger. When it's simple to increase load, you can avoid the necessity of doing endless reps, which is not only unproductive but can lead to overuse injuries.

Safety Considerations: The scapulae should be retracted, no movement should occur in the shoulders, elbows, hips or knees, and the movement should be isolated so that the ribs are being drawn toward the top of the pelvis. Work with control, keep tension in the abdominal muscles and maintain proper head/neck alignment throughout the exercise.

Key Point

Trunk flexion technique stays the same — the ribs are drawn toward the pelvis — regardless of equipment being used.

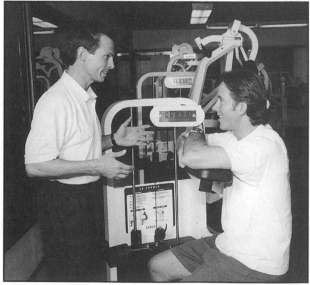

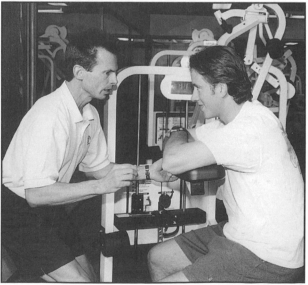

Fig. 38a

Fig. 38b

SUPINE REVERSE TRUNK FLEXION

Body Parts Targeted: Anterior trunk musculature/abdominal area
Joint Motion(s): Trunk flexion (posterior pelvic tilt)
Primary Muscles Strengthened: Rectus abdominis; external obliques

Fig. 39a

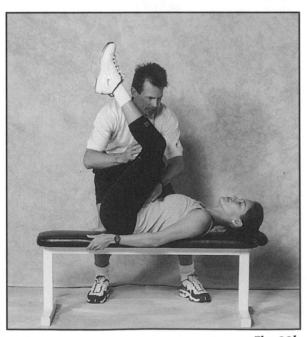

Fig. 39b

Setup and Alignment: Lie on a flat comfortable surface. Keep the scapulae and sacrum in firm contact with the padded surface, while maintaining neutral lumbar posture. Lifting one leg at a time, flex the hips to about 90 degrees and align the knees over the hips. Firmly grasp the sides or end of a bench or adjustable step platform with your hands, or place your hands on the floor at your sides. *See fig. 39a*

Performing the Exercise: Isometrically contract the abdominals before any movement occurs in the spine. Exhale and slowly flex the trunk, pulling the pelvis toward the bottom of the ribcage. Continue to pull the pelvis toward the ribcage until the abdominals have reached a full contraction, which is approximately 9 or 10 degrees of trunk flexion. At this point, the hips may roll slightly off the padded surface and the lower back will flatten. Return slowly to the starting position, and re-set neutral lumbar posture. *See fig. 39b*

Comments: Reverse trunk flexion represents the "other" 9 to 10 degrees of trunk flexion, and when combined with the ribcage to pelvis movement, accounts for the approximate 35 to 45 degrees of motion available in the lumbar spinal area. The posterior pelvic tilt is a very small movement where the back moves from a slightly arched (neutral lumbar posture) to a flat back position. Active hip flexion — drawing the knees up toward the chest — is often inadvertently added to increase range of motion. However, this added range of motion occurs only at the hip and does not require contraction of the targeted abdominal muscles. Active hip flexion can result in the lower region of the rectus abdominis not being challenged to any great degree. Any time the hips are lower than the head, this exercise becomes more challenging. At no time is the end-goal to lift or swing the knees or legs into the chest area. If this occurs, the hip flexors are being engaged. Instead, concentrate on drawing the pelvis up toward the ribcage, shortening the distance from point A (the top of the pelvis) to point B (the bottom of the ribcage). Movement in the lumbar trunk region occurs between the ribcage and pelvis and can be monitored with a "self-check." Place your thumbs in the 90-degree angle formed at the hip joint. As you perform a posterior pelvic tilt (trunk flexion), you should not feel the thumbs getting "pinched" at the hip joint. This "pinching" action lets you know that you are actively flexing the hips, rather than tilting the pelvis. A correctly performed posterior tilt will result in a hip angle that does not change throughout the motion.

Safety Considerations: Do not introduce extra motion of any kind. Excessive motion that includes active hip flexion or swinging of the legs, pushing down with the arms, or other uncontrolled movement are examples of poor exercise technique which may cause injury or lead to an end result where the abdominal muscles are not even engaged to any great extent. If the knees move below (inferior) the hip line, realize that this places more pull on the hip flexors and could cause the back to be forced into spinal hyperextension. On the other hand, positioning the knees below the hips makes the abdominals contract harder to maintain neutral. Work with control, keep tension in the abdominal muscles and maintain proper head/neck alignment throughout the exercise.

Exercise Variations: Reverse trunk flexion is known by a host of other names and represents dozens of "reverse curl" variations. These variations encompass simple floor exercises and the use of machines or other equipment. However, the core mechanics, in terms of performing reverse trunk flexion, do not change.

REVERSE TRUNK FLEXION EXERCISE VARIATIONS

Following are two more variations on the basic reverse trunk flexion exercise previously described. The joint motion(s) and primary muscles strengthened are the same. These variations are accomplished with different body positions and equipment.

1. STABILITY BALL REVERSE TRUNK FLEXION

Setup and Alignment: Lie in a supine position on a padded surface, with your hands resting by your sides or crossed over your chest. Drape your legs over the stability ball with a few degrees of external rotation at your hips. Grip the ball between the back of your thighs and your heels. Lift the ball off the floor as you flex your hips to approximately 90 degrees and align your knees directly over the hips. Keep the scapulae and sacrum in firm contact with the padded surface, while maintaining neutral lumbar posture. *See fig. 40a*

Performing the Exercise: Isometrically contract the abdominals before any movement occurs in the spine. Exhale and slowly flex the trunk, pulling the pelvis toward the bottom of the ribcage. Continue to pull the pelvis toward the

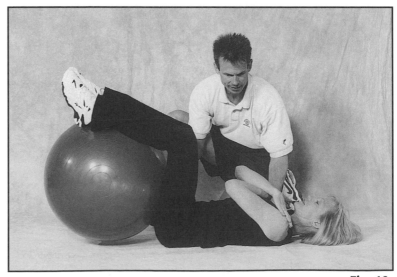

Fig. 40a

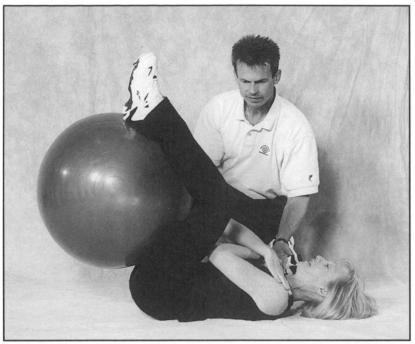

Fig. 40b

ribcage until the abdominals have reached a full contraction, which is approximately 9 or 10 degrees of trunk flexion. At this point, the hips may roll slightly off the padded surface and the lower back will flatten. Return slowly to the starting position, and re-set neutral lumbar posture. See *fig. 40b*

Comments: To increase stability challenge, place the hands across the chest. Holding the ball with the legs fixes the angle of the hips and knees, which limits the likelihood that the hip flexors will be used to assist the movement. At no time is the end-goal to lift or swing the knees or legs into the chest area. If this occurs, the hip flexors are being engaged. Instead, concentrate on drawing the pelvis up toward the ribcage, shortening the distance from point A (the top of the pelvis) to point B (the bottom of the ribcage). Use the reverse trunk flexion "self-check" described previously to monitor hip flexor activity.

Safety Considerations: Do not introduce extra motion of any kind. Excessive motion that includes active hip flexion, pushing down with the arms, or letting the weight of the stability ball create momentum are examples of poor exercise technique which may cause injury or lead to an end result where the abdominal muscles are not even engaged to any great extent. If the knees move below (inferior) the hip line, realize that this places more pull on the hip flexors and could cause the back to be forced into spinal hyperextension. On the other hand, positioning the knees below the hips makes the abdominals contract harder to maintain neutral. Work with control, keep tension in the abdominal muscles and maintain proper head/neck alignment throughout the exercise.

2. SUPPORTED REVERSE TRUNK FLEXION

Setup and Alignment: Using a dip stand or similar piece of equipment, assume a straight arm, supported position. Flex the knees and hips to an approximate 90-degree angle. Keep the scapulae retracted, while maintaining neutral lumbar and cervical posture. *See fig. 41a*

Performing the Exercise: Isometrically contract the abdominals before any movement occurs in the spine. Exhale and slowly flex the trunk, pulling the pelvis toward the bottom of the ribcage. Continue to pull the pelvis toward the ribcage until the abdominals have reached a full contraction, which is approximately 9 or 10 degrees of trunk flexion. At this point, the thighs will lift slightly and the hips will tuck under. Return slowly to the starting position, and re-set neutral lumbar posture. *See fig. 41b*

Comments: When this exercise is performed using hip flexion with bent legs, it is often called a "leg pull-in" or "knee tuck," and if done using hip flexion with straight legs, it is referred to as a "leg raise." In these exercises, the hip flexors are the prime movers, and the abdominals play an important role as stabilizers. The issue is not one of right or wrong, but whether you're targeting the rectus abdominis as a mover, or stabilizer, and whether or not the hip flexion exercises can be performed safely. The joint motion of this exercise — trunk flexion or posterior pelvic tilt — can be performed using seated, hanging, forearm supported, bent knee and straight leg variations. At no time is the end-goal to lift or swing the knees or legs into the chest area. If this occurs, the hip flexors are being engaged. Instead, concentrate on drawing the pelvis up toward the ribcage, shortening the distance from point A (the top of the pelvis) to point B (the bottom of the ribcage). Movement in the lumbar trunk region occurs between the ribcage and pelvis. The distance between these two points should become smaller as the abdominal muscles are contracted. During reverse trunk flexion, the entire pelvic bowl rotates posteriorly, but does so without active hip flexion occurring.

Safety Considerations: Do not introduce extra motion of any kind, especially active hip flexion. If the knees move below (inferior) the hips, realize this places more pull on the hip flexors and could cause the back to be forced into spinal hyperextension. On the other hand, positioning the knees below the hips makes the abdominals contract harder to maintain neutral. Work with control, keep tension in the abdominal muscles and maintain proper head/neck alignment throughout the exercise.

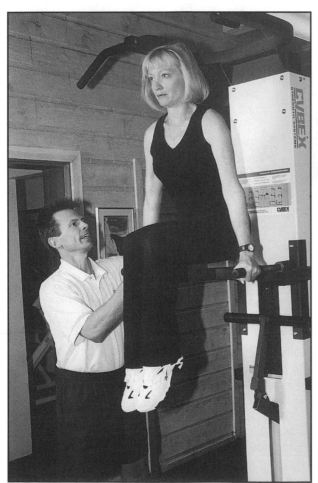

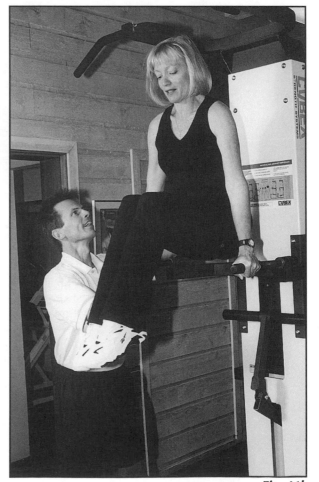

Fig. 41a   *Fig. 41b*

SUPINE TRUNK FLEXION WITH ROTATION

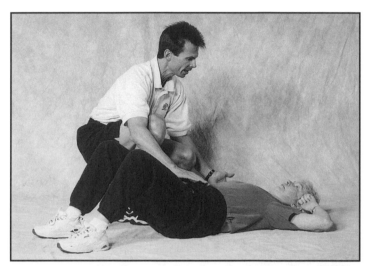

Fig. 42a

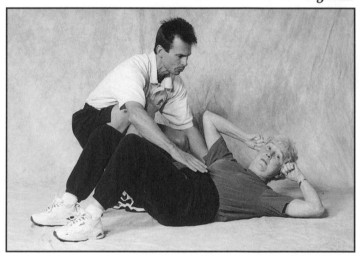

Fig. 42b

Body Parts Targeted: Anterior trunk musculature and "sides" of the abdominal area

Joint Motion(s): Trunk flexion; trunk rotation

Primary Muscles Strengthened: Rectus abdominis; internal and external obliques

Setup and Alignment: Lie supine on an inclined (gravity assisted), declined (gravity resisted) or flat surface with neutral lumbar posture. Rest the feet on the floor and flex the knees to form an angle which approximates 90 degrees. Arms may be placed at your sides, across the chest, behind your head, or the fists can be placed at the temples or under the chin (boxer position). Set scapular retraction to reduce the likelihood of protracting the scapula and introducing momentum into the movement. *See fig. 42a*

Performing the Exercise: Maintain scapular retraction and isometrically contract the abdominals. Exhale and slowly flex your spine, while simultaneously rotating the ribcage toward the same-side inner thigh. Placing the arms in the "boxer position" (fists under chin, elbows touching the ribcage) at first will facilitate correct rotation angles. For example, if you are rotating to your left, the right elbow and lower ribs should be directed toward the right thigh, without the fists leaving the chin. As you contract the abdominal muscles the low back will flatten and press firmly into the padded surface. Concentrate on drawing the lower ribcage toward the pelvis and same-side inner thigh. Rotation direction should not be toward the midline or across the midline of the body. Return to the start position with control. Repeat this unilateral exercise on both sides. *See fig. 42b*

Comments: Also known as "cross crunches," "oblique curls" or "trunk twists," a host of other names and variations exist for this simple exercise. However, trunk flexion with rotation amounts to pulling one side of the ribcage toward the same-side inner thigh. Why? Because the oblique fibers run more toward the same-side inner thigh, when compared to diagonally or horizontally across the body. Observing this simple anatomical fact — fiber direction — will tell you how the body should move when flexing and rotating the trunk. Oblique fibers can flex, laterally flex and rotate the trunk, due to their varied fiber attachments and resultant lines of pull. Beginning the movement with a few degrees of trunk flexion is the ideal way to perform this exercise. Trunk flexion then merges or blends into trunk rotation, where the ribcage pulls down toward the same-side inner thigh. The movement, though subtle, is forceful, and feels like oblique contractions that occur when pushing hard gears on a cycle or when aggressively turning during downhill skiing.

Safety Considerations: Do not introduce extra motion of any kind. Abdominal exercises are characterized by precise, controlled range-of-motion. Work with control, keep tension in the abdominal muscles and maintain proper head/neck alignment throughout the exercise.

TRUNK FLEXION WITH ROTATION EXERCISE VARIATIONS

Following are two more variations on the basic trunk flexion with rotation exercise previously described. The joint motion(s) and primary muscles strengthened are the same. These variations are accomplished with different body positions and equipment.

1. STABILITY BALL TRUNK FLEXION WITH ROTATION

Setup and Alignment: Begin in a supine position with the ball supported under the lumbar spine. An inclined position with the head higher than hips is easier (gravity assisted) when compared to a supine position with the ball placed under the lumbar spine. Establish neutral lumbar and cervical posture. Rest the feet on the floor about hip width apart and flex the knees to form an angle which approximates 90 degrees. Arms may be placed at your sides, across the chest, behind your head, or the fists can be placed at the temples or under the chin (boxer position). Set scapular retraction to reduce the likelihood of protracting the scapula and introducing momentum into the movement. *See fig. 43a*

Performing the Exercise: Maintain scapular retraction and isometrically contract the abdominals. Exhale and slowly flex your spine, while simultaneously rotating the ribcage toward the same-side inner thigh. Placing the arms in the "boxer position" (fists under chin, elbows touching the ribcage) at first will facilitate correct rotation angles. For example, if you are rotating to your left, the right elbow and lower ribs should be directed toward the right thigh, without the fists leaving the chin.

Fig. 43a

As you contract the abdominal muscles the low back will press into the ball. Concentrate on drawing the lower ribcage toward the pelvis and same-side inner thigh. Rotation direction should not be toward the midline or across the midline of the body. Return to the start position with control. Repeat this unilateral exercise on both sides. *See fig. 43b*

Fig. 43b

Comments: Performing trunk flexion with rotation on a stability ball will present balance and stabilization challenges as well as strength overload. A variety of positions are possible on the ball and can represent gravity neutral, assisted or resisted exercise. How you position the body on the ball determines the resistance. If the head is inclined higher than the hips, the exercise will be easier. Walking your feet back toward the ball, and letting the ball roll down your back toward the lumbar spine, will put your trunk in a position that is more parallel to the floor. Continuing to move the ball down under the hips will decline the head and upper trunk slightly. This progression — moving from incline toward supine or decline — represents easier to more difficult exercise. Since the ball is designed to be an unstable exercise surface, more muscular stabilization is required when compared to a bench or the floor. Controlling this lateral movement puts more demands on the obliques. Moving the feet to narrower positions also increases the stability challenge.

Safety Considerations: Do not introduce extra motion of any kind. Abdominal exercise is characterized by precise, controlled range-of-motion. Work with control, keep tension in the abdominal muscles and maintain proper head/neck alignment throughout the exercise.

2. Stability Ball Biased Trunk Flexion With Rotation

Setup and Alignment: Begin in a supine position with the ball supported under the lumbar spine. An inclined position with the head higher than hips is easier (gravity assisted) when compared to a supine position with the ball placed under the lumbar spine. Establish neutral lumbar and cervical posture. Rest the feet on the floor about hip width apart and flex the knees to form an angle which approximates 90 degrees. "Bias" the hips, pelvis and trunk by tilting them to one side. You should be halfway between a supine and sidelying position. Arms may be placed at your sides, across the chest, behind your head, or the fists can be placed at the temples or under the chin (boxer position). Set scapular retraction to reduce the likelihood of protracting the scapula and introducing momentum into the movement. *See fig. 44a*

Performing the Exercise: Maintain scapular retraction and isometrically contract the abdominals. Exhale and slowly flex your spine, drawing the ribcage toward the same-side inner thigh. Placing the arms in the "boxer position" (fists under chin, elbows touching the ribcage) when learning the exercise will facilitate the correct movement pattern. For example, if you are bringing the left elbow and left lower ribs toward the left thigh, concentrate on drawing the lower ribcage toward the pelvis and same-side inner thigh. Movement direction should not be toward the midline or across the midline of the body. Return to the start position with control. Repeat this unilateral exercise on both sides. *See fig. 44b*

Comments: This exercise, also called the "biased oblique curl," places the external obliques on a slight stretch and aligns the muscle fibers directly against the pull of gravity, thereby resisting the movement through a fuller range and with a direct line of resistance to oppose the movement. By allowing, for example, the left shoulder and hip to tilt to the right during set-up, the obliques can be effectively challenged without rotating the spine.

Safety Considerations: Do not introduce extra motion of any kind. Work with control, keep tension in the abdominal muscles and maintain proper head/neck alignment throughout the exercise.

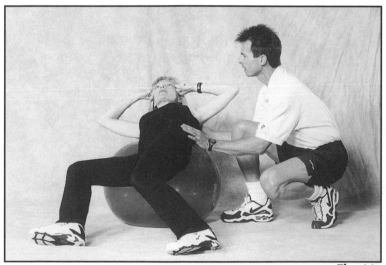

Fig. 44a

Fig. 44b

SIDELYING LATERAL TRUNK FLEXION

Body Parts Targeted: Anterior and posterior musculature of the trunk

Joint Motion(s): Trunk lateral flexion

Primary Muscles Strengthened: Rectus abdominis; internal and external obliques; quadratus lumborum; erector spinae

Setup and Alignment: Lie on your side and place a rolled-up towel under your waist. Placing a towel under the waist allows more lateral flexion to occur. Place your hands behind your head with one elbow pointing up and the other forward. Rest your head on your lower arm. Move your top leg slightly forward and the bottom leg slightly back, until you are in a "scissors" position. Your shoulders should be aligned with your hips. Do not flex the hips or waist. *See fig. 45a*

Performing the Exercise: From this sidelying position, laterally flex the trunk, drawing the bottom of the ribcage toward the top of the hip. Without letting your hips move forward or back, lift only as high as the trunk muscles will take you. Maintain neutral posture of the cervical spine, rather than laterally flexing the neck as you lift the trunk. Return with control to the starting position. *See fig. 45b*

Comments: Performing sidelying lateral flexion on the floor can be frustrating, due to the small range-of-motion (see Stability Ball Lateral Trunk Flexion for a solution), but the biggest technique flaw is usually an inability to maintain a neutral head/neck position. If the head is allowed to lead the movement, the result will be lateral neck flexion. The head should remain neutral and "go along for the ride," as the trunk laterally flexes. This movement is small and precise. Do not be tempted to use poor technique or momentum to create excessive motion. Keep the hips from moving forward or backward, as this puts more emphasis on either the anterior or posterior trunk musculature.

Safety Considerations: Do not tilt your neck or lead with your head as you laterally flex the trunk. Your ears should stay level with your shoulders as your trunk muscles pull your ribcage toward the hips and raise the upper body slightly off the floor. Keep your top hip and shoulder "stacked" directly over the bottom hip and shoulder. Maintain this setup and alignment throughout the movement.

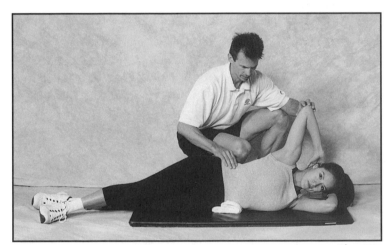

Fig. 45a

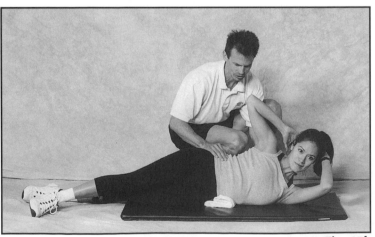

Fig. 45b

LATERAL FLEXION EXERCISE VARIATIONS

Following are two more variations on the basic lateral flexion exercise previously described. The joint motion(s) and primary muscles strengthened are the same. These variations are accomplished with different body positions and equipment.

1. STABILITY BALL LATERAL TRUNK FLEXION

Setup and Alignment: Drape your body over a stability ball in a sidelying position, with the ball supported under one hip. The legs are extended to the side in the "scissors" position described previously. Place your fists at the temples with your elbows open and your scapulae retracted. Allow the trunk to passively laterally flex over the ball. Your shoulders should be aligned with your hips so that you don't flex at the hips or waist. *See fig. 46a*

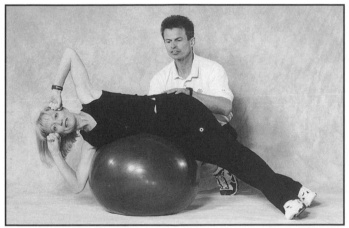

Fig. 46a

Performing the Exercise: From this sidelying position, maintain neutral alignment of the hips, not allowing the top hip to roll front or back. Laterally flex the spine, pressing the bottom hip into the ball as you lift the trunk. Concentrate on drawing the side of the top ribcage toward the side of the hip. Lift only as high as you are able to maintain correct alignment. Avoid laterally flexing the cervical spine or letting the head tip to the side. Return with control to the starting position. *See fig. 46b*

Comments: Using a stability ball allows for a greater resisted range-of-motion and increased mobility of the spine, since the trunk can start laterally flexed, pass through neutral and laterally flex on the opposite side of the torso — a result of the torso being able to drape over the ball. Lateral trunk flexion floor exercises do not allow for this stretched start position.

Safety Considerations: Do not lead with your head as you laterally flex your trunk. Your ears should stay level with your shoulders and "go along for the ride" as your trunk muscles pull the side of your ribcage toward the side of the hip. Keep the setup and alignment throughout the movement.

Fig. 46b

2. FLAT BENCH LATERAL TRUNK FLEXION

Setup and Alignment: Begin in a sidelying position on a flat bench. This exercise can also be done on a hyperextension machine. Position the body so that the hips and legs are supported, with the torso extended off the end of the bench. Place your lower arm down and rest the hand on the floor for support. The legs are on top of one another or slightly scissored. A trainer should firmly hold the legs in place by spotting at the hip and above the knee. Allow the trunk to slightly laterally flex over the end of the bench, 10 to 15 degrees. Now, place your hands behind your head. Your shoulders should be aligned with your hips.

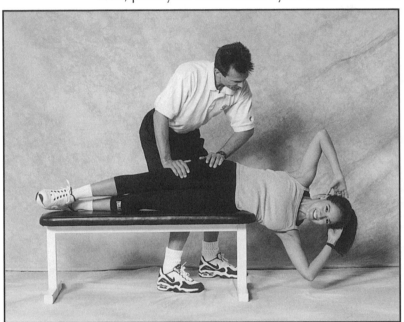

Fig. 47a

Do not flex the hips or waist. *See fig. 47a*

Performing the Exercise: From this sidelying position, maintain neutral alignment of the hips, not allowing the top hip to roll front or back. Laterally flex the spine, pressing the bottom hip into the bench as you lift the trunk. Concentrate on drawing the side of the top ribcage toward the side of the hip. Lift only as high as you are able to maintain correct alignment. Avoid laterally flexing the cervical spine or letting the head tip to the side. Return with control to the starting position. *See fig. 47b*

Comments: Using a piece of equipment like a flat bench, allows for a greater resisted range-of-motion and increased mobility of the spine when compared with the same exercise performed on the floor.

Safety Considerations: A fitness professional should spot this movement above the top knee and near the hip, to take lateral stress off of the knee joint. Do not laterally flex the cervical spine or lead with your head as you laterally flex the trunk. Maintain alignment of the top shoulder and hip over the bottom shoulder and hip. Avoid tipping forward or back as you laterally flex.

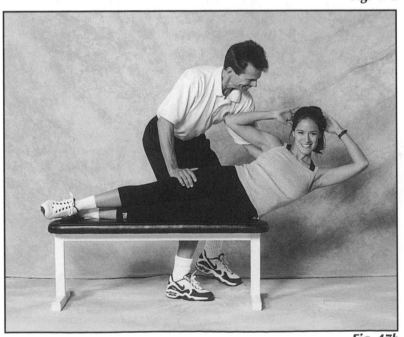

Fig. 47b

PRONE TRUNK EXTENSION

Body Parts Targeted: Posterior and lower trunk musculature
Joint Motion(s): Trunk extension

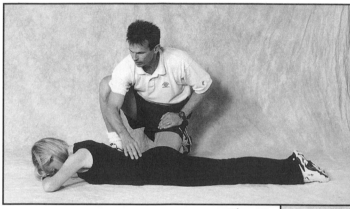

Fig. 48a

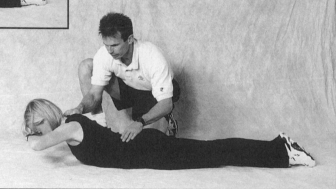

Fig. 48b

Primary Muscles Strengthened: Erector Spinae

Setup and Alignment: Position yourself face down with your legs straight and about hip width apart, with your hips externally rotated slightly. (This exercise can also be performed on inclined and declined surfaces.) Rest your forehead on your hands, keeping the neck in a neutral position and pointing your elbows out to the sides. Retract your scapulae. Note: Placing the arms at your sides (easier), near the head (harder), or overhead (hardest) will affect exercise difficulty and resistance. *See fig. 48a*

Performing the Exercise: Start the movement by slightly lifting the chest off the padded surface to provide tension in the low back muscles and to limit the likelihood of starting the exercise with momentum. Continue to smoothly lift your upper torso off the floor. Keep your shoulder blades retracted and depressed. Extend the spine to the point where the muscles are fully contracted, but the range-of-motion is still comfortable. *See fig. 48b*

Comments: Feeling the low back "work" and feeling muscle contraction is different than pain. I find it interesting to observe that many of my clients love to "feel" their biceps, but often are anxious about "feeling" sensations of any kind in the lower back region. Help your client to differentiate between discomfort and effective spinal extension exercise.

Safety Considerations: Keep the top of your feet and the front of your hips pressing firmly into the floor. Avoid excessive or forced hyperextension of the low back by lifting the upper torso off the floor with control. Maintain head and neck alignment throughout the movement. Do not allow the head to lead (i.e., cervical hyperextension) the movement. Perform the movement slowly and maintain muscle tension in the back extensors.

TRUNK EXTENSION EXERCISE VARIATIONS

Following are two more variations on the basic prone trunk exercise previously described. The joint motion(s) and primary muscles strengthened are the same. These variations are accomplished with different body positions and equipment.

1. FLAT BENCH PRONE TRUNK EXTENSION

Setup and Alignment: Position yourself face down on an adjustable step platform or flat bench, with your legs straight and about hip width apart, and your hips externally rotated slightly. (Note: A flat bench may not allow the legs to be placed hip width apart with external hip rotation.) Rest your forehead on your hands, keeping the neck in a neutral position and pointing your elbows out to the sides. Retract your shoulder blades. Placing the arms at your sides (easier), near the head (harder), or overhead (hardest) will affect exercise difficulty and resistance. The waist should be positioned toward the edge of the platform or bench, allowing for unrestricted movement of the lumbar spinal region, and a rounded or flexed spine starting position. *See fig. 49a*

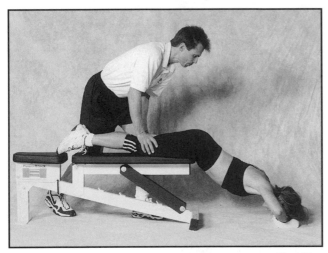

Fig. 49a

Performing the Exercise: Start the movement by extending the lumbar spine just enough to provide tension in the low back muscles and to limit the likelihood of starting the exercise with momentum. Continue to smoothly lift your upper torso away from the floor. Keep your shoulder blades retracted and depressed. Extend the spine to the point where the muscles are fully contracted, but the range-of-motion is still comfortable. *See fig. 49b*

Comments: Using equipment like a bench, adjustable step platform or hyperextension machine, allows for a greater resisted range-of-motion and increased mobility of the spine, since the trunk can start in a flexed position off the edge of the padded surface, pass through neutral and finally move into spinal hyperextension. Trunk extension exercises performed on the floor do not allow for this stretched/flexed start position. A common technique flaw is the inability to maintain a neutral head/neck position. If the head is allowed to lead the movement, the result is cervical hyperextension. The head should remain neutral as the trunk extends.

Safety Considerations: A fitness professional should spot this movement above the knees, near the hip or on the back of the thigh to avoid placing stress on the knee joint. If the movement is spotted at the heel, or the feet are fixed in a hyperextension machine without spotting above the knees, the knees can be forced into hyperextension. This exercise should not be performed without a spotter.

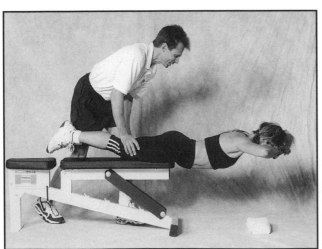

Fig. 49b

2. STABILITY BALL PRONE TRUNK EXTENSION

Setup and Alignment: Begin in a prone position on a stability ball with the ball supported under the hips and pelvis. The legs are extending behind your body with the knees slightly bent. Flex the trunk passively, bringing the forehead close to the ball. Maintain neutral cervical posture as you place your hands on the ball, in front of your forehead or your fists at your temples. *See fig. 50a*

Performing the Exercise: Start the movement by extending the lumbar spine just enough to provide tension in the low back muscles and to limit the likelihood of starting the exercise with momentum. Continue to smoothly lift your upper torso away from the floor. Keep your shoulder blades retracted and depressed. Extend the spine to the point where the muscles are fully contracted, but the range-of-motion is still comfortable. Note: Placing the arms at your sides (easier), near the head (harder), or overhead (hardest) will affect exercise balance challenges and overall difficulty and resistance. *See fig. 50b*

Comments: Performing trunk extension on the ball not only allows for the exerciser to begin in a position of trunk flexion over the ball — which increases the resisted range-of-motion — but also presents a stability challenge to other trunk muscles as they stabilize the rolling motion of the ball.

Safety Considerations: Avoid using momentum such as "bouncing" off of the ball to increase range-of-motion. Do not hyperextend your cervical spine as you extend the lumbar spine. Your ears should stay level with your shoulders as your trunk muscles pull the back of your ribcage toward the back of your hips. Control your movement speed in both directions.

Fig. 50a

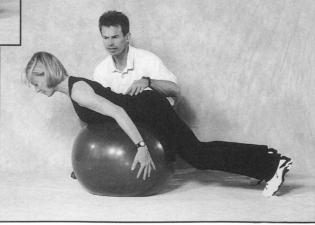

Fig. 50b

PRONE REVERSE TRUNK EXTENSION

Body Parts Targeted: Posterior and lower trunk musculature

Joint Motion(s): Trunk extension (anterior pelvic tilt)

Primary Muscles Strengthened: Erector spinae

Setup and Alignment: Lie face down on an adjustable step platform or other platform that is four to twelve inches off the floor. (The higher the step or bench, the more difficult the exercise.) The padded edge of the platform should be at or slightly below your waist. Placement of the hips on the adjustable step platform or flat bench should not interfere with pelvic motion. Rest your thighs on the platform and flex the knees so that your heels are directly above your knees. Wrap your arms around the sides and top edge of the platform and rest your forehead on it. Retract and depress your scapulae. *See fig. 51a*

Performing the Exercise: Keep your chest and forehead in contact with the platform and perform an anterior pelvic tilt. As a result of the pelvic bowl rotating in an anterior direction, your knees will lift. Use your lumbar extensor muscles to tilt the pelvis, rather than your hip extensor muscles. Continue to extend the spine to the point where the muscles are fully contracted, but the range-of-motion is still comfortable. *See fig. 51b*

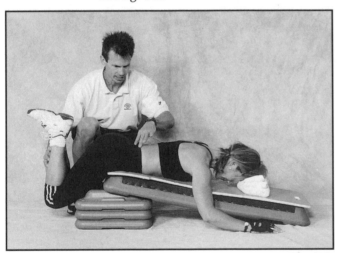

Fig. 51a

Comments: Also referred to as a "prone reverse hip lift," the exercise changes how the muscle attachments are stabilized. Rather than the insertion of the spinal extensors moving toward their origin, the direction of pull is reversed and the origin moves toward the insertion. The result is simply that the extensor muscles are challenged in a different way.

Safety Considerations: Using equipment such as an adjustable step platform or bench allows for a greater resisted range-of-motion and increased mobility of the spine, since the trunk can start in a flexed, rounded position, pass through neutral and finally move into spinal hyperextension (anterior pelvic tilt).

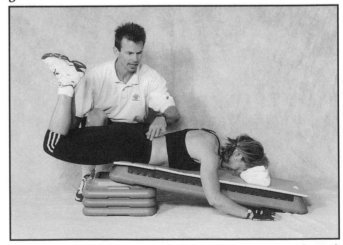

Fig. 51b

PRONE TRUNK EXTENSION WITH ROTATION

Body Parts Targeted: Posterior and lower trunk musculature

Joint Motion(s): Trunk extension; trunk rotation

Primary Muscles Strengthened: Erector spinae; deep spinal rotators

Setup and Alignment: Begin in a prone position on a padded surface, with your legs extended and about hip width apart, and your hips externally rotated slightly. This exercise can also be performed on inclined and declined surfaces to vary the intensity. Rest your forehead on your hands, keeping the neck in a neutral position and pointing your elbows out to the sides. Retract your scapulae. Note: Placing the arms at your sides (easier), near the head (harder), or overhead (hardest) will affect exercise difficulty and resistance. *See fig. 52a*

Performing the Exercise: Start the movement by extending the lumbar spine just enough to provide tension in the low back muscles and to limit the likelihood of starting the exercise with momentum. Continue to smoothly lift away from the floor, while simultaneously rotating your upper torso. Keep your scapulae retracted and depressed. Extend and rotate the spine to the point where the muscles are fully contracted, but the range-of-motion is still comfortable. *See fig. 52b*

Comments: Note that the oblique muscles do not rotate the trunk when extension is combined with rotation. Instead, the obliques are "on stretch" because of reciprocal innervation. The agonist muscles for this joint action are the trunk extensors and deep spinal rotators. Stated plainly, this is not an "oblique exercise." Start the movement with trunk extension and merge into rotation. The rotation is small and precise. If rotating to your right, for example, envision drawing the bottom of the right rib cage down toward the same-side hip.

Safety Considerations: Keep the tops of your feet and the front of your hips pressing firmly into the padded surface. Avoid excessive or forced hyperextension of the low back by lifting the upper torso off the floor with control. Maintain head and neck alignment throughout the movement. Do not allow cervical hyperextension during the movement.

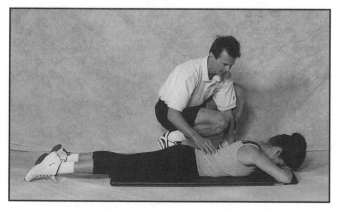

Fig. 52a

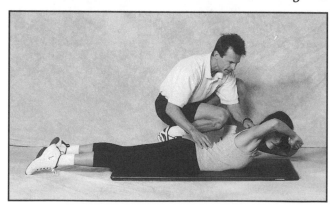

Fig. 52b

STABILITY BALL PRONE TRUNK EXTENSION WITH ROTATION

Fig. 53a

Fig. 53b

Body Parts Targeted: Posterior and lower trunk musculature

Joint Motion(s): Trunk extension; trunk rotation

Primary Muscles Strengthened: Erector spinae; deep spinal rotators

Setup and Alignment: Begin in a prone position on a stability ball with the ball supported under the hips and pelvis. The legs are extending behind your body with the knees slightly bent. Flex the trunk passively, bringing the forehead close to the ball. Maintain neutral cervical posture as you place your hands in front of your forehead or your fists at your temples. *See fig. 53a*

Performing the Exercise: Start the movement by extending the lumbar spine just enough to provide tension in the low back muscles and to limit the likelihood of starting the exercise with momentum. Continue to smoothly lift your upper torso away from the floor while simultaneously rotating your upper torso to one side. Keep your shoulder blades retracted and depressed. Extend and rotate the spine to the point where the muscles are fully contracted, but the range-of-motion is still comfortable. Note: Placing the arms at your sides (easier), near the head (harder), or overhead (hardest) will affect balance challenges and overall difficulty and resistance. *See fig. 53b*

Comments: Performing trunk extension on the ball not only allows for the exerciser to begin in a position of trunk flexion over the ball — which increases the resisted range-of-motion — but also presents a stability challenge to other trunk muscles as they stabilize the rolling motion of the ball.

Safety Considerations: Avoid excessive or forced hyperextension of the low back by lifting and rotating the torso away from the floor with control. Maintain head and neck alignment throughout the movement. Do not allow cervical hyperextension.

7

UPPER BODY EXERCISES

There is excellent evidence to suggest that upper body resistance training programs should initially focus on, and maintain the strength and endurance of muscles associated with the rotator cuff and upper back. Strong scapular and shoulder stabilizing muscles help to maintain shoulder joint and shoulder girdle integrity and function.

This chapter focuses on active exercises, but stabilization training for the upper body shouldn't be neglected. Many of the trunk stabilization exercises shown in Chapter 6 are useful not only for training the abdominal and back musculature functionally, but can be used to challenge the upper body in the same manner.

The ongoing principle of categorizing movement (Chapter 1) is captured by the following "rule": *After correctness and appropriateness of a particular movement has been determined, for the same or similar joint actions, the mechanics should remain unchanged — independent of body position or equipment used.*

Though every upper body exercise variation cannot be analyzed, any motion that is common to those analyzed in this chapter, will retain some degree of sameness with regard to correct exercise execution. Virtually all upper body resistance training exercise variations fit within the joint motions/actions demonstrated. Categorizing or grouping movement allows you to see the "big picture" related to movement analysis, and does not require that a "new" analysis be performed for each and every exercise variation, as long as the motion/joint actions are similar.

ROTATOR CUFF EXERCISES

SIDELYING DUMBBELL ROTATOR CUFF 3-PART SERIES

Body Part Targeted: Shoulder

Joint Motion(s): Part 1 - Shoulder abduction; Part 2 - Shoulder external rotation; Part 3 – Shoulder internal rotation

Primary Muscles Strengthened: Part 1 – Supraspinatus; Part 2 - Infraspinatus, teres minor and posterior deltoid; Part 3 - Subscapularis, anterior deltoid and pectoralis major

Setup and Alignment: Part 1 - Sidelying Shoulder Abduction: Lie on your side with a towel folded under your head. With a dumbbell in hand, rest your top arm on the side of the body. Place the lower arm in a comfortable position where it can help to support your head. Place the legs in a "scissors" position for balance, and maintain neutral spinal posture. Avoid lying directly on your shoulder by "cheating" it forward during the set-up. This positioning should allow you to be comfortable and stable. *See fig. 54a*

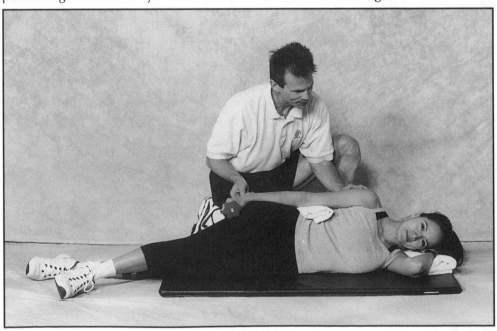

Fig. 54a

Performing the Exercise: Part 1 - From the stabilized set-up position, your top arm and wrist are kept straight. The wrist should not bend forward or back. Lift (abduct) your top arm toward the ceiling and away from the side, no higher than about 60 degrees. Going above 60 degrees is unnecessary because gravity no longer exerts a pull on the dumbbell and the supraspinatus works from zero to 60 degrees of shoulder abduction. Keep your top arm aligned over the side of the body throughout the exercise, making sure it does not move forward or back. Slowly return to the start position. *See fig. 54b*

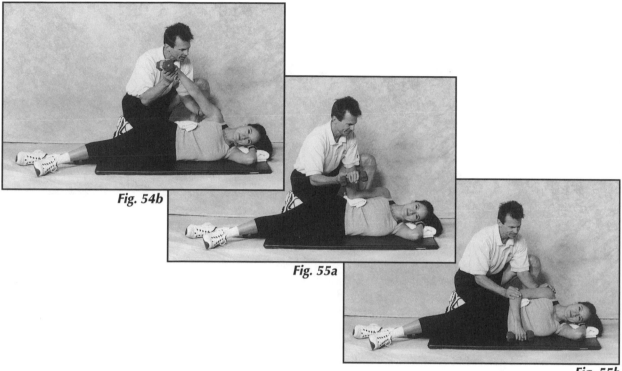

Fig. 54b

Fig. 55a

Fig. 55b

Setup and Alignment: Part 2 - Sidelying Shoulder External Rotation: Maintain the same set-up from sidelying shoulder abduction, but move the top hand so that the arm is flexed 90 degrees and the elbow is pressed into your body. Support the elbow with a folded towel at the waist if needed, in order to align the elbow directly under the shoulder. *See fig. 55a*

Performing the Exercise: Part 2 - From the stabilized set-up position, keep your top arm flexed at 90 degrees. The arm is pressed firmly into the side of your body and/or a towel. Lower the weight as far as possible, without letting your elbow lift from your side. The wrist is kept straight and it is important that the body does not roll forward or back. The concentric phase of this exercise begins with the arm internally rotated as far is possible, and the arm is returned to the start position by externally rotating the shoulder. *See fig. 55b*

Setup and Alignment: Part 3 - Dumbbell Sidelying Shoulder Internal Rotation: Maintain the sidelying set-up position, but move the weight from your top hand to the bottom hand and support your head with a folded towel. Return the top hand to a comfortable resting position on the side of your body. Position your bottom arm so that the elbow-shoulder line runs directly in front of the body from the shoulder and the elbow is flexed at 90 degrees. Position your lower hand just above the floor and support it with a folded towel or mat. Positioning the support under the hand can take potential stress off of the shoulder at this end point of external rotation. The elbow should not move up or down. *See fig. 56a*

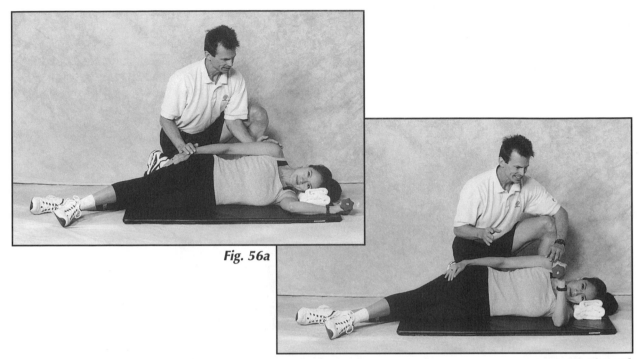

Fig. 56a

Fig. 56b

Performing the Exercise: **Part 3 -** From this "horizontal" shoulder position, keep the bottom elbow flexed at 90 degrees and the lower hand positioned just off the floor, but supported. Rotate the lower arm inwardly and toward the body, without the elbow moving from its start position. Avoid rotating the shoulder beyond 90 degrees (i.e., hand/elbow line perpendicular to the floor, as shown). *See fig. 56b*

Comments: An important aim of rotator cuff exercise is to develop shoulder joint strength and structural integrity of the shoulder. Often, the strength of the external rotators are overpowered by the muscles that assist in internal shoulder rotation, making it especially important to not only develop strength in the external rotators, but to maintain it throughout any program. The supraspinatus is not challenged to any great degree when performing standing shoulder abduction movements with dumbbells since the pull of gravity does not exert significant force until about 60 degrees of abduction. Challenging abduction from zero to 60 degrees is very important. This three-part series can be performed consecutively by first abducting the shoulder, followed by external rotation, and then switching the resistance to the lower hand and performing internal rotation. Then, turn the body to the other side and repeat the series.

Safety Considerations: Support the head so that proper neutral alignment of the cervical spine is maintained. Monitor the arm movement and stabilize the shoulder or assist the motion at the wrist, if needed. Limit movement to no more than 90 degrees of shoulder external or internal rotation, and 60 degrees of shoulder abduction. Not only are terminal end ranges of a joint potentially stressful (i.e., 90 degrees of internal or external rotation), but excessive range-of-motion is especially not warranted in situations where there is no gravitational pull on the dumbbell. Additionally, when performing *supine* shoulder internal rotation with the arm in a horizontal position, this positioning can cause shoulder impingement. A better choice would be the sidelying position discussed here. Rotator cuff movements should be comfortable and smooth, and if they are not, adjust the positioning of the working arm and/or path of motion.

STANDING CABLE SHOULDER INTERNAL ROTATION

Body Part Targeted: Shoulder
Joint Motion(s): Shoulder internal rotation
Primary Muscles Strengthened: Subscapularis, anterior deltoid and pectoralis major
Setup and Alignment: Stand in a "ready" position, with neutral spinal posture. The body is upright and the hips and knees are slightly flexed. Position the body so the force presented directly opposes the movement. Place a folded towel between your upper arm and side to use as a "pivot" point or to help align the elbow directly below the shoulder. Flex the elbow to an approximate angle of 90 degrees, and position the hand so that the thumb is oriented toward the ceiling. Firmly press your upper arm into the towel or side of your body, and actively externally rotate the arm "open" to about 70 to 80 degrees. *See fig. 57a*

Fig. 57a

Performing the Exercise: Press your upper arm firmly into the towel or side of your body, and from the externally rotated start position, internally rotate the shoulder. Keep your lower arm parallel to the ground. Hand position should not change (i.e,. do not pronate or supinate at the elbow). The arm should be drawn across and in front of the body as far as the musculature can actively move it. The upper arm should not lift from the towel or side of the body, nor move forward or back. Return to the start position with control. *See fig. 57b*

Comments: An important goal of rotator cuff exercise is to develop shoulder joint strength and structural integrity of the shoulder. Sufficient rotator cuff muscle strength is the basis for any upper body strength program or sporting activity that requires the use of the arms, chest and upper back. Shoulder flexibility and strength of the external and internal rotators will largely determine active range of motion (AROM) that can be attained.

Safety Considerations: The trainer can spot the movement by monitoring or physically stabilizing the shoulder and elbow start positions, and can direct the movement by assisting the path of motion near the wrist or forearm, as needed. Limit movement to no more than about 80 degrees of shoulder external rotation. The degree of internal rotation is determined by available AROM. Generally, terminal end range-of-motions can be potentially stressful to any joint, as is exhibited by approximately 80 degrees or greater of external rotation at the shoulder. Rotator cuff movements should be comfortable and smooth, and if they are not, adjust the positioning of the working arm and/or path of motion.

Exercise Variations: This exercise can be performed using any type of cable machine and can be performed in a seated position. It is also possible to position the arm with more or less shoulder flexion, or with more or less elbow flexion. Regardless of start position, the set up must be stabilized throughout the movement. These varied shoulder and elbow positions create different lines of pull and place different load requirements on the rotator cuff musculature. In simple terms, slightly altered joint motions help to challenge the same muscles in "different" ways.

Fig. 57b

STANDING CABLE SHOULDER EXTERNAL ROTATION

Body Part Targeted: Shoulder

Joint Motion(s): Shoulder external rotation

Primary Muscles Strengthened: Infraspinatus, teres minor and posterior deltoid

Setup and Alignment: Stand in a "ready" position, with neutral spinal posture. The body is upright and the hips and knees are slightly flexed. Position the body so the force presented directly opposes the movement. Place a folded towel between your upper arm and side to use as a "pivot" point or to help align the elbow directly below the shoulder. Flex the elbow to an approximate angle of 90 degrees, and position the hand so that the thumb is oriented toward the ceiling. Firmly press your upper arm into the towel or side of your body, and actively internally rotate the arm to a "closed" position. *See fig. 58a*

Performing the Exercise: Press your upper arm firmly into the towel or side of your body, and from the internally rotated start position externally rotate the shoulder. Keep the lower arm parallel to the ground. Hand position should not change (i.e,. do not pronate or supinate at the elbow). The arm should rotate away from the midline of the body, as far as the musculature can actively move it. Avoid exceeding about 80 degrees of external shoulder rotation. The upper arm should not lift from the towel or side of the body, nor move forward or back. Return to the start position with control. *See fig. 58b*

Comments: An important aim of rotator cuff exercises is to develop shoulder joint strength and structural integrity of the shoulder. Often, the strength of the external rotators are overpowered by the muscles that assist in internal shoulder rotation, making it especially important to not only develop strength in the external rotators, but to maintain it throughout any program. Shoulder flexibility and strength of the external and internal rotators will largely determine active range of motion (AROM) that can be attained.

Fig. 58a

Fig. 58b

Safety Considerations: The trainer can spot the movement by monitoring or physically stabilizing the shoulder and elbow start positions, and can direct the movement by assisting the path of motion near the wrist or forearm, as needed. Limit movement to no more than about 80 degrees of active shoulder external rotation. Generally, terminal end range-of-motions can be potentially stressful to any joint, as is exhibited by approximately 80 degrees or greater of external rotation at the shoulder. Rotator cuff movements should be comfortable and smooth, and if they are not, adjust the positioning of the working arm and/or path of motion.

Exercise Variations: This exercise can be performed using any type of cable machine and can be performed in a seated position. It is also possible to position the arm with more or less shoulder flexion, or with more or less elbow flexion. Regardless of start position, the set up must be stabilized throughout the movement. These varied shoulder and elbow positions create different lines of pull and place different load requirements on the rotator cuff musculature. In simple terms, slightly altered joint motions help to challenge the same muscles in "different" ways.

UPPER BACK EXERCISES

STANDING BARBELL SCAPULAR ELEVATION

Body Parts Targeted: Posterior neck, shoulder and upper back regions
Joint Motion(s): Scapular elevation
Primary Muscles Strengthened: Levator scapulae; upper and mid trapezius
Setup and Alignment: Stand in a "ready" position, with neutral spinal posture. The body is upright and the hips and knees are slightly flexed. Position the barbell *behind* the body, holding it with an over grip. The arms should be slightly flexed at the elbow. Retract the scapulae and keep the shoulders over the hips and feet. *See fig. 59a*

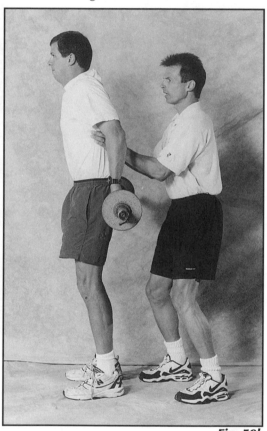

| *Fig. 59a* | *Fig. 59b* |

Performing the Exercise: Elevate the scapulae by pulling the shoulders up toward your ears. The arms will slide upward along the sides of your body. Be sure to keep the scapulae retracted. Lower the arms and scapular girdle to the start position by slowly depressing the scapulae from the elevated position. *See fig. 59b*

Comments: If the barbell is impeded by the protrusion of the gluteus maximus, use a dumbbell variation or place the barbell in front of the body. The trainer can facilitate the "shrug" movement by spotting the upper arms or the scapulae and directing the shoulder and arm movement upward. Positioning the bar behind the body, and setting scapular retraction prior to elevating the scapulae, helps to better align the pull and fiber direction of the targeted musculature against gravity and the load that has been placed in opposition to scapular elevation.

Safety Considerations: Do not let the shoulders rotate forward or backward after setting scapular retraction. This motion is not resisted and reduces the effectiveness of this exercise in targeting the trapezius and levator scapulae musculature. Maintain neutral lumbar and cervical spinal position.

Exercise Variations: When performing this movement using dumbbells, keep the dumbbells aligned at your sides. Good positioning is assisted by actively retracting the scapulae and by maintaining a stabilized shoulder position that does not allow the arms to move excessively forward of the midline of the body.

STABILITY BALL SCAPULAR DEPRESSION

Body Parts Targeted: Scapular and mid- to lower-back regions

Joint Motion(s): Scapular depression

Primary Muscles Strengthened: Pectoralis minor; subclavius; lower trapezius

Setup and Alignment: Sit upright on top of the ball with your hands placed on the sides of the ball slightly behind the hips, fingertips pointing down. Walk the feet forward one or two steps, letting the buttocks rest on the outer third of the ball. Retract the scapulae and slightly flex the elbows as your hips sink into the ball. Allow the scapulae to passively elevate, so that the shoulders are up near the ears. *See fig. 60a*

Performing the Exercise:
Push the hands down into the ball without hyperextending the elbows, and depress the scapulae. The shoulders will move downward and away from the ears. Keep the hips lightly in contact with the ball even after scapular depression has been completed. Then, flex your arms and let your hips sink deeper into the ball, allowing your shoulders to return to the elevated, start position. *See fig. 60b*

Comments: Scapular depression is an important postural exercise to perform since it opposes scapular elevation, and helps to balance this agonist/antagonist strength relationship. Setting scapular retraction prior to depressing the scapulae helps to better align the pull and fiber direction of the targeted musculature against gravity and the load that has been placed in opposition to scapular depression.

Fig. 60a

125

Safety Considerations: Do not let the shoulders rotate forward or backward after setting scapular retraction. This motion is not resisted, reduces the effectiveness of this exercise in targeting the trapezius and levator scapulae musculature, and can lead to shoulder injuries because of the unstable nature of performing this exercise on the stability ball. Keep the hips in contact with the ball at all times during this movement. Maintain neutral lumbar and cervical spinal position.

Exercise Variations: Scapular depression can be combined with a dip movement on the ball. Perform the dip movement first and follow it with scapular depression. During the dip movement, keep the back close to the ball and don't let the upper arm move deeper than about parallel to the ground. Do not assist the dipping movement with your legs. Additionally, seated "dip" machines, dip stands and seated triceps press machines can be used to challenge scapular depression.

Fig. 60b

STABILITY BALL SUPINE SCAPULAR RETRACTION

Body Parts Targeted: Mid-back musculature

Joint Motion(s): Scapular retraction (or adduction)

Primary Muscles Strengthened: Mid trapezius; rhomboids

Setup and Alignment: Begin seated on top of the ball and "walk" the body down to a supine position by the letting the ball travel up the spine. The ball supports the head, neck and shoulders. Extend the hips so that the upper thighs and torso are parallel to the floor, and maintain this stabilized position. Move your hands upward by flexing the shoulders until the arms are perpendicular to the floor. Protract your scapulae (scapular abduction) or round your shoulders off the ball. *See fig. 61a*

Performing the Exercise: Keeping your arms and hips lifted, retract the shoulder girdle by pulling the scapulae toward one another and pressing or "pinching" the upper back into the ball. Don't allow the elbows to flex as you retract the scapulae. Maintain neutral alignment of the lumbar and cervical spine throughout the retraction movement. Return to the start position by lowering the arms to your thighs or down toward the floor, and flex the trunk, "walking" the body back up to the upright starting position by letting the ball move down the spine. *See fig. 61b*

Comments: Scapular retraction is a key skill that can be combined with other strength exercises to help stabilize, as well as enhance training results and safety. Scapular retraction is also an important postural exercise, since it opposes scapular protraction that often accompanies ubiquitous pressing and reaching movements, and helps to improve the

Fig. 61a

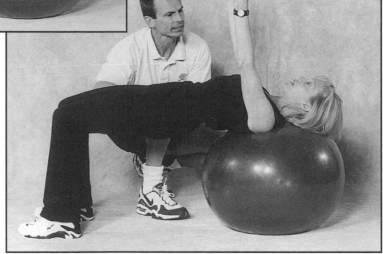
Fig. 61b

strength and flexibility balance between anterior shoulder/chest musculature and posterior shoulder/back musculature. Performed in isolation, this exercise can do a lot to counter poor posture and muscle imbalances that result in a rounded shoulder, chin jutted forward misalignment. Scapular retraction performed on the stability ball requires more balance and stability than many other scapular retraction variations.

Safety Considerations: Maintain neutral lumbar and cervical spinal position, and keep the hips lifted when performing scapular retraction. When moving from a seated position on the ball to the supine position, don't lean forward excessively with the upper torso or the ball can slip out from under the hips. Keep the shoulders over the ball at all times.

Exercise Variations: Scapular retraction can also be performed in a prone position on the stability ball. The ball is placed under your hips and abdomen, and your arms are hanging down in front of the ball with the hands clasping opposite elbows. Move your arms away from the floor by retracting the scapulae. Scapular retraction can be accomplished with a variety of equipment and in supine, prone, seated and standing positions. Elastic resistance, cables of any type, low or high pulley machines, and selectorized plate machines that specifically target shoulder horizontal abduction or extension, are a few examples of equipment that can be used to effectively target scapular retraction.

CHEST EXERCISES

SUPINE DUMBBELL CHEST PRESS

Body Parts Targeted: Chest; front of the shoulders; back of the upper arms
Joint Motion(s): Shoulder horizontal flexion (adduction); elbow extension
Primary Muscles Strengthened: Pectoralis majors; anterior deltoids; triceps
Setup and Alignment: Lie supine on a bench and place your feet on the floor, an elevated support or a platform. Use the foot positioning that allows you to simultaneously maintain neutral lumbar spinal position and stability. Maintain neutral cervical posture. Position the dumbbells so the hands are about shoulder width apart and directly above the shoulders. The elbows should be rotated outward, away from the body, and the thumbs are oriented toward one another. Keep your wrists neutral — avoid flexing, extending, abducting or adducting, and don't let the dumbbells tilt up or down. Retract the scapulae and attempt to keep this retracted position throughout the set of repetitions. Maintaining this alignment, press the dumbbells up until the elbows are almost straight. *See fig. 62a*

Fig. 62a

Performing the Exercise: Flex both elbows and lower the arms. Keep the arms rotated away from the body, maintaining the path of motion represented by horizontal abduction (lowering the arms) and horizontal flexion (raising the arms). Lower the arms until the upper arms are parallel to the floor and the elbows are flexed 90 degrees. The hands should be directly over the elbows. Return to the start position by extending the elbows, pressing the dumbbells up and drawing the arms toward one another. *See fig. 62b*

Comments: A bench that is too high may force the back into hyperextension, whereas placing the feet on top of the bench may not provide enough stability to perform the exercise safely. I prefer placing the feet on the floor, or if the bench is too high and nonadjustable, I raise the feet by placing blocks or another type of platform under the feet.

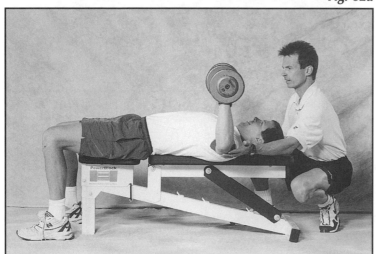

Fig. 62b

Keep the thumbs oriented to one another throughout the exercise. Rotating the thumbs in or out reduces the effectiveness of the exercise and can contribute to shoulder joint stress. Maintain the plane of movement by not allowing the shoulders to rotate in or out. Poor cues that cause joint stress and loss of proper path of motion include language that encourages the client to "bring their little fingers together" or to "turn their thumbs down." Avoid protracting the shoulder girdle by keeping your scapulae retracted. Using dumbbells or cables allows you to move the arms naturally and bring them toward one another as the shoulders go through the arc-motion of horizontal flexion. Envision moving your arms around a wide barrel. This is in contrast to limited movement ranges that are linear — straight versus arcing — that are characteristic of barbells, floor pushups and many chest press machines where the motion is predetermined and the hands are fixed.

Safety Considerations: Avoid flattening the lower back, as this is not the safest and strongest position for the spine. Maintain both cervical and lumbar neutral posture. The arms should not be lowered much deeper than the point where the upper arms are parallel to the floor. Cueing, "hands to the chest," may place the load too low and put the shoulders at risk for joint stress. Keep the wrists positioned strongly (no flexion or extension) so that the dumbbells are parallel to the floor. Do not externally or internally rotate the shoulders, and do not abduct (raise the elbow) or adduct (lower the elbow) the shoulder as this can change the focus for the targeted musculature, and can cause joint stress to the shoulder. Excessively wide or narrow hand positions contradict good movement mechanics. Keep the hands positioned in line with the elbow during pressing movements.

Exercise Variations: There are many variations of this dumbbell chest press. Similar movements are performed, using a variety of equipment and body positions, in the following section.

SUPINE DUMBBELL CHEST FLYE

Body Parts Targeted: Chest; front of the shoulders

Joint Motion(s): Shoulder horizontal flexion (adduction)

Primary Muscles Strengthened: Pectoralis majors; anterior deltoids

Setup and Alignment: Lie supine on a bench and place your feet on the floor, an elevated support or a platform. Use the foot positioning that allows you to simultaneously maintain neutral lumbar spinal position and stability. Maintain neutral cervical posture. Position the dumbbells so the hands are about shoulder width apart and directly above the shoulders. Press the dumbbells straight up, and hold a position with slightly bent elbows. The elbows should be rotated outward, away from the body, and the thumbs are oriented toward one another. Keep your wrists neutral — avoid flexing, extending, abducting or adducting, and don't let the dumbbells tilt up or down. Retract the scapulae and attempt to keep this retracted position throughout the set of repetitions. *See fig. 63a*

Performing the Exercise: Maintaining the same degree of flexion in the elbows as established in the start position, lower the arms in a controlled, arcing movement outward. Keep the arms rotated away from the body, maintaining the path of motion represented by horizontal abduction (lowering the arms) and horizontal flexion (raising the arms). Lower the arms until the upper arms are parallel to the floor and the elbows are flexed 90 degrees. Ideally, the hands should be directly over the elbows. Maintain an unchanging elbow position throughout the movement and keep the thumbs oriented to one another throughout the motion. Return to the starting position by arcing the arms back up in line with the shoulders and chest. *See fig. 63b*

Comments: With the exception of performing elbow extension, the chest flye exercise represents the same joint mechanics as chest pressing movements. In theory, the body cannot differentiate a flye movement from a chest press motion at the shoulder, since both use the identical joint motion of horizontal flexion. Because the arm is stabilized at the elbow during many flye variations, there is potentially more stress imparted to the wrist, elbow and shoulder. This is the result of a longer lever being used to challenge the chest and shoulder musculature. Ironically, the chest flye may not actually be a "great" chest exercise.

The limiting factor of this movement is often the strength of the elbow flexors that fix the arm in some degree of stabilized elbow flexion. Many times this exercise ends because of elbow flexor fatigue, not chest fatigue. A quick solution to this challenge is to use a machine (such as an Incline 10-Degree Chest Machine), where the padded arms of the equipment fit in the "crook" of the elbow. This eliminates the weak link, which is the ability of the elbow flexors to continue to stabilize the arm. Another solution is to work with cable type equipment, where the cable handles can be slid over the hand and attached to the arm in the elbow area when performing the flye movement.

Fig. 63a

Safety Considerations: A key concern during flye movement is related to the range-of-motion of the movement. The arms should not be drawn much deeper than the upper arms parallel to the floor. In other words, the line formed by the elbow and shoulder should not go much beyond parallel to the floor, or beyond the midline of the body. Do not use the hands as a gauge, because if the hands are lowered to chest depth, the elbow-shoulder line will be too deep. Keep the thumbs oriented to one another throughout the exercise. Rotating the thumbs in or out reduces the effectiveness of the exercise and can contribute to shoulder joint stress. Maintain the plane of movement by not allowing the shoulders to internally or externally rotate.

Exercise Variations: Use the Incline 10-Degree Chest Machine suggested previously, or attach a cable handle at, or above, the elbow to move past the limiting factor of elbow flexor strength, as well as to reduce overall joint stress on the wrists, elbows and shoulders. The flye movement can be performed standing, seated, supine and on a decline or incline, with a variety of equipment. Simply, make sure the resistance opposes the movement. The mechanics do not change.

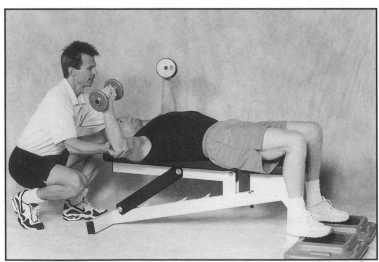

Fig. 63b

CHEST PRESS AND CHEST FLYE VARIATIONS

Following are six variations on the chest press and chest flye exercises previously described. The joint motion(s) and primary muscles strengthened are the same. These variations are accomplished with different body positions and equipment.

1. STANDING CABLE CHEST PRESS

Setup and Alignment: Stand upright with a slight straight-body forward lean. Maintain neutral spinal posture and place your feet about shoulder width apart, or in an astride position. Grasp the cable handles so the hands are about shoulder width apart and press them directly out in front of the shoulders. The elbows should be rotated outward, away from the body, and the thumbs are oriented to one another. The arms are parallel to the floor. Keep your wrists neutral — neither flexed, extended, abducted or adducted, and don't let the cable handles tilt up or down. Retract the scapulae and attempt to keep this retracted position throughout the set of repetitions. *See fig. 64a*

Performing the Exercise: Flex both elbows and draw the arms back. Keep the elbows rotated away from the body, maintaining the path of motion represented by horizontal abduction (drawing the arms back) and horizontal flexion (moving the arms forward). Bring the arms back until the line formed by the elbow and shoulder is no deeper than the midline of the body. The elbows are flexed approximately 90 degrees at this point. Keep the upper arms and forearms parallel to the floor. The hands should be directly in front of the elbows. Return to the start position by extending the elbows, pressing the cable handles forward and drawing the arms toward one another. *See fig. 64b*

Fig. 64a   *Fig. 64b*

Comments: Using any type of cable allows you to arc the arms naturally and bring them toward one another as the shoulders go through the arc-motion of horizontal flexion. Envision moving your arms around a wide barrel. This is in contrast to limited movement ranges that are linear — straight versus arcing — that are characteristic of barbells, floor pushups and many chest press machines where the motion is predetermined and the hands are fixed. This exercise can also be performed as a **Cable Chest Flye** by stabilizing the elbows in a slightly flexed position and focusing on the joint motions of horizontal flexion and extension.

Safety Considerations: Avoid flattening the low back, or rolling the hips under, as this is not the safest and strongest position for the spine. Maintain both cervical and lumbar neutral posture. The arms should not be drawn much deeper than the elbow-shoulder line and its intersection with the midline of the body. Cueing the hands back to the chest may place the load too deep, and put the shoulders at risk for joint stress. Position the wrists strongly so that the cable handles are parallel to the floor, and the wrists are neither flexed nor extended. Keep the thumbs oriented to one another throughout the exercise. Rotating the thumbs in or out reduces the effectiveness of the exercise and can contribute to shoulder joint stress. Maintain the plane of movement by not allowing the shoulders to rotate in or out. Avoid protracting the back by keeping your scapulae retracted.

2. Seated Incline Cable Chest Press

Setup and Alignment: Sit upright on the high-end of an adjustable platform or bench. Maintain neutral spinal posture and place your feet slightly wider than shoulder width apart. Securely attach the cable to the platform, or a point behind the bench. Grasp the cable handles and press them away from you, with hands about shoulder width apart and positioned slightly above the shoulders. (This places the line of pull of the clavicular portion of the pectoralis major in direct opposition to the resistance.) The elbows should be rotated outward, away from the body, and the thumbs are oriented to one another. Keep your wrists neutral — neither flexed, extended, abducted or adducted, and don't let the cable handles tilt up or down. Retract the scapulae and attempt to keep this retracted position throughout the set of repetitions. *See fig. 65a*

Performing the Exercise:
Flex both elbows and draw the arms back and slightly downward. The arms are at a slight angle to the floor during the movement. Keep the arms rotated away from the body, maintaining the path of motion represented by horizontal abduction (drawing the arms back) and horizontal flexion (moving the arms forward). Bring the arms back until the line formed by the elbow and shoulder is no deeper than the midline of the body. Keep the upper arms and

Fig. 65a

Fig. 65b

forearms at a slight angle to the floor, with the elbows flexed 90 degrees at this point. The hands should be directly in front of the elbows. Return to the start position by extending the elbows, pressing the cable handles forward and drawing the arms toward one another. *See fig. 65b*

Comments: Sitting on the incline bench makes it easier to maintain neutral posture. The same exercise, performed on the floor, tends to cause the hips to roll under, which flexes and loads the spine. The path of motion, determined by pressing the arms from the chest area upward and slightly higher than the shoulders, emphasizes the clavicular fibers of the pectoralis major muscles. Using any type of cable allows you to arc the arms naturally and bring them toward one another as the shoulders go through the arc-motion of horizontal flexion. Envision moving your arms around a wide barrel. This is in contrast to limited movement ranges that are linear — straight versus arcing — that are characteristic of barbells, floor pushups and many chest press machines where the motion is predetermined and the hands are fixed. This exercise can also be performed as a **Seated Incline Cable Chest Flye** by stabilizing the elbows in a slightly flexed position and focusing on the joint motions of horizontal flexion and extension.

Safety Considerations: Avoid flattening the low back, or rolling the hips under, as this is not the safest and strongest position for the spine. Maintain both cervical and lumbar neutral posture. The arms should not be drawn much deeper than the elbow-shoulder line and its intersection with the midline of the body. The upper arms should remain at a slight angle to the floor throughout the movement. Cueing the hands back to the chest may place the load too deep, and put the shoulders at risk for joint stress. Position the wrists strongly, so that the cable handles are parallel to the floor, and the wrists neither flexed nor extended. Keep the thumbs oriented to one another throughout the exercise. Rotating the thumbs in or out reduces the effectiveness of the exercise and can contribute to shoulder joint stress. Maintain the plane of movement by not allowing the shoulders to rotate in or out.

3. INCLINE DUMBBELL CHEST PRESS

Setup and Alignment: Adjust a bench so that it approximates a 50 to 60 degree angle from horizontal. Place the feet shoulder width apart on the floor or an elevated platform, depending on which set-up allows effective stabilization and a neutral lumbar spine. Maintain neutral cervical posture. Place a folded towel in the neck area to help with proper head and neck alignment. Press the dumbbells straight up from the shoulders, with the elbows rotated outward, away from the body. Flex your elbows slightly and keep your thumbs oriented to one another. Keep your wrists neutral — neither flexed, extended, abducted or adducted, and don't let the dumbbells tilt up or down. Retract the scapulae and attempt to keep this retracted position throughout the set of repetitions. *See fig. 66a*

Performing the Exercise: Flex both elbows and lower the arms. Keep the arms rotated away from the body, maintaining the path of motion represented by horizontal abduction (lowering the arms) and horizontal flexion (raising the arms). Lower the arms until the upper arms are parallel to the floor and the elbows are flexed 90 degrees. The hands should be directly over the elbows. Return to the start position by extending the elbows, pressing the dumbbells up and drawing the arms toward one another. *See fig. 66b*

Comments: Pressing upward from an inclined position places the line of pull of the clavicular portion of the pectoralis major in direct opposition to the resistance. The path of motion, determined by

Fig. 66a

Fig. 66b

pressing the arms from the chest area upward, and keeping the motion perpendicular to the floor, emphasizes the clavicular fibers of the pectoralis major muscles. How much you choose to incline or decline the bench should be dependent on the goal. As the bench is lowered toward a flat position, the joint motion and recruitment patterns begin to represent a supine dumbbell chest press, versus "upper" horizontal flexion. When the bench is moved toward vertical, the emphasis is placed on the anterior deltoid, to the point where very little pectoralis major contribution takes place. The path of motion — if the movement path is maintained while sitting on a bench that is inclined around 50 to 60 degrees from horizontal — emphasizes the clavicular fibers of the pectoralis major muscles. The entire muscle is active, but the line of pull and direction of force favors motor unit recruitment in the upper chest region. Using dumbbells allows you to arc the arms naturally and bring them toward one another as the shoulders go through the arc-motion of "upper" horizontal flexion. Envision moving your arms around a wide barrel. This is in contrast to limited movement ranges that are linear — straight versus arcing — that are characteristic of barbells, floor pushups and many chest press machines where the motion is predetermined and the hands are fixed. This exercise can also be performed as an **Incline Dumbbell Chest Flye** by stabilizing the elbows in a slightly flexed position and focusing on the joint motions of horizontal flexion and extension.

Safety Considerations: Avoid flattening the low back, as this is not the safest and strongest position for the spine. Maintain both cervical and lumbar neutral posture. The arms should not be drawn much deeper than the *upper* arms parallel to the floor. The hands and *lower* arms should remain perpendicular to the floor throughout the movement. Cueing the hands back to the chest may place the load too deep, and put the shoulders at risk for joint stress. Position the wrists strongly so that the dumbbells are parallel to the floor. Keep the thumbs oriented to one another throughout the exercise. Rotating the thumbs in or out reduces the effectiveness of the exercise and can contribute to shoulder joint stress. Maintain the vertical plane of movement by not allowing the shoulders to rotate in or out. Avoid protracting the shoulder girdle by keeping your scapulae retracted.

4. Decline Dumbbell Chest Press

Setup and Alignment: Adjust a bench so that it approximates a 10-degree angle from horizontal. This can be accomplished by placing a 4-inch platform under one end of the bench. Place the feet about shoulder width apart on the floor or an elevated platform, depending on which set-up allows effective stabilization and a neutral lumbar spine. Maintain neutral cervical posture. Holding the dumbbells, press the arms straight up from the shoulders, with the elbows rotated outward, away from the body. Flex your elbows slightly and keep your thumbs oriented to one another. Keep your wrists neutral — neither flexed, extended, abducted or adducted, and don't let the dumbbells tilt up or down. Retract the scapulae and attempt to keep this retracted position throughout the set of repetitions. *See fig. 67a*

Performing the Exercise: Flex both elbows and lower the arms. Keep the arms rotated away from the body, maintaining the path of motion represented by horizontal abduction (lowering the arms) and horizontal flexion (raising the arms). Lower the arms until the upper arms are parallel to the floor and the elbows are flexed 90 degrees. The hands should be directly over the elbows. Return to the start position by extending the elbows, pressing the dumbbells up and drawing the arms toward one another. *See fig. 67b*

Comments: Pressing upward on a decline places the line of pull of the "lower" portion of the pectoralis major in direct opposition to the resistance. The path of motion, determined by pressing the arms from the chest area upward, and keeping the motion perpendicular to the floor, emphasizes the "lower" fibers of the pectoralis major muscles, to some degree. Unlike the incline press, the bench needs to be raised only about 10 degrees from horizontal (i.e., place a 4 inch platform under one end of the bench) to create a decline set-up. During a flat press, the mid and lower motor units of the pectoralis major muscle are very active. It is not necessary to hang upside down "like a bat" to challenge the lower region of the pectoralis. In fact, an extreme decline position would have the exerciser performing shoulder adduction, versus shoulder horizontal flexion. This is not a case of right versus wrong, but one of defining what musculature of the chest you want to target, and determining what set-up position an average client can tolerate and stabilize effectively. When the bench is slightly declined and the head is place at its lower end, a slight emphasis is placed on the lower motor units of the pectoralis major muscles. The entire muscle is active, but the line of pull and direction of force favors motor unit recruitment in the "lower" chest region (Kendall, pg. 276). This exercise can also be performed as a **Decline Dumbbell Chest Flye** by stabilizing the elbows in a slightly flexed position and focusing on the joint motions of horizontal flexion and extension.

Fig. 67a

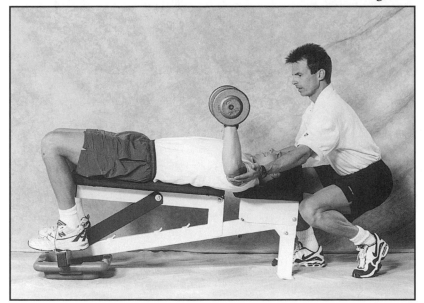

Fig. 67b

Safety Considerations: Avoid flattening the low back, as this is not the safest and strongest position for the spine. Maintain both cervical and lumbar neutral posture. The arms should not be drawn much deeper than the *upper* arms parallel to the floor. The hands and *lower* arms should remain perpendicular to the floor throughout the movement. Cueing the hands back to the chest may place the load too deep, and put the shoulders at risk for joint stress. Keep the wrists positioned strongly so that the dumbbells are parallel to the floor. Loss of neutral wrist positioning is evident by dumb-bells that are tilted or "laid" back. Keep the thumbs oriented toward one another throughout the exercise. Rotating the thumbs in or out reduces the effectiveness of the exercise and can contribute to shoulder joint stress. Maintain the vertical plane of movement by not allowing the shoulders to rotate in or out. Avoid protracting the shoulder girdle by keeping your scapulae retracted.

5. Machine Chest Press

Setup and Alignment: Adjust the machine seat so that the handles of the machine are positioned at about "chest" height. Maintain neutral spinal posture and place your feet about shoulder width apart, firmly on the ground. Place a folded towel in the neck area, if necessary, to help with proper head and neck alignment. Grasp the handles so that the hands are about shoulder width apart, and press them directly out in front of the shoulders. The elbows should be rotated outward, away from the body, and the thumbs are oriented toward one another. The arms are parallel to the floor. Keep your wrists neutral – neither flexed, extended, abducted or adducted. Retract the scapulae and attempt to keep this retracted position throughout the set of repetitions. *See fig. 68a*

Performing the Exercise: Flex both elbows and draw the arms back. Maintain the path of motion represented by horizontal abduction (drawing the arms back) and horizontal flexion (moving the arms forward). Bring the arms back until the line formed by the elbow and shoulder is no deeper than the midline of the body. Keep the upper arms and forearms parallel to the floor, with the elbows flexed 90 degrees at this point. The hands should be directly in front of the elbows. Return to the start position by extending the elbows, pressing the handles forward and drawing the arms toward one another. *See fig. 68b*

Comments: This particular machine actually allows you to arc the arms naturally and bring them toward one another as the shoulders go through the arc-motion of horizontal flexion. Envision moving your arms around a wide barrel. This is in contrast to limited movement ranges that are linear — straight versus arcing — that are characteristic of barbells, floor pushups and many chest press machines where the motion is predetermined and the hands are fixed.

Fig. 68a

Safety Considerations: Avoid flattening the low back, as this is not the safest and strongest position for the spine. Maintain both cervical and lumbar neutral posture. The arms should not be drawn back much deeper than the elbow-shoulder line and its intersection with the midline of the body. Limit depth range by using a "range-of-motion limiter" if the machine has this feature. The upper arms and forearms should remain parallel to the floor throughout the movement. Cueing the hands to the chest may place the load too deep, and put the shoulders at risk for joint stress. Position the wrists strongly so that the wrists neither flex nor extend. Loss of neutral wrist positioning is evident by wrists that are "laid" back. Keep the thumbs oriented to one another throughout the exercise. Rotating the thumbs in or out reduces the effectiveness of the exercise and can contribute to shoulder joint stress. Maintain the plane of movement by not allowing the shoulders to rotate in or out. Avoid protracting the back by keeping your scapulae retracted.

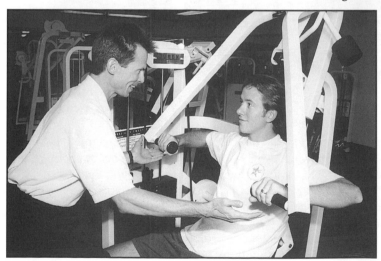

Fig. 68b

6. MACHINE "DIP" MOVEMENT

Setup and Alignment: Position yourself on the machine platform with an upright, neutral spinal posture. Place your hands on the support handles and slightly retract the scapulae. Keep your arms straight (not hyper-extended at the elbow) or slightly flexed. *See fig.* 69a

Performing the Exercise: Flex the arms at the elbow and lower to a position where the upper arm is about parallel to the floor. The elbow should not be flexed more than 90 degrees. Keep the head and shoulders aligned over the hips and ankles, and maintain a body position that is almost perpendicular to the floor. Return to the start position by flexing the shoulders and extending the elbows. Upon reaching the straight-arm start position, depress the scapulae without hyperextending the elbow. *See fig. 69b*

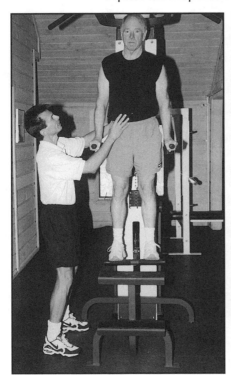 

Fig. 69a *Fig. 69b*

Comments: The dip can be characterized as a chest/shoulder exercise, although it is commonly thought of as a triceps exercise. The difference in joint motions is simply shoulder flexion rather than the shoulder horizontal flexion or adduction performed in the previous chest pressing exercises. For some clients, this exercise could be considered high-risk, depending on the type of equipment being used, and the ability of the client to perform this movement safely. Remember that this exercise simply targets the front of the shoulder, chest and back of the arms. If you have any concerns about using this exercise, many less complex exercise variations exist that can effectively and safely target this same musculature.

Safety Considerations: It is preferred that the dip be performed on a machine that can assist in lifting some of the participant's weight, so the ideal rep range can be attained. Body weight-type exercises tend to be too heavy or too light, rather than just right. Because extreme shoulder hyperextension and elbow flexion place both of these joints in vulnerable positions — being at the extreme end range of motion at both joints — it makes good sense to limit the depth to 90 degrees of elbow flexion, or where the upper arm is generally no deeper than parallel to the floor. Additionally, anterior shoulder joint capsule stress is a big concern as this can lead to shoulder instability and injury when the joint is heavily loaded at the extreme of shoulder hyperextension. When spotting the dip movement, watch for the torso moving forward or a body angle that reflects the chest moving in front and feet behind a centered position. This "lean" warns of imminent collapse.

UPPER BACK AND SHOULDER EXERCISES

KNEELING DUMBBELL HIGH ELBOW ROW

Body Parts Targeted: Back of the shoulder; front of the upper arm

Joint Motion(s): Shoulder horizontal extension (abduction); elbow flexion

Primary Muscles Strengthened: Posterior deltoid; elbow flexors

Setup and Alignment: Place one knee on a bench with the same-side hip aligned directly over it. The knee of the other leg should be at about the same height (i.e., make sure the bench is not too high) and slightly flexed. Take the hand on the side of the knee that is on the bench and place it just off the front edge of the bench, as a flat hand position puts more stress on the carpal bones of the wrist. Position the upper body so that it is parallel to the floor. Maintain neutral lumbar and cervical posture. The arm is hanging straight down from your shoulder and the elbow is straight or slightly flexed. Position the dumbbell so that it is above and parallel to the floor, and the palm of the hand faces back. Retract your scapulae and maintain retraction throughout the exercise. *See fig. 70a*

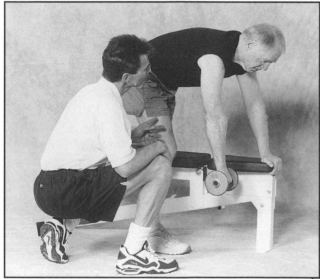

Fig. 70a

Fig. 70b

Performing the Exercise: Flex the elbow and pull the arm up until the upper arm is parallel to the floor or slightly higher, and the elbow forms an approximate angle of 90 degrees. The elbow should be rotated away from the side of the body, so that horizontal extension can be performed, and not shoulder extension. This movement should reflect a mirror image of the arcing-motion encouraged in the chest press exercises. As was true for these movements, it is critical to maintain the path of motion represented by horizontal shoulder extension. Return to the start position and when finished with the set, perform the exercise using the other arm. *See fig. 70b*

Comments: The "high-elbow" row is characterized as a shoulder exercise because it targets the shoulder horizontal abductors, specifically the posterior deltoid. Performed with scapular retraction, the high-row strengthens the upper back and back of the shoulder, which helps to create muscle balance between the chest and anterior shoulder musculature. I am often asked if you should begin the movement with shoulder extension and inwardly rotate the upper arm to the high-elbow position. Generally, I like to keep the joint motions "pure," meaning I don't blend actions at the same joint. Why? It's tough to effectively load rotation during a movement like this, so not only are you unable to strengthen the fibers responsible for rotation, but those fibers that were initially aligned favorably against the load, are now getting less force placed against them since their line of pull has changed. Keep joint motion simple. Keep it pure and effective when training to optimize strength. Training functional movement patterns where joint motion is often combined, and training with lighter loads or no load, represents a different training situation. Understand the distinction, that the two methods are simply "different."

Safety Considerations: Keep your chest square to the floor, versus "opening" it toward the ceiling. Control the movement and maintain start position throughout the exercise. Don't sit back on your heels. Keep the body weight evenly distributed between the supporting arm and legs, and keep the supporting arm slightly flexed. Maintain a neutral cervical spine, and don't let the shoulder internally or externally rotate. The hand should remain below the elbow and the forearm should remain perpendicular to the floor. It *is* appropriate to pull the upper arm slightly beyond the midline of the body, which is *not* true for pressing movements.

HIGH ELBOW ROW VARIATIONS

Following are two variations on the high elbow row previously described. The joint motion(s) and primary muscles strengthened are the same. These variations are accomplished with different body positions and equipment.

1. MACHINE HIGH ELBOW ROW

Setup and Alignment: Position the seat of the machine so the hand-grips are about chest high. Sit upright and maintain neutral lumbar and cervical posture. Grasp the handles with an over grip, and press the arms straight out in front of the shoulders. The palms face down and the elbows are slightly flexed and rotated away from the body. The arms should be parallel to the floor. Retract your scapulae and maintain retraction throughout the exercise. *See fig. 71a*

Performing the Exercise: Flex the elbows and pull the arms back until the shoulder-elbow line is at or slightly past the midline of the body. The elbows form an approximate angle of 90 degrees. The elbows should be rotated away from the sides of the body, so that horizontal extension can be performed, and not shoulder extension. This movement should reflect a mirror image of the arcing motion encouraged in the chest press exercises. As was true for these movements, it is critical to maintain the path of motion represented by horizontal shoulder extension. Return to the start position with control. *See fig. 71b*

Comments: The "high elbow" row is characterized as a shoulder exercise, because it targets the shoulder horizontal abductors, specifically the posterior deltoid. Performed with scapular retraction, the high-row strengthens the upper back and backs of the shoulders, which helps to create muscle balance between the chest and anterior shoulder musculature.

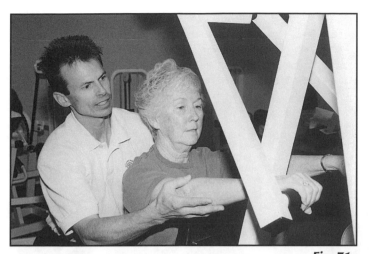

Safety Considerations: Keep your chest square to the machine, versus "opening" it toward the back wall. Control the movement and maintain start position throughout the exercise. Do not arch the back to assist the movement. Keep your head level and do not allow the shoulders to internally or externally rotate. The hands should remain in front of the elbows and the forearms should remain parallel to the floor. It *is* appropriate to pull the upper arms beyond the midline of the body, which is *not* true for pressing movements.

Fig. 71a

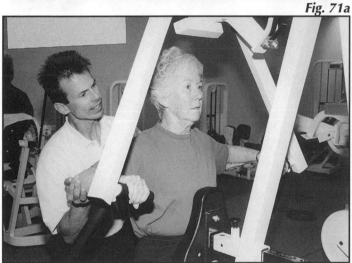

Fig. 71b

2. STANDING CABLE HIGH ELBOW ROW

Setup and Alignment: Securely attach an elastic resistance cable chest high. Move away from the attachment point with cable in hand. Stand in a "ready" position, with neutral spinal posture and tension on the cable. The body is upright and the hips and knees are slightly flexed. Hold the handles with the arms straight out in front of the shoulders, using an over grip. The palms face down and the elbows are rotated away from the body. The arms should be parallel to the floor. Retract your scapulae without flexing your elbows, and maintain retraction throughout the exercise. *See fig. 72a*

Performing the Exercise: Flex the elbows and pull the arms back until the shoulder-elbow line is at or slightly past the midline of the body. The elbows form an approximate angle of 90 degrees. The elbows should be rotated away from the sides of the body, so that horizontal extension can be performed, and not shoulder extension. This movement should reflect a mirror image of the arcing-motion encouraged in the chest press exercises. As was true for these movements, it is critical to maintain the path of motion represented by horizontal shoulder extension. Return to the start position with control. *See fig. 72b*

Fig. 72a   *Fig. 72b*

Comments: The "high elbow" row is characterized as a shoulder exercise because it targets the shoulder horizontal abductors, specifically the posterior deltoids. Performed with scapular retraction, the high-row strengthens the upper back and back of the shoulders, which helps to create muscle balance between the chest and anterior shoulder musculature.

Safety Considerations: Keep your chest square to the attachment point, versus "opening" it toward the back wall. Control the movement and maintain "ready" position throughout the exercise. Do not arch the back to assist the movement, or otherwise introduce momentum. Keep your head level and do not allow the shoulders to internally or externally rotate. The hands should remain in front of the elbows and the forearms should remain parallel to the floor. It *is* appropriate to pull the upper arms beyond the midline of the body, which is *not* true for pressing movements.

KNEELING DUMBBELL LOW ELBOW ROW

Body Parts Targeted: Side of the upper back; back of the shoulder; front of the upper arm

Joint Motion(s): Shoulder extension; elbow flexion

Primary Muscles Strengthened: Latissimus dorsi, teres major; posterior deltoid; elbow flexors

Setup and Alignment: Place one knee on a bench with the same-side hip aligned directly over it. The knee of the other leg should be at about the same height (i.e., make sure the bench is not too high) and slightly flexed. Take the hand on the side of the knee that is on the bench and place it just off the front edge of the bench, as a flat hand position puts more stress on the carpal bones of the wrist. Position the upper body so that it is parallel to the floor. Maintain neutral lumbar and cervical posture. The arm is hanging straight down from your shoulder and the elbow is straight or slightly flexed. Position the dumbbell so that it is above and parallel to the floor, and the palm of the hand faces inward. Retract your scapulae and maintain retraction throughout the exercise. *See fig. 73a*

Performing the Exercise: Flex the elbow and pull the arm up until the upper arm is parallel to the floor or slightly higher, and the elbow forms an approximate angle of 90 degrees. The elbow should be kept close to the side of the body, so that shoulder extension is performed and not shoulder horizontal extension. It is critical to maintain the path of motion represented by shoulder extension. Return to the start position and when finished with the set, perform the exercise using the other arm. *See fig. 73b*

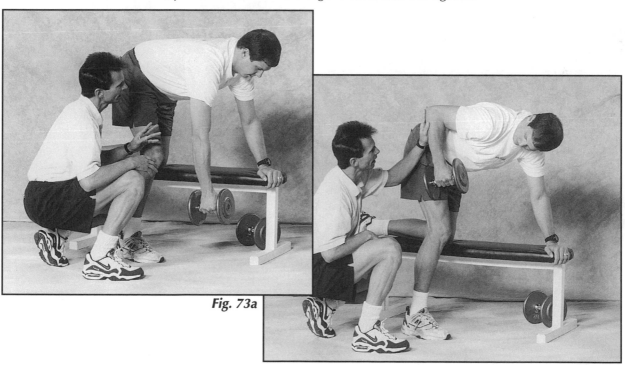

Fig. 73a

Fig. 73b

Comments: The "low-elbow" row is characterized as a "back" exercise, because it targets the shoulder extensors. The latissimus muscle, which helps to shape the side of the back, is very powerful when involved in shoulder extension. Performed with scapular retraction, the low-row strengthens the upper back and back of the shoulder, which helps to create muscle balance between the chest and anterior shoulder musculature. Cue the movement by telling the client to let the arm "slide" by the ribs until the upper arm is about parallel to the floor.

Safety Considerations: Keep your chest square to the floor, versus "opening" it toward the ceiling. Control the movement and maintain your start position throughout the exercise. Don't sit back on your heels. Keep the body weight evenly distributed between the supporting arm and legs, and keep the supporting arm slightly flexed. Keep your head level and don't let the shoulder internally rotate, where the elbow moves forward and away from the side. The hand should remain below the elbow and the forearm should remain perpendicular to the floor. It *is* appropriate to pull the upper arm beyond the midline of the body, which is *not* true for pressing movements.

Low Elbow Row Variations

The following is a variation on the low elbow row previously described. The joint motion(s) and primary muscles strengthened are the same. This variation is accomplished with a different body position and equipment.

1. Seated Cable Low Row

Setup and Alignment: Sit with your feet firmly placed on the floor or against the machine. Seat upright with neutral spinal posture. (A slight lean back is acceptable as long as the spine does not flex and the position is maintained throughout the exercise.) Grasp the handles of the bar, strap or split rope cable with the arms straight out in front of the shoulders, and the elbows straight or slightly flexed. Preferably, use a slightly supinated, neutral or under grip. (Grip choice will influence whether shoulder extension or shoulder horizontal extension is performed.) Orient the palms toward one another and keep the elbows at your sides. The arms should be straight, but not hyperextended. Retract your scapulae and maintain retraction throughout the exercise. *See fig. 74a*

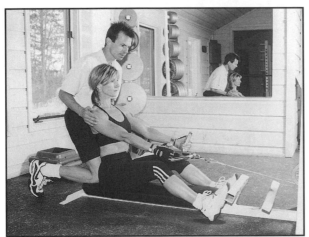

Fig. 74a

Fig. 74b

Performing the Exercise: Flex the elbows and pull the arms back until the shoulder-elbow line is at or slightly past the midline of the body. The elbows form an approximate angle of 90 degrees and the forearms are parallel to, or slightly higher than, the floor. The elbows should be kept close to the sides of the body, so that shoulder extension can be performed, and not shoulder horizontal extension. It is critical to maintain the path of motion represented by shoulder extension. Return to the start position with control and maintain scapular retraction. *See fig. 74b*

Comments: Often times performance of the seated cable low row represents a combination of elbow flexion and back hyperextension, with no shoulder extension, which is often the end result of using too much load. Choose an appropriate resistance that can be initiated without incorporating "cheat" or momentum into the movement. Keep the exercise "quiet" and "clean," meaning little or no movement occurs in the hip or spine. Initiate the movement with the latissimus muscles and shoulder extension. Elbow flexion will naturally follow.

Safety Considerations: Control the movement and maintain start position throughout the exercise. Do not arch the back to assist the movement. Keep your head level and do not allow the shoulders to internally rotate (elbows move or "flare" upward and outward). The hands should remain in front of the elbows and the forearms should remain just about parallel to the floor during most of the movement. It *is* appropriate to pull the upper arms beyond the midline of the body, which is *not* true for pressing movements.

SUPINE DUMBBELL PULLOVER

Body Parts Targeted: Sides of the upper back; backs of the shoulders; backs of the upper arms

Joint Motion(s): Shoulder extension

Primary Muscles Strengthened: Latissimus dorsi, teres majors; posterior deltoids; pectoralis majors (sternal portions); triceps (long head)

Fig. 75a

Fig. 75b

Setup and Alignment: Lie supine on a bench and place your feet on the floor, an elevated support or a platform. Use the foot positioning that allows you to simultaneously maintain neutral lumbar spinal position and stability. Maintain neutral cervical posture. Position the dumbbell over the chest, so the hands and arms are perpendicular to the chest, and press the dumbbell straight up. (Use a fixed or nonadjustable dumbbell so there is no chance, for example, that a retaining collar can work loose, causing weight plates to fall on the client's face.) The elbows are flexed slightly and the shoulders are slightly rotated inward, but don't let the elbows flare excessively outward, as a result of too much inward shoulder rotation. Use a "triangle" grip formed by the thumbs and forefingers touching one another, to securely hold the weight. Keep your wrists as neutral as possible. Be especially aware of the wrists excessively hyper-extending or being "laid" back. Retract the scapulae and attempt to keep this retracted position throughout the set of repetitions. *See fig. 75a*

Performing the Exercise: Keeping both elbows slightly flexed — don't let the degree of flexion change once the exercise starts — lower the arms toward an overhead position. Keep the arms in line with the sides of the body by not allowing the elbows to move outward. Maintain the path of motion represented by shoulder flexion and shoulder extension. Lower until the upper arms are about 20- to 30-degrees above parallel to the floor. As the arms flex overhead, keep tension in the abdominals to avoid back hyperextension. The hands and wrists should be in line with the elbows and shoulders. Return by extending the shoulders and pulling the arms back to the start position. *See fig. 75b*

Comments: Though not my "favorite" exercise, this is an excellent movement to analyze. With careful monitoring and a few adjustments, you can limit risk and the exercise can be performed "safely" by most people. A bench that is too high may force the back into hyperextension, whereas placing the feet on top of the bench may not provide enough stability to perform the exercise safely. This exercise can be tricky to stabilize and when the arms move overhead, tends to "force" the exerciser into excessive lumbar hyperextension. Because of these factors, I prefer placing the feet on the floor, or if the bench is too high and nonadjustable, I raise the feet by placing blocks or another type of platform under the feet.

Safety Considerations: Realize that this exercise uses a long lever, and almost straight arms. The lever can be shortened by flexing the elbow more, which reduces the shear force at the shoulders, but then the exerciser has very little clearance room for the dumbbell to pass the face. An easy solution is to use a cable attachment from the same supine position where the force presented more directly opposes the movement. Throughout the exercise, monitor for increased lordosis (indicator of weak abdominals or lack of stabilizing awareness) and don't let the shoulders flex to a position where the arms are parallel to the ground. Initiating the return before this extreme overhead position is reached, may reduce the likelihood of impingement pathology. Shear forces increase across the joint as shoulder flexion increases in this position.

Pullover or Pulldown Variations

The following exercise targets the "pullover" motion previously described. The joint motion(s) and primary muscles strengthened are the same. This variation is accomplished with a different body position and equipment.

1. Standing Straight Arm Cable Pull-Down

Setup and Alignment: Stand with your feet hip width apart, or in an astride stance. Regardless of stance, stand in a "ready" position, with neutral spinal posture. The body is upright, though a slight straight-body lean may be present from the hip to shoulder (i.e., the shoulders are slightly in front of the hips, but neutral lumbar posture is maintained) and the hips and knees are slightly flexed. Place your hands on the bar of the overhead cable machine, using an over grip. The arms are slightly flexed and about shoulder width apart. Position the angles of the arms so that the hands are about head height, in front of the body. You should be able to see your hands from this starting position by moving your eyes upward, but don't hyperextend your neck. The elbows are flexed slightly and the shoulders are slightly rotated inward, but don't let the elbows flare excessively outward, as a result of too much inward shoulder rotation and elbow flexion. Keep your wrists as neutral as possible. Especially be aware of the wrist excessively hyperextending or being "laid" back. Retract and depress the scapulae and attempt to keep this "set" position throughout the exercise. *See fig. 76a*

Performing the Exercise: Keeping both elbows slightly flexed — don't let the degree of flexion change once the exercise starts — pull the arms down toward the body. Keep the arms in line with the sides of the body by not allowing the elbows to move outward. Maintain the path of motion represented by shoulder flexion and shoulder extension. As the arms pull down toward the body (upper thigh), keep the scapulae depressed and retracted, and make sure the hips do not move forward or back. Keep tension in the abdominals to stabilize the start position and to avoid having the back hyperextend. The hands and wrists should be in line with the elbows and shoulders. Return by controlling the arms back to the overhead start position. *See fig. 76b*

Fig. 76a   *Fig. 76b*

Comments: The angle of the arms overhead in the start position represents the very functional daily activities of reaching overhead or removing an item from a kitchen cabinet. Starting from a partially flexed shoulder position, versus fully flexed or directly overhead — not only challenges the extensor muscles of the shoulder effectively, but reduces the risk of shoulder impingement, and avoids putting the joint at the extreme of shoulder flexion. Any time a joint is placed at an extreme joint motion position, more risk is presented to the joint in terms of injury potential.

Safety Considerations: Because this exercise uses the arms as a "long-lever," it is important to maintain a slight degree of elbow flexion. This will reduce cross-forces on the joints of the wrists, elbows and shoulders. Also, considerably less absolute weight will be used because of the long lever, especially when compared to pulling movements that utilize elbow flexion actively. Keep the wrist positioned strongly in neutral and don't let the elbows excessively flare up and out to the side, as this is an indicator that elbow flexion and inward shoulder rotation have been introduced into the movement.

SEATED CABLE LATISSIMUS PULLDOWN

Body Parts Targeted: Sides of the upper back; backs of the shoulders; fronts of the upper arms

Joint Motion(s): Shoulder adduction; elbow flexion

Primary Muscles Strengthened: Latissimus dorsi; teres majors; posterior deltoids; elbow flexors

Setup and Alignment: Stand and place your hands on the bar overhead, with the hands placed in an over grip and slightly wider than the elbows. It is important to carefully set the width of the hands, so that when the elbows flex during the movement the hands will move in line with the elbows and retain a position that is close to being directly above the wrists at the endpoint of the pull downward. Pulling the bar downward, sit with your feet firmly placed on the floor and knees under the pad. Maintain a neutral spinal posture and lean backward from the hip (don't flex the spine) about 20- to 30-degrees. Retract and depress your scapulae and maintain this "set" position throughout the exercise. *See fig. 77a*

Fig. 77a

Fig. 77b

Performing the Exercise: Initiate the movement by contracting the lats, and flexion of the elbows will naturally follow. As you flex the elbows, envision pulling the arms out (arc to the outside) and down toward your sides (shoulder adduction). At all times during the movement, keep the line from the wrists to the elbows (the forearms), perpendicular to the floor. At no point should the forearms rotate toward the floor, which is caused by inward shoulder rotation, and results from drawing the elbows *past* the sides of the body, rather than down and into the sides of the body. Keep tension in the abdominals to stabilize the start position and to avoid back hyperextension. The torso should *not* move forward or back. Return by controlling the arms back to the overhead start position. *See fig. 77b*

Comments: The slight backward lean from the hip and pull of the bar toward the chest, places the direction of force (the load presented by the cable-pulley system) in perfect opposition to the movement and the line of pull presented by the latissimus muscles. The latissimus fiber direction is oblique, or one of a slight angle that runs from the lumbo-sacral area of the low-back, at a slight angle to its insertion point in the upper, medial aspect of the humerus. Not only is pulling behind the neck likely to cause trauma to the shoulder joint (Chapter 9), but it does not best load the latissimus muscles, since their fiber direction is *not* vertical. As the straight-body lean backward becomes more pronounced, at some point the shoulder joint motion will become pure shoulder horizontal extension, which targets the posterior deltoids as the prime mover. It is important to maintain a more upright seated position — still avoiding the pulldown behind-the-neck — to effectively target shoulder adduction and keep the latissimus muscle as the prime mover.

Safety Considerations: Many times when this exercise is performed, it looks more like elbow flexion plus back hyperextension. To keep the exercise safe and to retain the goal of the exercise which is to target the latissimus, stabilize the start position, don't allow the angle of the upper body to change during the exercise, and initiate the movement with shoulder adduction and latissimus contraction. Keep the arms/elbows pulling outward, down and into the sides of the body. A common technique error is to pull the elbows past the sides, which can put considerable stress on the wrists, elbows and shoulders. The motion of this exercise stops when the elbows are pulled into the sides or the forearms rotate from their perpendicular orientation toward the floor, to one where they are moving toward parallel. If the hands are not placed wide enough and outside the elbows in the start position, toward the end-range of the motion the wrists are likely to adduct (evident by the little finger moving outward). This places unnecessary stress on the wrists, and too much elbow flexion (hands moving toward the shoulders) can limit the degree of shoulder adduction possible.

Exercise Variations: Use of an under-grip, neutral-grip (i.e., "hammer-grip") or over-grip (shown in this exercise) hand position will effect the contribution provided by the elbow flexors, though all are activated with any grip position. An under-grip places the biceps brachii in a more advantageous position to exert force, whereas the neutral-grip favors the brachioradialis. The brachialis is the prime mover in the over-grip because it attaches on the ulna, and its line of pull is unaffected by pronation. But, the mechanics of the overall pull-down exercise should not change. It is arguable that the under grip has the most potential to create elbow and shoulder stress when performing the exercise using a straight bar because of the extreme externally rotated position of the shoulder. Be sure to monitor this grip choice for any discomfort in the wrist, elbow or shoulder regions.

MACHINE LATISSIMUS PULL-UP

Body Parts Targeted: Sides of the upper back; backs of the shoulders; fronts of the upper arms

Joint Motion(s): Shoulder extension; elbow flexion

Primary Muscles Strengthened: Latissimus dorsi, teres majors; posterior deltoids; elbow flexors

Setup and Alignment: Place your hands on the parallel grips overhead, with the hands directly in line with slightly flexed elbows, and using a neutral-grip. Stand with your feet firmly placed on the platform, with the knees and hips slightly flexed. Maintain a neutral spinal posture and lean slightly backward without flexing your spine (i.e., a slight, straight-body lean), so that a more favorable line of pull is presented to the muscles. This also allows you to pull the chest toward the hands, rather than vertically toward the tops of the shoulders. Retract and depress your scapulae and maintain this "set" position throughout the exercise. *See fig. 78a*

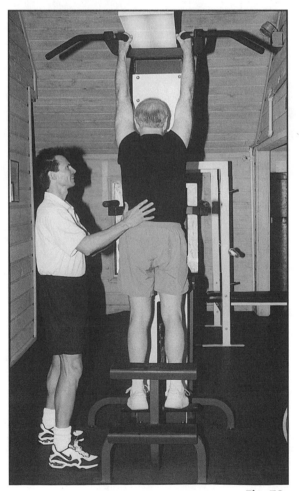

Fig. 78a

Performing the Exercise:

Initiate the moving by contracting the lats, and flexion of the elbows will naturally follow. As you flex the arms, envision arcing the elbows out in front of you and down toward the sides of the body (shoulder extension). Continue the motion until the elbows are at the sides. At all times during the movement, keep the line from the wrist to the elbow (the forearms), perpendicular to the floor. Don't attempt to draw the elbows *behind* body. Keep tension in the abdominals and scapular muscles to stabilize the start position. The body should *not* swing forward or back. Return by controlling the arms back to the overhead start position. *See fig. 78b*

Fig. 78b

Comments: With regard to latissimus work, I set a goal to target shoulder adduction and shoulder extension because these are the two most powerful joint motions to which the latissimus muscles contribute. I can target shoulder extension, for example, with one-arm rows, straight-arm cable pulldowns and by using a netural- or under-grip when performing pulldown or pull-up movements. Shoulder adduction can be targeted with the seated cable pulldown previously described.

Safety Considerations: I prefer to use the neutral-grip hand position because it potentially provides less stress to the wrist, elbow and shoulder since the shoulder is not forced to externally rotate, which does occur when using the under-grip. Either grip will allow the client to perform shoulder extension, but the neutral-grip may reduce the risk of joint-related stress.

Exercise Variations: Use of an under-grip, neutral-grip (i.e., "hammer-grip") or over-grip (shown in this exercise) hand position will effect the contribution provided by the elbow flexors, though all are activated with any grip position. An under-grip places the biceps brachii in a more advantageous position to exert force, whereas the neutral-grip favors the brachioradialis. The brachialis is the prime mover in the over-grip because it attaches on the ulna, and its line of pull is unaffected by pronation. But, the mechanics of the overall pulldown exercise should not change. It is arguable that the under grip has the most potential to create elbow and shoulder stress when performing the exercise using a straight bar because of the extreme externally rotated position of the shoulder. Be sure to monitor this grip choice for any discomfort in the wrist, elbow or shoulder regions.

SHOULDER EXERCISES

STANDING DUMBBELL SHOULDER FLEXION

Body Parts Targeted: Front of the shoulders

Joint Motion(s): Shoulder flexion

Primary Muscles Strengthened: Anterior deltoids; clavicular portion of the pectoralis major

Setup and Alignment: Stand in a "ready" position, with neutral spinal posture. The body is upright and the hips and knees are slightly flexed. Let the arms hang naturally, with the hands slightly forward of your sides. The palms of the hands should face the sides of your body, and your elbows should point back throughout the movement. Keep your wrists neutral — neither flexed, extended, abducted or adducted, and don't let the dumbbells tilt up or down. Retract and depress the scapulae and attempt to keep this position throughout the set of repetitions. *See fig. 79a*

Performing the Exercise: With slightly flexed elbows, lift the arms out and up until they are about parallel to the floor. The hands should remain just outside of the shoulders, wrists stay neutral, and the thumbs are oriented to the ceiling. Avoid rotating the shoulder in or out, or supinating or pronating the elbows. Lower the arms back down to the start position with control. *See fig. 79b*

 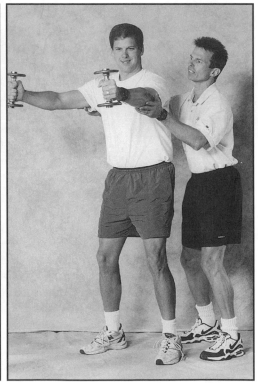

Fig. 79a   *Fig. 79b*

Comments: The "front delt raise," is another exercise that targets the anterior shoulder and chest musculature. Make sure you balance this type of training by training muscles that counter anterior shoulder and chest strength, such as the posterior shoulder and upper back muscles.

Safety Considerations: A common pattern of movement — scapular elevation and protraction of the scapulae — often leads to shoulder impingement. In light of this observation, it makes sense to maintain scapular depression and retraction during shoulder flexion.

Exercise Variations: Shoulder flexion can be performed in supine and standing positions, and with a variety of equipment such as cables, elastic tubing and machines. Make sure the type of resistance being used opposes the path of motion.

STANDING DUMBBELL SHOULDER ABDUCTION

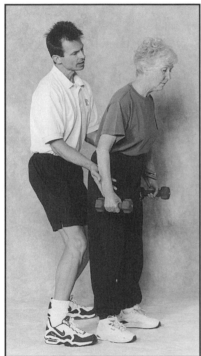

Fig. 80a

Body Parts Targeted: Shoulders

Joint Motion(s): Shoulder abduction

Primary Muscles Strengthened: Medial deltoids

Setup and Alignment: Stand in a "ready" position, with neutral spinal posture. The body is positioned with a slight straight-body lean from the hips, and the hips and knees are slightly flexed. The slight lean forward should allow the medial deltoid to more effectively be resisted by the pull of gravity. Let the arms hang naturally, with the hands slightly forward of your sides. The palms of the hands should face the sides of your body, and your elbows should point back throughout the movement. Keep your wrists neutral — neither flexed, extended, abducted or adducted, and don't let the dumbbells tilt up or down. Stabilize scapular position and attempt to keep this stabilized position throughout the set of repetitions. *See fig. 80a*

Performing the Exercise: With slightly flexed elbows, "push" the arms out and up until they are about parallel to the floor. The hands should remain in front of the shoulders, with the elbows directly in line with the shoulders. Keep the wrists neutral, and the palms oriented to the floor at the end range of motion. Avoid rotating the shoulder in or out, or supinating or pronating the elbow. Lower the arms back down to the start position with control. *See fig. 80b*

Comments: Generally, the "lateral raise" is performed in an upright position, which puts the anterior deltoid in a perfect line of pull against gravity. To more effectively target the medial deltoid, simply lean forward 10 to 30 degrees. *Note:* The client used as a model in these photos has kyphosis of the thoracic spine. While it appears that she is rounding her shoulders and pushing her head forward, this represents her "current" neutral posture in the cervical and thoracic spine. This current posture is significantly better than her posture prior to a year of strength training.

Safety Considerations: Maintain neutral position in the shoulders. Allowing the shoulder to externally rotate to a "thumbs up" position puts the anterior

Fig. 80b

deltoid back on top of the shoulder, and external rotation is not effectively resisted by dumbells and gravity. Inward rotation of the shoulder also cancels out the goal of targeting the medial deltoid, and can cause impingement, as well as limiting abduction range-of-motion. Abduct to 90 degrees or below, to avoid shoulder impingement.

Exercise Variations: This same exercise can be performed in a supine inclined position with elastic tubing attached to the bottom of an adjustable step platform or looped under the foot. The head should be slightly higher than the hips. Shoulder abduction can be performed in several other positions, using a variety of equipment such as cable or machines. Regardless of the position or equipment used, make sure the type of resistance you are using directly opposes the movement motion.

PRONE DUMBBELL BACK FLYE

Body Parts Targeted: Backs of the shoulders

Joint Motion(s): Shoulder horizontal extension (abduction)

Primary Muscles Strengthened: Posterior deltoids

Setup and Alignment: Position yourself prone on a bench, knees bent with your ankles aligned over your knees. The head should be placed comfortably, either face down or turned to either side of the body. Maintain neutral lumbar and cervical posture. The arms are hanging down toward the floor, with the hands outside of the elbows. This abducted position of the arms, as opposed to the hands being positioned directly under the shoulders, provides some resistance from the pull of gravity on the dumbbells at the start of the movement. Grasp the dumbbells with the palms facing *back*, and keep the elbows slightly flexed. Retract your scapulae and maintain retraction throughout the exercise. *See fig. 81a*

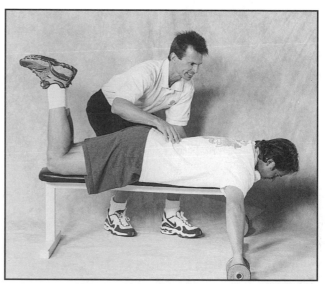

Fig. 81a

Performing the Exercise: Keeping the elbows slightly flexed and stabilized, pull (use an arcing motion) the arms up until the upper arms are parallel to the floor or slightly higher. The hands

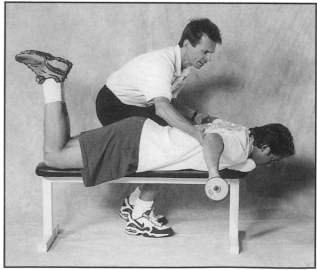

Fig. 81b

153

should remain outside the elbows. The elbows should be kept away from the sides of the body, so that shoulder horizontal extension can be performed, and not shoulder extension. This movement should reflect a mirror image of the arcing-motion encouraged in the chest press and flye exercises. As was true for these movements, it is critical to maintain the path of motion represented by horizontal shoulder extension. Return to the start position. *See fig. 81b*

Comments: The "high-elbow flye" or "rear delt flye" is characterized as a shoulder exercise, because it targets the shoulder horizontal abductors, specifically the posterior deltoids. The flye is stabilized at the elbow by the triceps (the opposite of what happens during a chest flye, when the elbow flexors stabilize the arm as a long lever). When performed with scapular retraction, the back-flye strengthens the upper back and backs of the shoulders, which helps to create muscle balance between the chest and anterior shoulder musculature. Use of a flat bench (where the bench surface is parallel to the floor) is desirable when using dumbbells, rather than an incline of any degree, because the force of gravitational pull on the dumbbells directly opposes the movement from a prone position.

Safety Considerations: Control the movement and maintain start position throughout the exercise. Don't let the shoulders internally or externally rotate. The hands should remain outside of the elbows, and the forearms should *not* rotate toward a position where the forearms begin to be oriented parallel to the floor (this would indicate that shoulder external rotation had been introduced to the movement). The elbows should remain oriented to the ceiling. It *is* appropriate to pull the upper arms beyond the midline of the body, which is *not* true for pressing movements.

Exercise Variations: The back flye can be performed from prone, supine, seated and standing positions, with a variety of equipment such as cable, elastic tubing or machines. Independent of equipment, technique does not change. But, as always, it is important to make sure the resistance is placed in direct opposition to the movement for effective overload to take place, and that the desired path of motion is maintained.

SEATED DUMBBELL PRESS OVERHEAD

Body Parts Targeted: Front and medial aspects of the shoulders; backs of the upper arms; back of the neck and mid-back regions

Joint Motion(s): Shoulder flexion and abduction; scapular rotation upward; elbow extension

Primary Muscles Strengthened: Anterior deltoids; trapezius; triceps

Setup and Alignment: Set the incline bench at 10 to 20 degrees of incline, from a vertical position. Place the feet about shoulder width apart on the floor or elevated platform, depending on which set-up allows effective stabilization and a neutral lumbar spine. Maintain neutral cervical posture. Place a folded towel in the neck area to help with proper head and neck alignment. Raise the dumbbells to shoulder height and split the difference between having your elbows pointed out to the sides in the frontal plane (extremely open/external shoulder rotation) and your elbows oriented forward in the sagittal plane (close to your sides/inward shoulder rotation). Orient your thumbs to one another, palms facing predominantly forward, though the lower forearms should be partially supinated for natural alignment. Keep your wrists neutral — neither flexed, extended, abducted or adducted, and don't let the dumbbells tilt up or down. (They should remain parallel to the floor throughout the movement.) Stabilize the scapular region and avoid excessive scapular motion. *See fig. 82a*

Fig. 82a

Fig. 82b

Performing the Exercise: Press the weight up and *slightly* forward, and as if you were pressing around a barrel. Finish the pressing movement by bringing the thumbs toward each other. The dumbbells may or may not touch. Keep the elbows from moving forward (inward) or back (outward). You should be able to see the hands overhead. Look with your eyes, but don't tilt your head back. The hands should be positioned overhead, just in front of the shoulders at the endpoint of the exercise. Return to the start position with control, keeping the hands aligned over the elbows. *See fig. 82b*

Comments: How much you choose to incline or decline the bench should be dependent on the goal. As the bench is lowered toward a flat position, the joint motion and recruitment patterns begin to represent a supine dumbbell chest press, versus shoulder flexion/abduction. When the bench is moved toward vertical, the emphasis is placed on the anterior deltoid, to the point where very little pectoralis major contribution takes place. Completely vertical presses overhead are undesirable because more stress is placed on the shoulder joints, so generally, 10 to 20 degrees of incline from the vertical accomplishes the training goal of strengthening the anterior deltoids, trapezius and triceps. Using dumbbells allows you to arc the arms naturally and bring them toward one another as the shoulders go through the upward arcing-motion of shoulder flexion and abduction. This is in contrast to a limited movement range that occurs, for example, when using a straight bar.

Safety Considerations: Avoid flattening the low back against the back of the bench, as this is not the safest and strongest position for the spine. Maintain both cervical and lumbar neutral posture. Position the wrists strongly so that the dumbbells are parallel to the floor. Keep the thumbs oriented to one another throughout the exercise. Rotating the thumbs in or out reduces the effectiveness of the exercise and can contribute to shoulder joint stress. Maintain the vertical and slightly forward plane of movement by not allowing the shoulders to rotate in or out. Avoid protracting the back by keeping the scapulae area stabilized to minimize excessive scapular movement.

Exercise Variations: The press overhead can be performed from seated and standing positions, with a variety of equipment such as cable, elastic tubing or machines. Independent of equipment, technique does not change. Avoid presses behind the head or positioning a straight-bar behind the head and pressing overhead (See Chapter 9, *Understanding Resistive Training Exercise Controversy*).

Upper Arm Elbow Flexor Exercises

Standing Dumbbell "Curl"

Body Parts Targeted: Front of the upper arms
Joint Motion(s): Elbow flexion
Primary Muscles Strengthened: Biceps brachii; brachioradialis; brachialis

Fig. 83a

Fig. 83b

Setup and Alignment: Stand in a "ready" position, with neutral spinal posture. The body is upright with your head and shoulders over your hips, and the hips and knees are slightly flexed. Let your arms hang naturally to your sides. Your palms are forward, the upper arms close to your sides, and the lower arms are angled away from the body. This arm placement represents anatomical position or a natural "carrying angle" and can be described as an upright position, arms relaxed at the sides with the hands wider than the hips, and palms facing forward with an under-grip (supinated). Anatomical position places the shoulder in a more "neutral" position and helps to maintain the true hinge-joint action of the elbows. Keep your wrists neutral — neither flexed, extended, abducted or adducted, and don't let the dumb-bells tilt up or down. (They should remain parallel to the floor throughout the movement.) Retract your shoulder blades and keep the same shoulder position throughout the exercise. *See fig. 83a*

Performing the Exercise: Maintain neutral spinal posture and begin with the elbows aligned directly under the shoulders and the hands slightly forward of the elbows. The tendency when performing an upright arm curl is to lean backward and push the pelvis forward to get the weight moving. Stabilize internally by using the abdominal musculature, and initiate arm movement by moving the lower arms "outward" and "upward." Maintain the natural carrying angle of the arms. The lower arms are placed wider than the shoulders and hips. Keep the wrists straight throughout the movement and do not lift the elbows or change the position of the shoulder. Bring the hands toward the shoulder and flex the elbow through its full AROM. Slowly return to the start position. *See fig. 83b*

Comments: In relation to other muscle groups, the arms, and especially the biceps, are probably unnecessarily over-empha-sized in strength training routines. The triceps and biceps are both used in a functional, push-pull capacity in daily activities. Realize that the biceps receive a lot of work, for example, in rowing and latissimus pull-down movements, whereas the triceps are chal-lenged in any pushing or pressing movement. Retracting the scapulae prior to movement, "fixing" the upper arms by firmly pressing them into your sides, and not allowing the shoulder to move forward or backward into shoulder flexion or extension, are excellent set-up/stabilization steps to take to assure that the shoulder position that you started in, will be the position in which you end. Keep the motion at the elbow joint "pure," by *not* adding rotation at the joint. For example, do not start in a neutral grip (partially supinated) and end the movement in an under-grip (fully supinated).

Safety Considerations: Keep the set-up and alignment throughout the movement. Stay upright, don't flex or extend the spine, don't rotate the shoulder inward or outward, and don't let the elbows move up or down (as a result of flexing or extending the shoulder). Keep the shoulders positioned back or in their starting position by keeping the scapulae retracted.

Exercise Variations: Standing or seated arm curl variations can be used with a variety of equipment, that include machines, cables and elastic tubing, and can be performed with different grip positions to activate specific elbow flexors, more or less (see the special section, *Anatomical Facts About The Elbow Flexors*). Regardless of grip choice, follow the same technique described in all of the elbow flexor exercises.

UPPER ARM ELBOW FLEXOR VARIATIONS

Following are two variations on the elbow flexor exercise previously described. The joint motion(s) and primary muscles strengthened are the same. These variations are accomplished with different body positions and equipment.

1. SEATED INCLINE DUMBBELL "CURL"

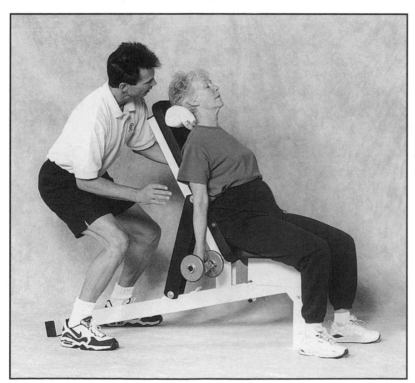

Fig. 84a

Setup and Alignment: Angle an incline bench slightly, to about 20- to 30-degrees from vertical. Holding dumbbells, sit with the arms hanging down naturally by your sides, perpendicular to the floor and with an extended shoulder position. This position places the biceps musculature in a stretched position since the heads (tendinous attachment points) of the biceps cross the shoulder joint. Place the feet shoulder width apart on the floor or an elevated platform, depending on which set-up allows effective stabilization and a neutral lumbar spine. Maintain neutral cervical posture. Place a folded towel in the neck area to help with proper head and neck alignment. Keep your palms facing forward, the upper arms close to your sides, and the lower arms angled away from the body. This arm placement represents anatomical position or a natural "carrying angle." Anatomical position places the shoulder in a more "neutral" position and helps to maintain the true hinge-joint action of the elbows. Keep your wrists neutral — neither flexed, extended, abducted or adducted, and don't let the dumbbells tilt up or down. Retract your shoulder blades and keep the same shoulder position throughout the exercise. *See fig. 84a*

Performing the Exercise: Maintain neutral spinal posture, and begin with the elbows aligned directly under the shoulders and the hands slightly forward of the elbows. The tendency when performing a seated arm curl is to lean forward or to arch the back. Stabilize internally by using the abdominal musculature, and initiate arm movement by moving the lower arms "outward" and "upward." Maintain the natural carrying angle of the arms. The lower arms are placed wider than the shoulders and hips. Keep the wrists straight throughout the movement and do not lift the elbows or change the position of the shoulder. Bring the hands toward the shoulder and flex the elbow through its full AROM. Slowly return to the start position. *See fig. 84b*

Comments: Retracting the scapulae prior to movement, "fixing" the upper arms by firmly pressing them into your sides, and not allowing the shoulder to move forward or backward into shoulder flexion or extension, are excellent set-up/stabilization steps to take to assure that the shoulder position that you started in, will be the position in which you end. Keep the motion at the elbow joint "pure," by *not* adding rotation at the joint. For example, do not start in a neutral grip (partially supinated) and end the movement in an under-grip (fully supinated). Rotation generally is not easily resisted and the fibers that flex the elbow with the hands in a chosen starting position are not loaded as effectively through the entire range of motion.

Safety Considerations: Keep the set-up and alignment throughout the movement. Maintain neutral spinal posture, don't flex or extend the spine either at the neck or in the lumbar region, don't rotate the shoulder inward or outward, and don't let the elbows move up or down (as a result of flexing or extending the shoulder). Keep the shoulders positioned back or in their starting position by keeping the scapulae retracted.

Fig. 84b

2. Seated Unilateral Dumbbell "Concentration Curl"

Fig. 85a

Fig. 85b

Setup and Alignment: Sit on a flat bench and hinge forward from the hip without changing neutral posture of the cervical and lumbar regions, and "tuck" or position the working arm against the inside of the leg. Place your feet slightly wider than shoulder width apart. Do not rotate the arm inward (this places the shoulder in an extreme inward rotated position). Instead, keep the upper arm and lower arm angled in a direction that closely parallels the support leg. This also replicates the "carrying angle." The elbow of the working arm should be placed near the support leg knee, which places the shoulder in a flexed position. Keep the palm facing forward. This position places the biceps musculature in a shortened position since the heads (tendinous attachment points) of the biceps cross the shoulder joint. Keep your wrist neutral — neither flexed, extended, abducted or adducted, and don't let the dumbbell tilt up or down. Retract your shoulder blades and keep the same shoulder position throughout the exercise. *See fig. 85a*

Performing the Exercise: Initiate arm movement by moving the lower arm "out" and "upward." Maintain the natural carrying angle of the arm. The lower arm is turned out slightly from the shoulder. Keep the wrist straight throughout the movement and do not lift the elbow or change the position of the shoulder. Bring the hand toward the shoulder and flex the elbow through its full AROM. Slowly return to the start position and when the set is finished, repeat using the other arm. *See fig. 85b*

Comments: Keep the motion at the elbow joint "pure," by *not* adding rotation at the joint. For example, do not start in a neutral grip (partially supinated) and end the movement in an under-grip (fully supinated). Rotation generally is not easily resisted and the fibers that flex the elbow with the hands in a chosen starting position are not loaded as effectively through the entire range of motion.

Safety Considerations: Keep the set-up and alignment throughout the movement. Don't rotate the shoulder inward or outward, and don't let the elbow move up or down (as a result of flexing or extending the shoulder). Keep the shoulders positioned in their starting position by keeping the scapulae retracted.

Anatomical Facts About The Elbow Flexors

The degree of elbow flexor contribution from the biceps brachii, brachioradialis and brachialis, depends to some degree on grip position. But, regardless of hand position, the same muscles (biceps, brachialis and brachioradialis) are used in elbow flexion.

The *biceps* is most powerful when elbow supination (palm up) is maintained throughout elbow flexion range of motion (Basmajian, 1985; Thompson, 1989). When the palms face down (pronation), this position results in decreased effectiveness of the biceps brachii because of the disadvantageous line of pull.

The *brachialis* muscle is used in combination with other elbow flexors to the same degree, regardless of whether the hand is pronated or supinated. Its attachment just below the elbow on the ulna is significant because its pull on the ulna, which does not rotate, allows its effectiveness to be *undiminished* regardless of hand position. In a pronated position during an arm curl, the brachialis shows the highest EMG activity, when compared to the brachioradialis and biceps brachii. It is not that the brachialis' EMG activity changes because of various arm positions, but instead, the EMG activity of the biceps and brachioradialis decreases because of this mechanically, disadvantageous position for these two muscles (Kendall et. al., 1993, pg. 268).

The *brachioradialis'* strongest action in elbow flexion occurs with the forearm in a mid or neutral position. This position can be described as in-between full supination and prona- tion, and is often referred to as a hammer or neutral grip.

Should a client start a curl in a hammer grip (in-between supination and pronation) and finish in a supinated or palms-up position? Technically, in terms of EMG activity and maximizing a muscle's response, combining joint actions may compromise the results. The highest degree of muscle activity does *not* occur when combination of movements, is compared to pure movement. Instead, it is probably preferable to rotate the forearm to the desired grip position *before* the exercise motion begins and maintain pure movement.

Can one head of the biceps work more than the other head? By positioning the shoulder in flexion (i.e., concentration or preacher curl) or extension (i.e., seated on an incline bench with the shoulder fixed in extension), it is often claimed that the "long" or "short-head" of the biceps can be worked either more, or less. It is true that the muscle will be put on more or less stretch in these situations and some research supports this contention (Basmajian and DeLuca, 1985). But generally, from a functional and application standpoint, it must be concluded that both heads of the biceps work together, for the most part, to stabilize the shoulder joint. There is little differentiation, in terms of muscle contribution or "head" activity, based on a supinated or pronated hand position, or the position of the shoulder during the execution of elbow flexion. The most important role, concerning the heads of the biceps, might be their function of working together, as opposed to independently, as shoulder stabilizers. The significance of changing exercise shoulder position when perform- ing elbow flexion does not boil down to, "which head is working," but instead, a focus on which muscle fibers related to the two heads of the biceps, are more or less active, and generally, the fibers of both heads are active.

UPPER ARM ELBOW EXTENSOR EXERCISES

KNEELING UNILATERAL DUMBBELL TRICEPS PRESS

Body Parts Targeted: Back of the upper arm

Joint Motion(s): Elbow extension

Primary Muscles Strengthened: Triceps brachii; anconeus

Setup and Alignment: Place one knee on a bench with the same-side hip aligned directly over it. The knee of the other leg should be at about the same height (i.e., make sure the bench is not too high) and slightly flexed. Take the hand on the side of the knee that is on the bench and place it just off the front edge of the bench, as a flat hand position puts more stress on the carpal bones of the wrist. Position the upper body so that it is parallel to the floor. Maintain neutral lumbar and cervical posture. Flex the elbow and extend the shoulder until the upper arm is parallel with the floor. Position the dumbbell so that the palm of the hand faces the ribcage, and the wrist is aligned under the elbow. Retract your scapulae and maintain retraction throughout the exercise. *See fig. 86a*

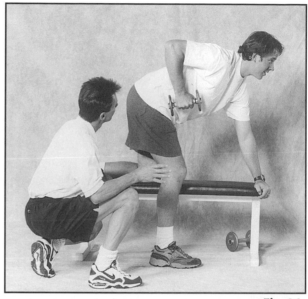

Fig. 86a

Performing the Exercise: Keeping the shoulder and elbow starting positions, slowly extend the elbow until the forearm is parallel to the floor. Keep the wrist stabilized, not allowing the dumbbell to tip toward the floor. The upper and lower arm should remain parallel and close to the body, rather than opening (abducting) to the side. Extend the elbow through its full AROM, then flex the elbow and return to the start position. *See fig. 86b*

Fig. 86b

Comments: It is easier to perform this movement kneeling and using one weight, when compared to the stabilizing challenge of performing the elbow extension movement supine with both arms holding dumbbells, a straight bar or an E-Z curl bar. Retracting the scapulae prior to movement, and not allowing the shoulder to move forward or backward into shoulder flexion or extension, are excellent set-up/stabilization steps which insure that the shoulder position you started in, will be the position in which you end. Shoulder position must be maintained by keeping the elbow pointed back during the entire ROM. If the elbow drops down, the action of the triceps will be weakened greatly since the resistance will not be in direct opposition to the movement.

Safety Considerations: Don't let your elbow flare out (a result of inward shoulder rotation) by keeping the elbow oriented back and the upper arm parallel to your side. Keep the motion at the elbow joint "pure," by *not* adding rotation at the joint. For example, do not *start* in a neutral grip and *end* the movement in a fully pronated or supinated position. Rotation generally is not effectively resisted, and the fibers that extend the elbow with the hands in a chosen starting position are not loaded as effectively through the entire range of motion, if rotation is added.

Exercise Variations: Standing, supine or seated elbow extension variations can be used with a variety of equipment, that includes machines and cables, and can be performed with different grip positions (see the special section, *Anatomical Facts About The Elbow Extensors*). Regardless of grip choice, follow the same technique described in all of the elbow extensor exercises.

UPPER ARM ELBOW EXTENSOR VARIATIONS

Following are two variations on the elbow extensor exercise previously described. The joint motion(s) and primary muscles strengthened are the same. These variations are accomplished with different body positions and equipment.

1. STANDING CABLE OVERHEAD TRICEPS PRESS

Setup and Alignment: Stand in a ready position with feet shoulder width apart or in an astride position. Use the foot positioning that allows you to maintain stability. Keep the hips and knees slightly flexed and allow the upper torso to flex forward from the hip about 30- to 50-degrees from a vertical position. Keep neutral lumbar and cervical spinal position. Grasp the handles and extend the elbows to a fully extended or slightly flexed position. The upper arms should be slightly above parallel to the floor to place more stretch on the long head of the triceps, and to shift the recruitment focus to the long head. The shoulders should not flex or extend, nor should they rotate inwardly (elbows flare away from body). The arms are parallel to each other. Keep your wrists neutral – neither flexed, extended, abducted or adducted. Retract the scapulae and keep this retracted position throughout the set of repetitions. *See fig. 87a*

Performing the Exercise: Keeping the shoulder and elbow starting positions, slowly flex the elbows and allow the handles to move back toward the body until an approximate angle of 90 degrees of elbow flexion is attained. Keeping the wrists stabilized, extend the elbows through their full AROM, and return to the start position. *See Fig. 87b*

Comments: In relation to other muscle groups the triceps are often unnecessarily over-emphasized in strength training routines. The triceps are used in a functional, push/press away from the body capacity in daily activities. Realize that the elbow extensors receive a lot of work, for example, in any pushing or pressing movement. Retracting the scapulae prior to movement, and not allowing the shoulder to move forward or backward into shoulder flexion or extension, are excellent set-up/stabilization steps which insure that the

Fig. 87a

shoulder position you started in, will be the position in which you end. Shoulder position must be maintained by keeping the elbow oriented toward the front during the entire ROM. The starting shoulder position (i.e, more or less flexed) creates a different recruitment emphasis that enhances long head involvement. It is more difficult to maintain this flexed shoulder position in both standing and supine positions, compared to a more moderate angle.

Safety Considerations: Don't let the elbows flare out (a result of inward shoulder rotation) by keeping the elbows oriented forward and the upper arms just above parallel to the floor.

Fig. 87b

2. STANDING CABLE TRICEPS PRESS

Fig. 88a

Fig. 88b

Setup and Alignment: Stand in a ready position with feet shoulder width apart or in an astride position. Use the foot positioning that allows you to maintain stability. Grasp the handles and place your elbows alongside your body, keeping the elbows aligned under the shoulders. Extend the elbows, positioning the arms so that the elbows are fully extended or slightly flexed in the starting position, with the hands near the front of the thighs. Keep your wrists neutral — neither flexed, extended, abducted or adducted. The shoulders should not flex or extend, nor should they rotate inward (elbows flare away from the body). Retract the scapulae and keep this retracted position throughout the set of repetitions. *See fig. 88a*

Performing the Exercise: Keep the shoulder setup position and slowly flex the elbows. Allow the handles to move up toward the chest until an approximate angle of 90 degrees of elbow flexion is attained. Keep the wrists stabilized as you flex the elbows through their full, AROM. Return to the start position by extending the elbows and pressing the hands toward the floor with control. *See fig. 88b*

Comments: Do not change the starting position of the elbows or shoulders. If the movement is initiated by pulling the shoulders back (shoulder extension) or hunching over (spinal or hip flexion), momentum has been gained into the movement, and the overload will not be as great. This technique flaw tends to occur when too much resistance is used. Full range elbow extension work requires a wider grip than is typically used for press-downs, especially if a straight bar is used. Using a split rope or cable allows you to start in a neutral grip, with the hands placed about shoulder width apart. As you extend the elbows, the hands can separate, and a full degree of elbow extension can be attained.

Safety Considerations: Because of the mechanical stress to the wrists and elbow that a pronated grip often causes when, for example, using a straight bar, many participants will have a natural tendency to reduce this stress by inwardly rotating the shoulder. This is not a desired movement and is alleviated by using a neutral grip and having the hands naturally move away from one another as the elbow moves toward full extension.

Anatomical Facts About
The Elbow Extensors

During elbow extension against resistance, the lateral and long heads of the triceps, or the muscle fibers related to these tendinous attachments, are recruited. The medial head, however, is *always* active and appears to be the prime extensor of the elbow (Basmajian, 1985, pg. 281). The medial head of the triceps is like the brachialis muscle. Both are the "workhorses" for their respective joint action of either elbow extension or flexion (brachialis). The lateral and long heads of the triceps are held in reserve until needed. However, significant resistance against elbow extension will call all three heads into play.

In contrast to elbow flexion, the triceps and associated elbow extension is affected very little by grip position. Whether using a pronated grip (i.e., palms down from a standing postion), or reverse grip (supinated or palms up from a standing position), only the radius is involved in supination and pronation. Since the olecranon process of the ulna articulates with the humerus, the triceps musculature and elbow extension are largely unaffected by the action of supination and pronation.

Should you use a variety of grips during elbow extension? The answer is, "Yes." Pronated, neutral, and supinated grips may be correctly used. Since the grip does not directly affect the action of elbow extension and the triceps' involvement, what is the rationale behind a variety hand positions? The decision to use a particular grip is related to the type of equipment being used (for example: straight bars or dumbbells), maintaining stabilization throughout the entire movement, and a minimization of orthopedic stress. A variety of grips offers no real advantage with regard to muscle line of pull, and may be accompanied by mechanical disadvantages. My preference, whenever possible, is to maintain a neutral grip for triceps work. This neutral position of the forearm is between full supination and pronation.

Neutral position allows my clients to easily stabilize and maintain their starting position from start to finish. Unnecessary mechanical stress on the wrists, elbows and shoulders is minimized, if not eliminated. Often, in an attempt to alleviate discomfort in these areas of the body when using other grips, the individual compensates by inwardly rotating shoulders or flaring elbows. This seems to especially hold true when using a pronated grip with a straight bar.

8

LOWER BODY EXERCISES

There is excellent evidence to suggest that resistance training programs for the lower body should initially focus on trunk strength, followed by stabilization training for the muscles of the upper and lower legs. Also, it is important to develop isolated hip strength in every plane of movement. Hip rotator strength is as important to the lower body as shoulder rotator strength is to the upper body. Additionally, strong scapular and shoulder stabilizing muscles help to maintain correct lower body positioning during lower body stabilization exercises and active isolation training.

While this chapter focuses predominantly on active exercises, don't neglect stabilization training for the lower body. Several exercises, which include squats, lunges and leg presses — represent closed chain activity that effectively train the lower body in a dynamic, functional fashion.

The ongoing principle of categorizing movement (Chapter 1) is captured by the following "rule": *After correctness and appropriateness of a particular movement has been determined, for the same or similar joint actions, the mechanics should remain unchanged — independent of body position or equipment used.*

Though every lower body exercise variation cannot be analyzed, any motion that is common to those analyzed in this chapter will retain some degree of sameness with regard to correct exercise execution. Virtually all lower body resistance training exercise variations fit within the joint motions/actions demonstrated. Categorizing or grouping movement allows you to see the "big picture" related to movement analysis, and does not require that a "new" analysis be performed for each and every exercise variation, as long as the motion/joint actions are similar.

Hip Exercises

Standing Machine Hip Flexion

Fig. 89a

Body Parts Targeted: Front of the hip and upper leg

Joint Motion(s): Hip flexion

Primary Muscles Strengthened: Iliopsoas; rectus femoris

Setup and Alignment: Stand upright with neutral spinal alignment. Grasp the stabilizing bar of the machine with straight arms and slightly flexed elbows. The supporting leg (outside leg) is slightly flexed and the hip joint should be aligned with the axis of rotation of the machine. The resistance pad should be placed just above the knee on the front of the thigh, of the inside leg. The start position (degree of hip extension) is determined by your ability to maintain proper starting position while keeping an upright (don't lean forward, backward or to the sides), stabilized position. *See fig. 89a*

Performing the Exercise: Raise the leg by contracting the hip flexors and drawing the leg forward and up until the thigh is approximately parallel to the floor. The lower leg will bend naturally and clear the platform as the hip flexes. Do not allow the hip to rotate outward or inward, and avoid trunk rotation. Maintain neutral spinal posture and do not lean back. Hold the end position, supporting this posture

Fig. 89b

with the stabilizing leg and trunk musculature. Return with control to the start position and when finished with the set, perform the exercise using the other leg. *See fig. 89b*

Comments: The hip flexors, while usually having adequate strength for daily activities, often require stretching. Tight hip flexors can result in spinal misalignment resulting from an anterior pelvic tilt that places the back in a chronically, misaligned position. Not only are the hip flexors of the inside leg being challenged as primary movers during the exercise, but the supporting leg receives an excellent functional challenge to maintain body stabilization as required by this single-leg stance. This is a good hip, leg and pelvic stabilization exercise.

Safety Considerations: Do not lean back, or otherwise rotate or hyperextend the spine. Perform both the concentric hip flexion and eccentric hip extension with control.

Exercise Variations: Hip flexion can be

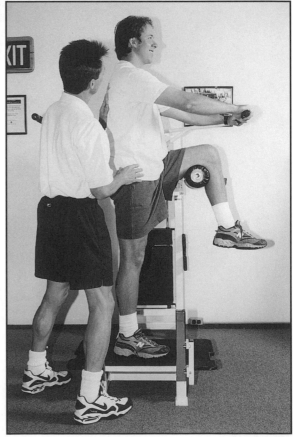

Fig. 90a

performed in supine, sidelying and standing positions. Independent of equipment and position, follow the same stabilization, alignment and exercise range-of-motion principles.

Standing Machine Hip Extension

Body Parts Targeted: Back of the hip and upper leg
Joint Motion(s): Hip extension
Primary Muscles Strengthened: Gluteus maximus; hamstrings
Setup and Alignment: Stand upright with neutral spinal alignment. Grasp the stabilizing bar of the machine with straight arms and slightly flexed elbows. The supporting leg (outside leg) is slightly flexed and the hip joint should be aligned with the axis of rotation of the machine. The

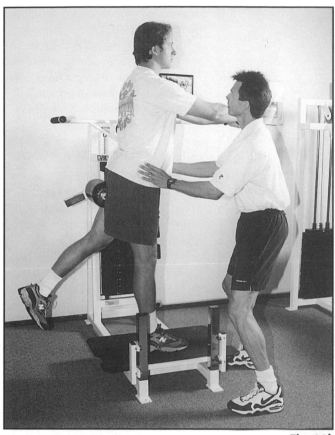

Fig. 90b

resistance pad should be placed at the knee on the back side of the inside leg. The start position (degree of hip flexion) is determined by your ability to maintain proper starting position while keeping an upright (don't lean forward, backward or to the sides), stabilized position. *See fig. 90a*

Performing the Exercise: Extend the leg by contracting the hip extensors and drawing the leg back and up until the upper leg is even with or past the stationary, stabilizing leg. Extend the hip actively as far as you can without deviating from the set-up position. Do not allow the hip to rotate outward or inward, and avoid trunk rotation. Maintain neutral spinal posture and do not lean excessively forward. Hold the end position, supporting this posture with the stabilizing leg and trunk musculature. Return with control to the start position and when finished with the set, perform the exercise using the other leg. *See fig. 90b*

Comments: The more the knee is flexed, the less contribution from the hamstrings, because they are a two joint muscle group. A flexed knee version (i.e., 90 degrees of knee flexion) will place more load on the gluteus maximus. Not only are the hip extensors of the inside leg being challenged as primary movers during the exercise, but the supporting leg receives an excellent functional challenge to maintain body stabilization as required by this single-leg stance. This is a good hip, leg and pelvic stabilization exercise.

Safety Considerations: Do not lean back, or otherwise rotate or hyperextend the spine. Perform both the concentric hip extension and the eccentric hip flexion with control and maintain proper body alignment throughout the exercise.

Exercise Variations: Hip extension can be performed in prone, sidelying and standing positions. Independent of equipment and position, follow the same stabilization, alignment and exercise range-of-motion principles.

PRONE HIP EXTENSION

Body Parts Targeted: Back of the hips and upper legs

Joint Motion(s): Hip extension

Primary Muscles Strengthened: Gluteus maximus; hamstrings

Setup and Alignment: Lie face down on a platform or bench that is at least four inches off the ground (the higher the bench, the greater range-of-motion that is available, thus making the exercise harder). The edge of the bench should be at or slightly below the waist, which corresponds to the axis of rotation in the body presented by the hip joints. Rest your knees or feet (depending on the height of the platform) on the floor. Wrap your arms around the sides and/or top edge of the bench and rest your chin or forehead on it, or turn the head

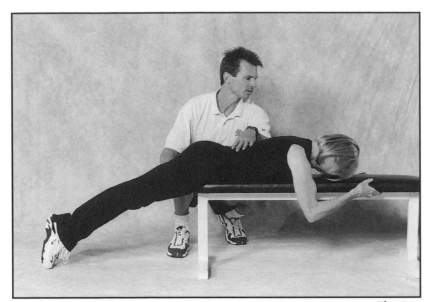

Fig. 91a

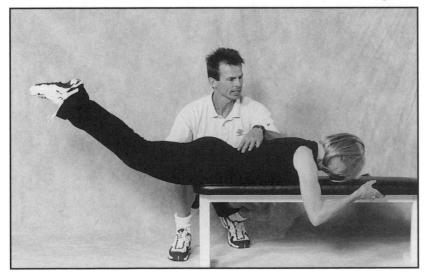

Fig. 91b

to one side. Retract your shoulder blades and stabilize spinal neutral posture, and begin the exercise with your knees or feet just off the floor to minimize any momentum that might be introduced at the start of the motion. If the feet are touching the floor (rather than your knees), keep the legs straight throughout the movement. *See fig. 91a*

Performing the Exercise:

Extend the legs by contracting the hip extensors and drawing the legs upward until the upper legs are about parallel to, or slightly higher when compared to the floor. Extend the hips actively as far as you can without deviating from the set-up position. Do not allow the hips to rotate out or inward (force cannot be placed in opposition to rotation using the pull of gravity), and keep the trunk or torso from rotating to either side or away from the bench. Maintain neutral spinal posture and do not let the head lift. Hold the end position, using the low back muscles to sustain spinal stabilization. Return with control to the start position. *See fig. 91b*

Comments: Extending the hips and holding this "lifted" position allows the low back muscles to work very effectively as spinal stabilizers. The more the knee is flexed, the less contribution from the hamstrings, because they cross two joints (hip and knee). A flexed knee version (i.e., 90 degrees of knee flexion) would place more load on the gluteus maximus and lessen the contribution of the hamstrings.

Safety Considerations: Use no momentum. Control your movements. Do not lift your head or arch your back. Keep the stabilized set-up and alignment throughout the movement.

Exercise Variations: Isolated hip extension can be challenged from prone, standing and seated positions, with a variety of equipment. Independent of these choices, follow the same principles set forth in this and other hip extension exercises to safely and effectively target hip extension. When performing, for example, squats, lunges, leg presses and dead lifts the hip extensors are also targeted very effectively.

Fig. 92a

MODIFIED "DEAD LIFT"

Body Parts Targeted: Back of the hips and upper legs
Joint Motion(s): Hip extension
Primary Muscles Strengthened: Gluteus maximus; hamstrings
Setup and Alignment: Stand upright with the ankles, knees and hips slightly flexed. The shoulders and hips should be aligned over the ankles. Stabilize the cervical and lumbar spine in neutral posture. Grasp the bar with an over grip, placing it at the thighs, in front of the body. The hands should be slightly wider than the hips with the scapulae retracted. *See fig. 92a*

Performing the Exercise: Maintain the setup position of the upper body throughout the movement. Begin to lower the torso by pushing your hips back ("leaning" over without pushing back can place excessive shear force on the spine). Flex or "hinge" from the hips, and make sure the spine does not flex or round. Lower the torso until you feel a slight stretch in your hamstrings or at about 30- to 40-degrees of hip flexion. Generally, I cue my clients to lower their hands to about knee level, as this often approximates a 30-degree

hip angle. Then, extend the hips and return to the upright starting position with control, while concentrating on "driving the heels into the ground." While extending the hips, simultaneously maintain slightly flexed knees and spinal neutral posture. *See fig. 92b*

Comments: See Chapters 4 and 9 for in-depth discussion of the dead lift and unsupported forward flexed positions of the spine and torso that occur during exercise. This exercise leaves very little room for execution error, and is not for everyone. It is arguable that significant shear forces are placed

Fig. 92b

across the spine, even when this lift is performed perfectly and the range-of-motion is limited. If you have any doubts about your client's ability to perform the movement safely, realize there are many exercises that can target the gluteus maximus and hamstrings with lower risk.

Safety Considerations: Many people immediately release scapular retraction (shoulders round forward or protract), neutral neck (head lifts up and back or hyper-extends) and lumbar posture (low back flexes or rounds) when moving into hip flexion. Maintain your setup position throughout the exercise. Keep the bar close to the body and under the shoulders. This keeps you from having the upper torso end up parallel to the ground, which puts the spine at risk for excessive shear forces. If available, use an adjustable "hang/clean" stand so that the weight does not have to be picked-up from and returned to the floor.

Exercise Variations: When using dumbbells, the technique remains the same. The dumbbells are positioned naturally at the sides of the body. Make sure the weight does not move forward as you flex at the hips and lower the torso.

STANDING MACHINE HIP ABDUCTION

Body Parts Targeted: Side of the hip

Joint Motion(s): Hip abduction

Primary Muscles Strengthened: Gluteus medius; gluteus minimus; tensor fasciae latae

Setup and Alignment: Stand upright with neutral spinal alignment, facing the machine. Grasp the stabilizing bars of the machine with the arms out to the side. The supporting leg is slightly flexed at the knee, and the hip joint of the working leg should be aligned with the axis of rotation of the machine. Place the resistance pad at, just below, or preferably, just above the knee of the working leg. The start position (degree of hip adduction) should have the leg in neutral adduction (ankle and knee positioned in line with the hip) or slightly

Fig. 93a

Fig. 93b

adducted (leg crossed over the midline). Minimize hip flexion as much as possible to keep the gluteus medius and minimus targeted. *See fig. 93a*

Performing the Exercise: Contract the hip abductors and move the leg outward and up until the leg is about 35 to 45 degrees abducted. Abduct the hip actively as far as you can without deviating from the set-up position. Do not allow the hip to rotate out or inward, and keep the trunk from rotating. Maintain neutral spinal posture and do not lean forward or to either side. Hold the end position, supporting this posture with the stabilizing leg and trunk musculature. Return with control to the start position and when finished with the set, perform the exercise using the other leg. Beginning and ending positions of this exercise should be determined by your ability to maintain neutral spinal alignment and upright stabilized position. *See fig. 93b*

Comments: The hip abductors and adductors are adequately challenged in a functional, stabilizing manner when, for example, standing on one leg or performing squats or lunges. Not only are the hip abductors of the non weight bearing leg being targeted as primary movers during the exercise, but the supporting leg receives a functional challenge to maintain body stabilization as required by this single-leg stance. This is an excellent hip, leg and pelvic stabilization exercise. The extended hip (versus flexed hip) version of hip abduction, as seen in this exercise, primarily targets the gluteus medius and minimus muscles. The tensor fasciae latae muscle comes more into play when the leg is abducted from a horizontal position (the hip is flexed and horizontally abducted or moved to the side). A good example is provided by a seated, horizontal abduction exercise.

Safety Considerations: Do not lean back, rotate or hyperextend the spine, or lean to either side. Perform hip abduction with control and maintain proper body alignment throughout the exercise.

Exercise Variations: Hip abduction can be performed in supine, sidelying and standing positions. Independent of equipment and position, follow the same stabilization, alignment and exercise range-of-motion principles.

SEATED MACHINE HORIZONTAL HIP ABDUCTION

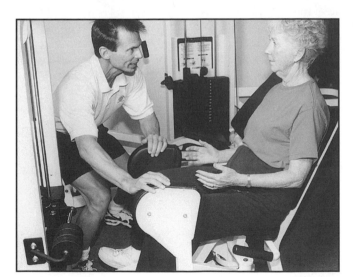

Fig. 94a

Body Parts Targeted: Sides of the hips
Joint Motion(s): Hip horizontal abduction
Primary Muscles Strengthened: Gluteus medius; gluteus minimus; tensor fasciae latae
Setup and Alignment: Sit comfortably with neutral spinal alignment. Sitting more upright or leaning back with the body supported by the machine *does* have an impact on abductor recruitment. The more extended the hips, the better the line of pull for the gluteus minimus and medius muscles. Choose the position that is in line with your training goals, and most comfortable. The upper leg should be parallel to the floor with the knee flexed 90 degrees. The resistance pads should be placed at the knees, and the feet placed flat on the support pegs of the machine. The start position (degree of hip adduction) should have the legs positioned so the knees are directly in front of the hips. *See fig. 94a*

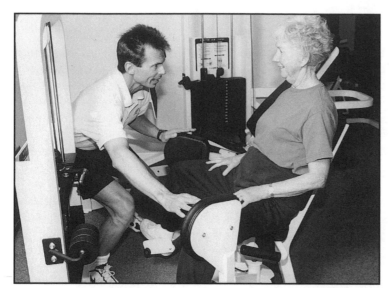

Fig. 94b

Performing the Exercise: Contract the hip abductors and move the legs away from the midline of the body until the knees are outside of the hip line. Abduct the hips actively as far as you can without deviating from the set-up position. Do not allow the hips to rotate outward or inward, and keep the trunk from rotating, excessively arching or flexing. Maintain neutral spinal posture and do not lean forward or to either side. Hold the end position and return with control to the start position. Beginning and ending positions of this exercise should be determined by your ability to maintain neutral spinal alignment (the tendency is to let the hips slide forward and to arch the back) and upright stabilized posture. *See fig. 94b*

Comments: The gluteus medius and minimus are very important in walking, running and many other functional activities encountered in daily life and sport. I often modify the seated abduction machine so that the hips are extended, which in turn better activates these two important muscles. Or, I use a standing, sidelying or supine version so it is easier to work with an extended hip, versus flexed hip. The flexed hip version of hip abduction, as seen in this exercise, efficiently recruits the tensor fasciae latae, when compared to a seated, standing or supine position with an open or extended hip. In this case, position of the hip — either flexed (i.e., seated more upright) or extended — *does* affect abductor recruitment because the abductors do in fact cross the hip, which is not true of hip adductors, as discussed.

Safety Considerations: Do not lean back (unless it is intentional and stabilized from the start position to better recruit the gluteal muscles), or otherwise rotate, flex or hyperextend the spine, or lean to either side. Perform hip abduction with control and maintain proper body alignment throughout the exercise. Never force the movement outward or introduce momentum to gain range-of-motion. The intent of this exercise is to strengthen the abductors through an active range-of-motion, and not to stretch the adductors with a ballistic stretch.

Exercise Variations: This same exercise can be performed with the knees extended, but will have little affect on the hip abductors. Hip abduction can be performed in supine, sidelying and standing positions. Independent of equipment and position, follow the same stabilization, alignment and exercise range-of-motion principles.

STANDING MACHINE HIP ADDUCTION

Body Parts Targeted: Inside of the thigh

Joint Motion(s): Hip adduction

Primary Muscles Strengthened: Adductor magnus; adductor brevis; adductor longus; pectineus; gracilis

Setup and Alignment: Stand upright with neutral spinal alignment, facing the machine. Grasp the stabilizing bars of the machine with the arms out to the side. The supporting leg is

Fig. 95a

Fig. 95b

slightly flexed at the knee and the hip joint of the working leg should be aligned with the axis of rotation of the machine. The resistance pad should be placed at, just below, or preferably, just above the knee of the working leg. The start position (degree of hip abduction) should have the leg abducted about 30- to 45-degrees. Beginning and ending positions of this exercise should be determined by your ability to maintain neutral spinal position and upright stabilized position. *See fig. 95a*

Performing the Exercise: Contract the hip adductors and move the leg toward the midline of the body until the ankle and knee are in front of the working hip, or slightly past the midline of the body. Adduct the hip actively as far as you can without deviating from the set-up position. Do not allow the hip to rotate out or inward, and keep the trunk from rotating. Maintain neutral spinal posture and do not lean forward or to either side. Hold the end position, supporting this posture with the stabilizing leg and trunk musculature. Return with control to the start position and when finished with the set, perform the exercise using the other leg. *See fig. 95b*

Comments: The hip adductors and abductors are adequately challenge in a functional, stabilizing manner when, for example, standing on one leg or performing squats or lunges. Not only are the hip adductors of the non weight bearing leg being targeted as primary movers during the exercise, but the supporting leg receives a functional challenge to maintain body stabilization as required by this single-leg stance. This is an excellent hip, leg and pelvic stabilization exercise. The straight leg (versus flexed knee) version of hip adduction, as seen in this exercise, efficiently recruits the long leg adductors, when compared to a seated position with a flexed knee. In this case, position of the hip (either flexed or extended) does not affect adductor recruitment because none of the adductors cross the hip, which is not true of hip abductors, as previously discussed.

Safety Considerations: Do not lean back, rotate or hyperextend the spine, or lean to either side. Perform hip adduction with control and maintain proper body alignment throughout the exercise.

Exercise Variations: Hip adduction can be performed in supine, sidelying and standing positions. Independent of equipment and position, follow the same stabilization, alignment and exercise range-of-motion principles.

SEATED MACHINE HORIZONTAL HIP ADDUCTION

Fig. 96a

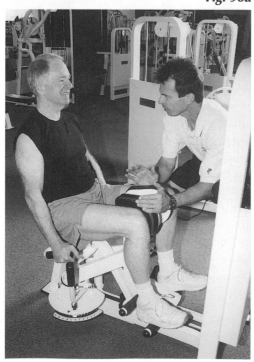

Fig. 96b

Body Parts Targeted: Insides of the thighs

Joint Motion(s): Hip horizontal adduction

Primary Muscles Strengthened: Adductor magnus; adductor brevis; adductor longus; pectineus; gracilis

Setup and Alignment: Sit comfortably with neutral spinal alignment. Sitting more upright or leaning back with the body supported by the machine does not impact adductor recruitment. Choose the position that is most comfortable. The upper leg should be parallel to the floor with the knee flexed 90 degrees. The resistance pads should be placed inside the knees, with the feet placed flat on the support pegs of the machine. The start position (degree of hip abduction) should have the leg abducted about 30- to 45-degrees, or more important, wide enough to provide a light stretch on the adductors. Beginning and ending positions of this exercise should be determined by your ability to maintain neutral spinal posture (tendency is to let the hips slide forward and arch the back) and an upright stabilized position. *See fig. 96a*

Performing the Exercise: Contract the hip adductors and move the legs toward the midline of the body until the ankles and knees are aligned with the hips. Adduct the hips actively as far as you can without deviating from the setup position. Do not allow the hips to rotate out or inward, and keep the trunk from rotating, excessively extending or flexing. Maintain neutral spinal posture and do not lean forward or to either side. Hold the end position and return with control to the start position. *See fig. 96b*

Comments: The flexed knee version of hip adduction, as seen in this exercise, efficiently recruits the short leg adductors, when compared to a seated or standing position with an extended knee. In this exercise, position of the hip — either flexed (i.e., seated more upright) or extended — does not affect adductor recruitment because none of the adductors cross the hip, which is not true of hip abductors, as previously discussed.

Safety Considerations: Do not lean back, or otherwise rotate, flex or hyperextend the spine, or lean to either side. Perform hip adduction with control and maintain proper body alignment throughout the exercise. Be careful to start the legs in an abducted position that does not strain the adductor musculature. The intent of this exercise is to strengthen the adductors, not to place them on significant stretch.

Exercise Variations: This same exercise can be performed with the knees extended, which will challenge the long adductors to a greater degree. Hip adduction can be performed in supine, sidelying and standing positions. Independent of equipment and position, follow the same stabilization, alignment and exercise range-of-motion principles.

Fig. 97a

Fig. 97b

SEATED HIP INTERNAL ROTATION

Body Parts Targeted:
Outside of the hip
Joint Motion(s):
Hip internal rotation
Primary Muscles Strengthened:
Gluteus medius; gluteus minimus; tensor fasciae latae
Setup and Alignment: Sit upright with neutral spinal alignment, placing one leg on the floor and the other so that the knee can flex over the edge of the bench. Use your hands for support and to assist with stabilizing the upright position and neutral lumbar posture. Elevate the bench so that the working leg swings freely, or support the underside of the knee with a towel so that the foot of the flexed knee does not touch the ground. Attach elastic tubing to the ankle and rotate the hip externally to its starting position. When the hip rotates outwardly the ankle/heel will move toward the midline of the body. *See fig. 97a*

Performing the Exercise: From an externally rotated hip position, begin to internally rotate the leg. The ankle/heel will move away from the midline of the body outward. Internally rotate the leg as far as you can actively, without flexing the hip (i.e., lifting the leg from the bench), or without abducting the leg (i.e., moving the upper leg out). With control, return the hip to its starting position, and when finished with the set, repeat using the other leg. *See fig. 97b*

Comments: Isolated hip rotation work is very important for the integrity of the hip joint. Often, the hip receives many functional conditioning challenges when the legs are weight bearing, but rarely is hip rotation resisted in isolation during daily movements, sports and resistance training sessions. Internal hip rotation is especially important to counter and balance the strength of the powerful external hip rotators.

Safety Considerations: Maintain the setup position, and don't force or attempt to create a range of motion that goes beyond your active range-of-motion capabilities.

Exercise Variations: Generally, it is difficult to effectively place resistance in opposition to hip rotation with machines or free weights of any kind. Elastic resistance and other types of cables that provide resistance via cable attachments are very practical and effective.

Fig. 98a

Fig. 98b

SEATED HIP EXTERNAL ROTATION

Body Parts Targeted: Back of the hip

Joint Motion(s): Hip external rotation

Primary Muscles Strengthened: Gluteus maximus; obturator externus and internus; gemelli; piriformis; pectineus

Setup and Alignment: Sit upright with neutral spinal alignment, placing one leg on the floor and the other so that the knee can flex over the edge of the bench. Use your hands for support and to assist with stabilizing the upright position and neutral lumbar posture. Elevate the bench so that the working leg swings freely, or support the underside of the knee with a towel so that the foot of the flexed knee does not touch the ground. Attach the tubing to the ankle and rotate the hip internally to its starting position. When the hip rotates inwardly the ankle/heel will move away from the midline of the body. *See fig. 98a*

Performing the Exercise: From an internally rotated hip position, begin to externally rotate the leg. When the hip rotates externally the ankle/heel will move toward the midline of the body. Externally rotate the leg as far as you can actively, without flexing the hip (i.e., lifting the leg from the bench), without abducting the leg (i.e., moving the upper leg out) or without adducting the leg (i.e., moving the upper leg past the midline of the body). With control, return the hip to its starting position, and when finished with the set, repeat using the other leg. *See fig. 98b*

Comments: Isolated hip rotation work is very important for the integrity of the hip joint. Often, the hip receives many functional conditioning challenges when the legs are weight bearing, but rarely is hip rotation resisted in isolation during daily movements, sports and resistance training sessions.

Safety Considerations: Maintain the setup position, and don't force or attempt to create a range of motion that goes beyond your active range-of-motion capabilities.

Exercise Variations: Generally, it is difficult to effectively place resistance in opposition to hip rotation with machines or free weights of any kind. Elastic resistance and other types of cables that provide resistance via cable attachments are very practical and effective.

COMPOUND LEG EXERCISES

STANDING BARBELL SQUAT

Body Parts Targeted: Back of the hips; fronts and backs of the thighs

Joint Motion(s): Hip extension; knee extension

Primary Muscles Strengthened: Gluteus maximus; quadriceps; hamstrings

Setup and Alignment: Stand upright with your weight evenly centered over both feet. Place your feet hip width or slightly wider, with your toes pointing straight ahead or slightly turned out. Slightly flex your hips and position your knees in a fully extended (not hyper-extended) or slightly flexed starting stance. Grasp the barbell and place it comfortably behind the neck, below cervical vertebrae number seven, but keep the bar above the tops of the scapulae. Use a padded bar or place a towel in the

Fig. 99a

Fig. 99b

neck region if necessary. (It is best to use a safety rack to help to position the weight when beginning the exercise, as well as to unload the weight upon completion.) Use an over grip and place the hands wide enough for stability, but not so wide you cannot retract the scapulae. Retract the scapulae and position the cervical and lumbar spine in neutral. Keep the weight centered over the ankles, by keeping the barbell, shoulders and hips aligned over the ankles. *See fig. 99a*

Performing the Exercise: Flex your knees and hips and slowly move your hips back. Maintain neutral posture and keep your "chest lifted" by maintaining scapular retraction. Lower to about 60- to 90-degrees of knee flexion. The trunk should have a slight, straight-body forward lean from the hips. The knees should not move inside of your big toes or outside of your little toes, nor should the knees travel beyond the toes. Knees should always follow the direction the feet are pointing. Keep the barbell and shoulders aligned over the ankles as the hips push back, which limits forward lean. Too much forward lean begins to look like a "dead lift," which is a different exercise and not the intended motion of a squat. Extend the hips and knees, and press back up to the starting position. *See fig. 99b*

Comments: Performing a squat correctly, in its simplest form, is simply a matter of finding the right combination of knee and hip flexion. Too much knee flexion causes the knees to travel forward of the toes and creates shear force at the knees. Too much hip flexion causes the shoulders to move forward of the ankles and places unnecessary stress on the spine. See Chapter 9 for an in-depth discussion on depth of knee flexion and squatting movements. It is not a requirement to attain 90 degrees of knee flexion, when training from a health and fitness perspective, to receive significant training benefits. Risk of knee injury is minimized by limiting the degree of knee flexion. Note that competitive power lifters are required by their sport to achieve a 90-degree or deeper squat, and as a result, increase the likelihood of knee injury.

Safety Considerations: Generally it is a good idea to end the exercise when a depth of 60- to 90-degrees of knee flexion is attained, or when the movement becomes uncomfortable, the heels lift, the knees move inside or outside of the foot, or the knees travel beyond the toes. Additionally, if the scapulae protract or the low back flexes or rounds, "the exercise is over." Keep the hands wide enough to stabilize the movement, but not so wide you place stress on the shoulders or are unable to retract the scapulae. If the grip on the bar is too narrow, it is hard to balance and stabilize the bar. Keep the heels in contact with the floor at all times and keep the weight centered between the front and back of the foot. More experienced lifters can focus on returning to the start position by "pressing out of the heels," but there is a risk of getting the weight too far back. Pressing out of the heels helps to mentally focus on initiating the return movement by using the gluteus maximus. Raising or "blocking the heels" with some kind of lift being placed under the heels, is simply a bad idea. Blocking the heels does place more load on the quadriceps because the hips don't flex as much and become less of a "player" in the movement, but this slight recruitment emphasis is gained at the expense of the knee. The knee travels excessively forward of the toes if the heels are blocked as little as 4 inches, and causes significant shear forces at the knees and ankles, in addition to potential lower-back stress. The squat is a combination of hip flexion and hip extension. Blocking the heels effectively takes an outstanding closed chained exercise and turns it into a high risk exercise that places stress *across* the joint.

Exercise Variations: If the behind-the-neck position with a barbell is uncomfortable for the neck or shoulders, consider using dumbbells, or train the same motion using a machine leg press variation. A number of compound leg exercises performed in a variety of positions and using different equipment, can effectively challenge hip and knee extension. The mechanics and concerns for most "leg press" variations that use these two joint actions — independent of equipment or body position — should be implemented.

SQUAT VARIATIONS

Following are variations on the squat exercise previously described. The joint motions and primary muscles strengthened are the same. These variations are accomplished with different body positions and equipment.

Fig. 100a

Fig. 100b

STANDING TUBING SQUAT

Setup and Alignment: Stand upright with your weight evenly centered over both feet. Place your feet hip width or slightly wider, with your toes pointing straight ahead or slightly turned out. Slightly flex your hips and position your knees in a fully extended (not hyper-extended) or slightly flexed starting stance. Grasp the handles of the tubing and securely place the cord under your feet. Lower your body into a squat position by flexing the hips and knees to about 60- to 90-degrees. Pull the handles of the tubing up to the shoulders, with palms facing in, until you feel tension on the tubing. Though squat technique stays the same, when using tubing it is necessary to load and unload (release) the tubing resistance at shoulder height with the body in the *lowered* position. It is unlikely that you would want to start a squat with a barbell in the lowered position, but with tubing, this procedure reduces the tension on the tubing and makes it easier to load the movement effectively and to get in and out of position. *See fig. 100a*

Performing the Exercise: Extend the hips and knees, pressing into a standing position. Do not let the resistance of the tubing pull the spine into flexion of extension. Maintain a neutral position of the wrists, not allowing them to flex, extend, abduct or adduct. Slowly lower back down to the starting position. *See fig. 100b*

Comments: Add resistance by using thicker tubes, multiple strands of tubing or by wrapping the cord around your hands. Performing a squat correctly, in its simplest form, is simply a matter of finding the right combination of knee and hip flexion. Too much knee flexion causes the knees to travel forward of the toes and creates shear force at the knees. Too much hip flexion causes the shoulders to move forward of the ankles and places unnecessary stress on the spine. It is not a requirement to attain 90 degrees of knee flexion, when training from a health and fitness perspective, to receive significant training benefits. Risk of knee injury is minimized by limiting the degree of knee flexion.

Safety Considerations: Keep the wrists neutral throughout the exercise. The tendency is for the wrists to be pulled into hyperextension. Generally it is a good idea to end the exercise when a depth of 60- to 90-degrees of knee flexion is attained, or when the movement becomes uncomfortable, the heels lift, the knees move inside or outside of the foot, or the knees travel beyond the toes.

HORIZONTAL MACHINE LEG PRESS

Fig. 101a

Setup and Alignment: Sit in the machine with the hips and torso firmly supported. Focus on centering your weight evenly over both feet. Place your feet slightly wider than hip width, with your feet pointing straight ahead or slightly turned out. Flex your hips and position your knees in a fully extended (not hyper-extended) or slightly flexed starting stance. Place your hands where they are comfortable and secure. Retract the scapulae and position the cervical and lumbar spine in neutral. *See fig. 101a*

Performing the Exercise: Flex your knees and hips, letting the thighs move toward the chest. Maintain neutral posture and keep your "chest lifted" by maintaining scapular retraction. Lower to about 60- to 90-degrees of knee flexion and return to the start position by extending the knees and hips. The knees should not move inside of your big toes or outside of your little toes, nor should the knees travel beyond the toes. Your knees should always

follow the direction the feet are pointing. Feel as though the weight is centered over the ankles. The knees should be over or slightly behind the ankles (less than 90 degrees of knee flexion) at the end point of the leg press. *See fig. 101b*

Comments: Too much knee flexion causes the knees to travel forward of the toes and creates shear force at the knees. See Chapter 9 for an in-depth discussion of knee flexion and depth of knee extension and squatting movements.

Safety Considerations: Keep the heels in contact with the press plate of the machine at all times and the weight centered between the front and back of the foot. More

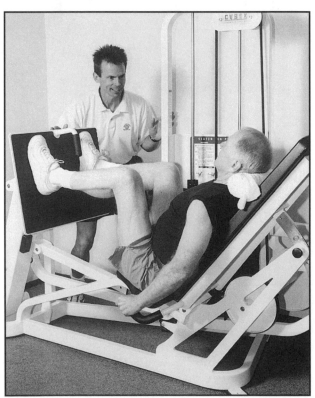

Fig. 101b

experienced lifters can focus on returning to the start position by "pressing out of the heels." Pressing out the heels helps to mentally focus on initiating the return movement by using the gluteus maximus. Generally it is a good idea to end the exercise when a depth of 60- to 90-degrees of knee flexion is attained, or when the movement becomes uncomfortable, the heels lift, the knees move inside or outside of the foot, or the knees travel beyond the toes.

STANDING STATIONARY BARBELL LUNGE

Fig. 102a

Body Parts Targeted: Back of the hips; fronts and backs of the thighs

Joint Motion(s): Hip extension; knee extension

Primary Muscles Strengthened: Gluteus maximus; quadriceps; hamstrings

Setup and Alignment: Stand upright using an astride stance, with your weight evenly centered over both feet. Place your feet hip width apart (in line with your hips, not wider) with your feet pointing straight ahead, and slightly flex your knees and hips. Grasp the barbell and place it comfortably behind the neck, below cervical vertebrae number seven, but keep the bar above the tops of the scapulae. Use a padded bar or place a towel in the neck region if necessary. (For heavy loads it is best to use a safety rack to help position the weight when beginning the exercise, as well as to unload the weight upon completion.) Use an over grip and place the hands wide enough for stability, but not so wide you cannot retract the scapulae. Retract the scapulae and position the cervical and lumbar spine in neutral. Keep the weight centered over the shoulders and hips, and focus on keeping the weight loaded on the front leg. The trail or back leg is used to stabilize the movement. *See fig. 102a*

Performing the Exercise: Flex your knees and hips and slowly lower your hips straight down. Maintain neutral posture and keep your "chest lifted" by maintaining scapular retraction. The shoulders should remain *over* the hips. Lower to

Fig. 102b

about 60- to 90-degrees of knee flexion on the front leg and return to the start position by extending the knees and hips. (Since the back leg is not loaded, don't worry about the degree of knee flexion.) The knee of the front or working leg should remain over or slightly behind the ankle at all times. The front knee should not move inside of your big toe or outside of your little toe, nor should the knee travel past the ankle. *See fig. 102b*

Comments: The barbell lunge is essentially a one-legged squat. The key technique difference is that the hips aren't pushed back, but otherwise the joint actions and muscle recruitment are the same. Common technique flaws include looking down at the floor during the movement and starting with a base of support that is too narrow. Keep the chin level to the floor and look straight ahead and position the feet in what could be characterized as "narrow railroad tracks," where the feet are in line with the hips. Also, be sure the client does not step toward the midline of the body during set-up, as it will be hard to stabilize the movement if the feet are in line with one another. Perform the movement from a stationary stance rather than stepping into the movement each time. There is no need to make this a dynamic exercise by stepping into the movement and returning to the start position, if your focus is strength development. Instead, set the movement up, and challenge the lead leg from a stationary set up, changing to the other side when the first leg is fatigued. Generally, I always load the front leg to avoid client confusion.

Safety Considerations: Maintain a stable stance with the feet in line with the hips, the shoulders over the hips and the hips level. Keep the head lifted, eyes looking forward and don't allow the knee to travel beyond the ankle.

Exercise Variations: Dynamic *reverse* lunges typically are less stressful to the knee, when compared to dynamic *forward* lunges, as the knee of the loaded "front" leg is less likely to move beyond the ankle. But, when setting up the exercise as a stationary lunge, as this exercise demonstrates, it makes little difference how you move into the lowered position, as long as the leg being loaded, has a set-up where the knee is placed over the ankle at the lowest part of the movement.

MACHINE REVERSE LUNGE

Body Parts Targeted: Back of the hips; fronts and backs of the thighs

Joint Motion(s): Hip extension; knee extension

Primary Muscles Strengthened: Gluteus maximus; quadriceps; hamstrings

Setup and Alignment: Stand upright on an elevated platform with your feet under your hips and pointed forward. Flex one hip and draw the leg upward until it is parallel to the floor, and the knee is flexed 90 degrees. Grasp the

Fig. 103a

Fig. 103b

barbell and place it comfortably behind the neck, below cervical vertebrae number seven, but keep the bar above the tops of the scapulae. Use a padded bar or place a towel in the neck region if necessary. Use an over grip and place the hands wide enough for stability, but not so wide you cannot retract the scapulae. Retract the scapulae and position the cervical and lumbar spine in neutral. Keep the trunk upright and the shoulders aligned over the hips. *See fig. 103a*

Performing the Exercise: Flex your knee and hip of the weight bearing leg and slowly lower your hips down by stepping back with the trail leg. Move the non-weight bearing leg behind you and contact the ball of the foot with the floor. Keep the hips level and directly under the shoulders. Maintain neutral posture and keep your "chest lifted" by maintaining scapular retraction. Lower to about 60- to 90-degrees of knee flexion on the front leg and return to the start position by extending the knee and hip. (Since the back leg is not loaded, don't worry about the degree of knee flexion.) The knee of the front or working leg should remain over or slightly behind the ankle at all times, or at the least, should not travel beyond the toes. The front knee should not move inside of your big toe or outside of your little toe. *See fig. 103b*

Comments: The reverse lunge is essentially a one-legged squat. The key technique difference is that the hips aren't pushed back, but the joint actions and muscle recruitment are the same.

Safety Considerations: Maintain a stable stance, keep the shoulders over the hips and the hips level. Keep the eyes up and looking forward without hyperextending the neck. The trail leg should stay slightly flexed with the toes pulling up toward the shin, so the foot can be placed in contact with the floor on the ball of the foot, rather than the toe or side of the foot.

UPPER LEG KNEE EXTENSION AND FLEXION EXERCISES

SEATED MACHINE KNEE EXTENSION

Body Parts Targeted: Fronts of the thighs
Joint Motion(s): Knee extension
Primary Muscles Strengthened: Quadriceps group (rectus femoris, vastus lateralis, vastus intermedius, vastus medialis)
Setup and Alignment: Adjust the seat so the knee joints are aligned with the machine's axis of rotation. (The true axis of rotation of the knee is slightly posterior to the "middle" of the knee joint.) The lower leg pad should contact the shins, just above the ankles. Sit upright or slightly back with your buttocks pressed firmly against the back pad. Set neutral spinal posture and retract your scapulae. Position the knees with between 60- and 90-degrees of knee flexion. Keep your knees in line with your hips and keep your patellae oriented

Fig. 104a

forward. *See fig. 104a*

Performing the Exercise: Relax your ankles (don't plantar or dorsi flex) and begin to slowly straighten or extend the knees. Stop short of full knee extension by 10 to 20 degrees, as this is less stressful to the knee, and can reduce shear forces across the knee. Return the legs slowly to their start position. *See fig. 104b*

Comments: Since the action of knee extension occurs in any squat, lunge or leg press exercise, it is not necessary to perform this exercise to challenge the quadriceps musculature, and may not be appropriate for some people to perform. See Chapter 9 for an in-depth discussion of knee flexion and extension, and the impact of extending the knee to zero (straight) or flexing the knee beyond 60- to 90-degrees. Sitting forward, with the hips flexed to a greater degree, places the rectus femoris on "slack,"

meaning it is not on stretch. Because of this, it is less effective at producing force, and as a result, places more load on the vastus group, which may play an important role in keeping the patella properly tracking. The ability to flex the hip to a greater degree is dependent on hamstring flexibility.

Safety Considerations: When performing isolated knee extension, it is preferable to have equipment where you can set start and end position range-of-motion. The patella

Fig. 104b

should be oriented forward or up throughout the exercise, avoiding internal or external rotation of the legs.

Exercise Variations: Isolated knee extension can be performed using a variety of positions, including standing and prone, and can be resisted with elastic resistance and other cable arrangements. Regardless of equipment or body position, the concerns and parameters remain the same.

SEATED MACHINE KNEE FLEXION

Fig. 105a

Fig. 105b

Body Parts Targeted: Backs of the thighs

Joint Motion(s): Knee flexion

Primary Muscles Strengthened: Hamstrings group (biceps femoris, semimembranosus, semitendinosus)

Setup and Alignment: Adjust the seat so the knee joints are aligned with the machine's axis of rotation. (The true axis of rotation of the knee is slightly posterior to the "middle" of the knee joint.) The lower leg pad should contact the back of the legs, just above the heels or ankles. Sit upright or slightly back with your buttocks pressed firmly against the back pad. If your hamstrings are tight, it will be difficult to sit upright and requires that the back support pad be moved back to allow more hip extension. Adjust the upper thigh retainer pad so that it firmly contacts the upper thighs above the knees, but allows for the knees and hips to be slightly flexed. Set neutral spinal posture and retract your scapulae. Position the knees with between 10- to 20-degrees of knee flexion. Keep your knees in line with your hips and don't let the ankles move out of line with the buttocks (i.e., don't let the hips rotate in or out). *See fig. 105a*

Performing the Exercise: Relax your ankles (don't plantar or dorsi flex) and begin to slowly flex the knees. Continue to pull the legs back toward the buttocks as far as you can, without using momentum or losing neutral spinal posture. Return the legs slowly to their start position. *See fig. 105b*

Comments: It is preferable to have equipment where you can set start and end position range-of-motion. This will help prevent hyper-extended knees in the start position and excessive flexion at the end of the range.

Safety Considerations: Maintain a slight degree of knee flexion in the start position of the movement to avoid hyperextending the knees and to avoid excessive shear forces across the knees. Keep the knees from rotating in or out, and don't rotate the lower legs (toes moving in or out create tibial torsion stress) during knee flexion. Hold a contraction or maintain light tension in the abdominals and avoid hyperextending the spine.

Exercise Variations: Knee flexion can be performed from standing and prone positions using a variety of equipment. But, independent of body position and type of equipment being use, the mechanics and principles remain unchanged.

PRONE MACHINE KNEE FLEXION

Body Parts Targeted:
Backs of the thighs
Joint Motion(s):
Knee flexion
Primary Muscles Strengthened:
Hamstrings group (biceps femoris, semi-membranosus, semiten-dinosus)
Setup and Alignment: Lie face down on a "leg curl" machine so the knee joints are aligned with the machine's axis of rotation, and the kneecaps are just off the edge of the bench. (The

Fig. 106a

Fig. 106b

true axis of rotation of the knee is slightly posterior to the "middle" of the knee joint.) The lower leg pad should contact the back of the leg, just above the heels or ankles. The knees should be slightly flexed. Set neutral spinal posture and retract your scapulae. Position the knees with between 10- to 20-degrees of knee flexion. Keep your knees in line with your hips and don't let the ankles move out of line with the buttocks (i.e., don't let the hips rotate in or out). *See fig. 106a*

Performing the Exercise: Relax your ankles (don't plantar or dorsi flex) and begin to slowly flex the knees. Continue to pull the legs toward the buttocks as far as you can, without using momentum or losing neutral spinal posture. The lower leg pad may, or may not, touch the buttocks and will be defined by attainable active range-of-motion (AROM). Don't let the hips raise (as a result of hip flexion) or back arch (hyperextend). Return the legs slowly to their start position. *See fig. 106b*

Comments: It is preferable to have equipment where you can set start, and end, position range-of-motion. If you're unsure of how far the heels should travel toward the buttocks, determine AROM by having the client perform the movement with no resistance.

Safety Considerations: Maintain a slight degree of knee flexion in the start and end positions of the movement to avoid hyperextending the knees and creating excessive shear forces across the knees. Keep the knees from rotating in, or out, and don't rotate the lower legs (toes moving in or out create tibial torsion stress) during knee flexion. Keep tension in the abdominals and avoid hyperextending the spine or flexing the hips (i.e., as a result the hips will lift upward).

Exercise Variations: Knee flexion can be performed from standing and seated positions using a variety of equipment. But, independent of body position and type of equipment being use, the mechanics and principles remain unchanged.

LOWER LEG PLANTAR AND DORSI FLEXION EXERCISES

STANDING MACHINE HEEL RAISE

Body Parts Targeted: Backs of the lower legs
Joint Motion(s): Ankle extension (plantar flexion)
Primary Muscles Strengthened: Gastrocnemius; soleus
Setup and Alignment: Stand upright with neutral spinal alignment. Grasp the stabilizing bars of the machine with flexed elbows. The legs are straight, but not hyper-extended. The shoulders and hips are aligned over the ankles, and the feet are pointing forward. Line the ankles up with one another to make sure one foot is not forward or behind the other. Stabilize the lower leg to keep the ankles from falling off center. Distribute the weight across all the toes and set scapular retraction. Begin with the heels below the toes, but don't force the range of motion and over stretch in this dorsi-flexed position. *See fig.107a*

Performing the Exercise: Without pulling with the arms or moving the hips forward or backward, lift the body vertically by contracting the gastrocnemius and soleus muscles. Continue to pull the heels up until full, active range-of-motion has been reached. At the end of the movement, when the heels are fully lifted (ankle extension), maintain weight across all the toes to avoid rolling the ankles in or out, and do not hyperextend the knees. Return with control to the start position. *See fig. 107b*

Comments: When the knees are extended, the gastrocnemius is the prime mover, because it is fully stretched and is more effective at producing force in this extended knee position, when compared to a flexed knee position. The flexed knee, or seated heel raise, places the gastrocnemius on "slack" (it's not fully stretched) and the soleus, which does not cross

Fig. 107a

Fig. 107b

the knee and is unaffected by knee position, takes most of the load.

Safety Considerations: Determine how far the heels should be positioned below the toes in the start position by actively dorsi flexing the foot in a non-weight bearing position. Don't inwardly or outwardly rotate the hips. Not only does this not work the "outer" or "inner" calf muscles (they don't exist), these positions tend to cause the foot to evert and invert. What people "feel" when performing these "maneuvers" is misalignment stress in the areas of the "outer" or "inner" calf region. This type of positioning can cause the ankles to "fall off center" and could result in ankle injury or compromise the stability of the ankles when working against heavy loads. Not only is turning the toes in and out unsafe, it's ineffective. The toes are "turned" by rotating the hips, and hip rotation has no effect on the line of pull between the common tendinous attachment of the gastrocnemius and soleus muscles at the Achilles tendon, and their attachments below (soleus) and above (gastrocnemius) the knee. This could be termed "variety-for-the-sake-of-variety" and compromises the intention of the exercise. Keep the hips and lower legs from rotating to provide a safer and more effective exercise.

Exercise Variations: Standing and seated "heel raises" can be performed using a variety of equipment. Include both standing (knee extended) and seated (knee flexed) ankle extension exercises to fully challenge the "calf" musculature.

SEATED MACHINE HEEL RAISE

Body Parts Targeted: Backs of the lower legs

Joint Motion(s): Ankle extension (plantar flexion)

Primary Muscles Strengthened: Gastrocnemius; soleus

Setup and Alignment: Sit upright with neutral spinal alignment. Grasp the stabilizing handles of the machine with flexed elbows, and a relaxed grip. The knees are flexed at an approximate angle of 90-degrees, and the ankles are directly below the knees. Align the shoulders over the hips. Keep the feet under the ankles and pointing forward, but in line with the hips (not too wide or narrow). Distribute the weight across all the toes and set scapular retraction. Line the ankles up with one another to make sure one foot is not forward or behind the other. Stabilize the lower leg to keep the ankles from falling off center. Begin with the heels below the toes, but don't force the range of motion and over stretch in this dorsi-flexed position. *See fig. 108a*

Performing the Exercise: Without pulling with the arms or moving the hips forward or backward, lift the heels vertically by contracting the gastrocnemius and soleus muscles. Continue to pull the heels up until full, active range-of-motion has been reached. At the end of the movement, when the heels are fully plantar flexed, maintain weight across all the toes

Fig. 108a   *Fig. 108b*

to avoid rolling the ankles in or out and return with control to the start position. *See fig. 108b*

Comments: When the knee is extended, the gastrocnemius is the prime mover because it is fully stretched and is more effective at producing force in this extended knee position, when compared to a flexed knee position. The flexed knee, or seated heel raise, places the gastrocnemius on "slack" (it's not fully stretched) and the soleus, which does not cross the knee and is unaffected by knee position, takes most of the load.

Safety Considerations: Determine how far the heels should be positioned below the toes in the start position by actively dorsi flexing the foot in a non-weight bearing position. Keep the hips and lower legs from rotating to provide a safer and more effective exercise.

Exercise Variations: Standing and seated "heel raises" can be performed using a variety of equipment. Include both standing (knee extended) and seated (knee flexed) ankle extension exercises to fully challenge the "calf" musculature.

SEATED TIBIALIS ISOLATION

Body Parts Targeted: Front of the lower leg
Joint Motion(s): Ankle flexion (dorsi flexion)
Primary Muscles Strengthened: Tibialis anterior
Setup and Alignment: Sit upright with neutral spinal alignment, placing one leg on the

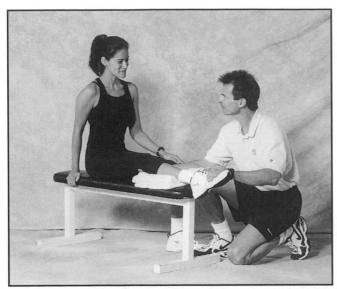

Fig. 109a

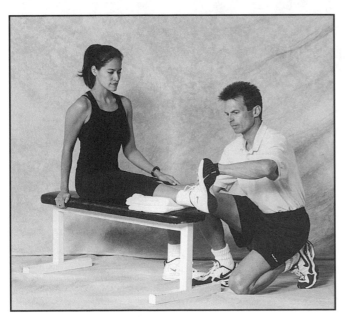

Fig. 109b

floor and the other straight on top of the bench so that the ankle can freely flex and extend off the front edge of the bench. Place a towel under the back of the knee to help stabilize the leg. Use the hands for support and to assist with maintaining the upright position and neutral lumbar posture. Begin with the ankles plantar flexed or the toes pointed away from the body, with manual resistance placed on top of the foot. *See fig. 109a*

Performing the Exercise: Slowly pull the foot up and back against the manual resistance. Envision pressing the heel of the foot away from you in an arcing motion. Continue to pull the toes toward the shin until the ankle is fully flexed. Return to the start position with control and continue to resist the force placed against the top of the foot. Avoid rotating the hip, flexing or extending the knee, or inverting or everting the foot. *See fig. 109b*

Comments: Activities such as walking have very little effect on the strength of the anterior compartment muscles of the lower leg. Targeting this area of the body helps to balance the strength differential between ankle flexors and extensors (gastrocnemius, soleus). Functionally, strengthening these muscles is very important because the action of drawing the toes up during walking or other activities is important to avoid falling and for skilled performance.

Safety Considerations: If manual resistance is being applied to the top of the exercising foot, do so in a controlled, steady manner through the full range-of-motion.

Exercise Variations: In addition to manual resistance, it is easy to load ankle flexion with resistance by attaching elastic tubing to the foot. Commercial products can be purchased that utilize weight plates (i.e., Dard) or hydraulic cylinders (i.e., Wicko Ankle Machine) to challenge ankle flexion and extension, as well as other foot motions such as inversion and eversion (the Wicko machine has this capability).

Quick Index:

Chapter 9, For an in-depth discussion of lower body exercise performance controversies

9

UNDERSTANDING RESISTIVE TRAINING EXERCISE CONTROVERSY

Controversy, or at least spirited discussion and differing opinions, abounds with regard to resistance training exercise technique. Some convictions are factual and backed by science. Others represent a viewpoint that comes from nothing more than observation, or years of experience doing something incorrectly, or less than optimal. Many other perspectives on resistance training exercise mechanics have risen out of the gym-dust and are based on anecdotal, "cause and effect" rationalization. In reality, biased opinion that is based only on "experience" and "observation" often perpetuate myth-conceptions and adds to the volumes of inaccurate gym folklore that just won't go away.

Quick Index:

Chapter 4, The "Any Exercise Drill" provides a process for an objective exercise analysis

Is it correct to state that an exercise is outdated, right or wrong, contraindicated or safe? Or, should exercise labeling be more centered on the degree of appropriateness for each specific situation? The bigger picture is simply a matter of truly understanding what the exercise can, or cannot, do in terms of accomplishing the strength/rehabilitation goal, and evaluating the risk versus effectiveness ratio. Adopting the "big picture" motive moves your evaluation into the realm of "relative-risk," rather than a hard-edge "right" or "wrong."

Key Point

The concept of "relative-risk" takes analysis into a more sophisticated and useful realm that evaluates the degree of appropriateness as it relates to the training goal, the individual and human anatomy.

If you agree with this philosophy, it then becomes important that you determine the relative-risk of any exercise by considering the individual you are working with, and placing all of the information you have gathered in proximity to:

1. The resistance training goal you're trying to accomplish

2. Human anatomy

TO DO, OR NOT TO DO

Following is a sampling of the confusing and seemingly contradictory thoughts that abound in the arena of resistance training. These most often relate to how exercises should, or should not, be performed.

- Should you adduct or retract the scapula during pulling and pushing movements always, some of the time, or never?
- Is an upright row or dipping movement always safe to perform, sometimes safe to perform or contraindicated?
- How deep should you allow the arms to go during a dumbbell, cable or machine press?
- Should the arms be placed behind the shoulders during press overhead movements or pulled behind the head/neck during latissimus pull downs?
- How far should the knee flex when performing a seated leg extension or squat?
- Is the best kind of training functional, stabilization, open chain or closed chain training?
- Is there a better way to classify a potentially dangerous exercise, other than contraindicated?

Key Point

During your study of resistive exercise training technique and exercise performance, if you see or hear the words "never," "always," "only-way," "best-way," "wrong," "right" or "contraindicated," a yellow caution flag should be raised in your evaluative brain. You may not be getting accurate information, or the whole story.

Effective and safe exercise design requires you to weigh all of the pros and cons of each exercise — risk versus benefit — and then to personalize each exercise choice to the unique individual client or patient. Using this type of approach, you avoid one-size-program-design that fits no one!

Establishing Exercise Technique Ground Rules

On the other hand, it is important to establish general exercise guidelines that are wide-ranging and in the best interest of a large segment of the population that chooses to strength train, and who are apparently asymptomatic and healthy. Needless to say, it would be overwhelming for most fitness professionals to start from scratch with exercise analysis and design for every client.

In my teachings, I try to qualify and present every possibility for a given situation. But when I've completed the presentation, the audience is usually very clear on how I would dictate execution for a given situation. I am not so vague that my message is ambiguous, or communicates "anything goes."

Ultimately, the decision of how clients will perform certain exercises comes back to each individual fitness professional. Do not jump on a bandwagon unless you are excited about, and believe in, what is being proposed. I always ask my audiences to "not make me the bad guy" as it relates to presenting information that goes against traditionally accepted gym "wisdom." I query them: "Does the information make sense? Does the science and anatomy support it? Now, make a decision. You have three choices: Accept what I've said and implement it. Put it on the back burner so you can gather more information or take more time to process the concept to a point where you understand it. Or, reject it." Take ownership of your decision, and regardless of your choice, at least know why you made it!

Though it is important to perceive the whole picture, and to be open to different applications and views, it is equally important to take a strong stand with regard to how you and your clients/patients will perform resistance training exercise. In my opinion, it is *not* true that, "There is no such thing as a bad strength training exercise." At the least, there are better and worse exercises, depending on the individual and training goals! Taking a strong stand on exercise technique should have more to do with the safety of your client and a results oriented program, as opposed to being "right" or "wrong." Once you've made your decision, remain open to the "winds-of-change" as it seems nothing is written in stone, and that's the way it should be as exercise interpretation evolves!

Key Point

It is not so much a matter of "to do, or not to do," but an issue of appropriateness.

Taking A Closer Look At High-Risk Exercises

Years ago, exercises fell into one of two categories: "good" or "bad." Today, it's important to broaden your perspective and match exercises to population specific needs and what is known about human anatomy.

Contraindicated Exercise

The term "contraindicated exercise" was established when the fitness industry began setting standards for exercise. This label proved a useful tool for identifying exercises that posed a high-risk and included exercises that could present an increased risk of joint structure damage or soft tissue injury, or might increase the likelihood of a specific population having, for example, a heart attack or stroke.

Situations still exist that merit the use of the term "contraindicated." Ask any cardiac rehabilitation specialist, or other professional that works with high-risk clients, and they will tell you that, "certain situations dictate that exercise be done in a very specific manner or at specific intensity, and it is contraindicated for the client, at this given time, to move beyond these set parameters." Physical therapists often pinpoint certain strength exercises as "off-limits" during, for example, the initial stages of knee rehabilitation. The point is, don't think that someone who uses the term "contraindicated" is outdated. Instead, use it as is appropriate.

Degree Of Appropriateness

As the fitness industry grew in size, applied knowledge and sophistication, it became evident that placing exercises into lists of "dos" and don'ts" created a few problems. For example, an exercise that was considered contraindicated for the average, deconditioned individual, might be appropriate (and even necessary) for an athlete with sport-specific needs. Degree of appropriateness is in contrast to giving an exercise a black and white, thumbs-up or thumbs-down rating. Many resistance training exercises resist easy categorization. A move or position that is extremely risky for some populations may actually be very appropriate for other populations. And an exercise characterized as "safe for everyone" probably isn't.

"One-size-fits-all" categorization can not provide optimal health or fitness benefits, for every training situation. For example, you might agree that forced hyperextension of the trunk, or excessive back extension is risky. But, telling a world-class gymnast that she shouldn't be doing back walk-overs on the balance beam is laughable. Or, you might think there is good evidence that suggests it is not a sound idea to use full squat movements (buttocks near the floor) with the average client. However, tell a competitive Olympic lifter or power lifter they should limit knee flexion to about 90 degrees (thighs parallel to the floor), and they realize you don't understand the requirements of his or her sport.

Key Point

Fitness professionals often want that black-and-white answer that holds true all of the time. It doesn't exist. Instead, the reality is that there are cases and situations where professionals have to carefully weigh the advantages and risks — and make a decision!

The Concept Of Relative-Risk

The basis for categorizing movement as high- or low-risk lies in joint mechanics, mechanisms of injury and injury predisposition. Unfortunately, there is little scientific evidence to help establish a specific threshold at which injuries will occur in any population. However, when joint biomechanics research indicates that certain movements produce significant stresses and those same motions are involved in common injury mechanisms, it is sensible that an exercise would be labeled high-risk for specific populations and various training scenarios.

Once you characterize an exercise as high-risk, it's time to provide modifications that make the exercise more appropriate, or choose different exercises that are lower risk and meet the set goals. Exercise analysis needs to be accomplished by applying the facts and by considering individual client circumstance. Human anatomy must also be considered, and when known orthopedic risks exist, it makes sense that a corrective change should be instituted.

Key Point

Always seek to understand why the relative-risk of an exercise is high for a given person or population, and how it can be lowered.

STRENGTHS AND WEAKNESSES OF DIFFERENT TYPES OF TRAINING

There are many arguments to advocate the exclusivity of one type of training over others. Let's look at four different types of training, their benefits, how they compare with each other, and the strengths and weaknesses of each.

Stabilization Training And Functional Training

To simplify the idea of *stability or stabilization training*, you might think of this type of training as nothing more than the use of isometric, or stabilizing contractions, in order to maintain a body position or desired alignment. Stability training is important because it will enhance the safety and performance of most strength exercises by creating isometric strength in the muscles that are holding the body in correct alignment throughout the path of motion of a given exercise. *Functional training* incorporates the concepts of stability training and closed chain exercise (CCE) by requiring the body's natural motor reflexes to react as an integrated unit. In other words, the whole body is challenged to participate in order to maintain correct posture and balance while moving. The inclusion of activities that involve the entire body in a dynamic and coordinated fashion represents the development of functional fitness. This type of fitness is easily transferred to daily tasks, recreation and sport. Stabilization and functional training can both be integrated with closed chain and open chain exercise as explained in the following sections.

Quick Index:

Chapter 5, Trunk stabilization and functional movement
Chapter 6, Exercises that challenge trunk stability

Closed Chain And Open Chain Exercise

To best understand whether you are performing a closed chain exercise (CCE) or open chain exercise (OCE), it is useful to view your body as a length of chain. Envision your arms and legs as opposite ends of the chain.

Open chain exercise occurs when an end segment of the chain (arms or legs) is not fixed and does not support the weight of your body. An example of OCE is a seated knee extension or an arm curl.

Closed chain exercise occurs if either set of limbs (hands or feet) is involved in supporting the weight of your body. A squat or lunge movement is a good illustration of CCE. The legs and feet bear the weight of your body. CCE requires a dynamic response from the whole body to perform the movement correctly, safely and most efficiently.

Though not classically defined as CCE, any exercise that partially supports your body weight and requires an integrated response from the body's musculature, can be characterized as CCE. A push-up position that is held with your legs placed on a stability ball is a good example. Your arms and hands partially bear the weight of your body and an end segment of the chain (your hands) is "closed," "fixed" or weight bearing.

Many experts believe that effective rehabilitation and strengthening exercise is *not* best developed by stabilizing one part of the body in a non-weight bearing position, and then isolating another body part, as is exemplified by the seated leg extension and OCE. While there are certainly many proper applications of OCE, this traditional approach may not stimulate the body to react in a natural way. OCE is best characterized by isolation, whereas CCE is best referred to as dynamic, functional, and working in concert with the body as a whole, integrated unit. Both types of training, depending on application and participant needs, are considered excellent ways to condition the body. The best results will be realized when you use both approaches.

Natural and functional movement is directly related to the harmonious workings of joints, muscles and the neurological system. Our neurological systems interact with our musculoskeletal system in a coordinated and complex manner. Using stability or balance training, and CCE, is the perfect way to stimulate and train this complex interaction of the body. After all, this is the way we normally function every moment of our lives. Think about common activities and you'll realize that most of your movements are dependent on coordinated balance and force output throughout the body. *See fig. 110*

Fig. 110, Different methods used to stimulate stability, balance and to present a CCE challenge

Demands placed on the body during stability training, balance training and close chain exercise vary dramatically, but replicate daily life and sport situations. From moment to moment, the body strives to maintain balance and to integrate the responses into safe, skilled movement. This mirrors daily activities where our bodies constantly perform in many planes of movement. Because of this, we need to challenge our bodies on a regular basis with these types of training.

A Review Of Open And Closed Chain Exercise

Open chain exercise (OCE)
- OCE is often described as less functional or less "usable" muscle strength
- If the end segment of chain is not fixed, but instead free, and not supporting the weight of your body, the exercise is termed OCE

Closed chain exercise (CCE)
- CCE is often described as functional or "usable" muscle strength
- If either set of limbs is involved in supporting your weight, the effort is referred to as an example of a CCE
- An end segment of a CCE is said to be closed, fixed or weight-bearing

Arguments For CCE And OCE
1. CCE is generally said to be more functional, more effective in the healing/ rehabilitation process.
2. CCE allows your body (i.e., joints, muscles, neurological system) to function as it normally does in day-to-day activities as it coordinates stabilization forces with dynamic movement.
3. CCE represents functional training that increases strength of the muscles and ligaments in a manner specific to natural movement, and trains balance, proprioception and coordination.
4. CCE is especially applicable for lower body, weight bearing exercise, though CCE applications for the upper body are available.
5. OCE can help optimize upper body multi-joint function since you cannot challenge multi-function joint movements if the chain is fixed (i.e., push-up, barbell press). A dumbbell press overhead is a good example of OCE challenging dynamic joint motion.
6. OCE exercises strengthen weak muscles in isolation and may be important before more complex (CCE) exercise can be attempted.

Key Point

Isolated movement patterns (OCE) strengthen weak muscles. Combined movement patterns (CCE) maintain or reestablish function. Functional movement patterns, stabilization training, OCE and CCE are all important to a balanced program.

CONTROVERSIAL RESISTANCE TRAINING EXERCISES AND THEORIES

The art of application (i.e., educated guess work based on a factual framework) and individualized fitness program design requires that you consider textbook information, current research, throw in a dose of your own experience, and choose a methodology that you believe will work and is in the best interest of your client.

In the following sections, we'll examine a few of the strength training exercise controversies that seem to be common today.

SCAPULAR STABILIZATION OR FIXATION CONTROVERSIES

When performing some exercises which involve the shoulder joint, full (complete) or partial stabilization of the scapulae may allow for a more effective and safe exercise. Full scapular fixation is accomplished by completely retracting (also referred to as scapular adduction) or drawing the scapulae together, *before* movement into the exercise occurs. *See fig. 111*

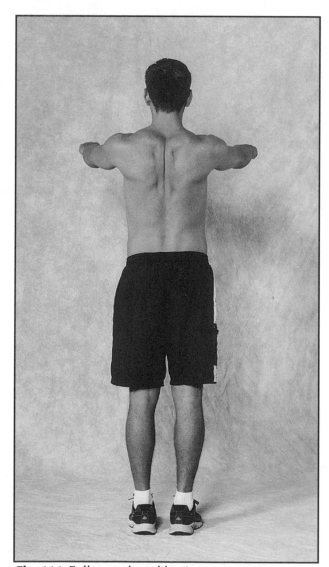

When combining scapular retraction with other joint movement, step one is to retract the scapulae, and step two is performance of the trunk, upper or lower body movement. The scapulae remain contracted throughout the exercise and may be released between each repetition, or maintained for the duration of the set.

Why Use Scapular Adduction Or Retraction?

Full scapular fixation stabilizes the shoulder girdle. Stabilization enhances the ability of the muscles crossing the shoulder joint to exert force. Scapular retraction (fixation) transforms the trunk into a rigid, solid platform. This allows the muscles to exert force more effectively. By initiating movement with scapular stabilization you can get a complete shortening of the scapular muscles. These key postural muscles, the mid-trapezius and rhomboids, are often ineffectively isolated if scapular stabilization is not initiated prior to shoulder joint movement.

Fig. 111, Full scapular adduction or retraction

Posture And Scapular Retraction

Even if you choose not to utilize scapular retraction in an exercise, it's important to view scapular adduction as a strength exercise in its own right. Poor posture that is exemplified by rounded shoulders and upper back can be corrected with scapular adduction in isolation, since this action counters the rounded upper torso posture by "pulling the shoulders backward."

When not executing a full retraction of the scapulae, maintaining a partial stabilizing contraction (i.e., neutral scapular position) in the mid-trapezius and rhomboid muscles will facilitate proper postural alignment throughout each exercise and in daily posture. A partial stabilizing contraction expands the chest and slightly draws the shoulders back. This position could be described as a neutral scapular position or partially retracted scapular position.

FIVE REASONS TO USE SCAPULAR RETRACTION

1. Train Key Postural Muscles And Avoid Momentum

Scapular retraction "isolates" key postural muscles in the upper body that counter a rounded shoulder position. Many times, these muscles are not targeted if retraction is attempted *after* the movement (pulling or pushing) has been completed. Trying to add retraction of the scapulae after the press, or pull, encourages "cheat" or an introduction of momentum into the movement. During trunk exercises, scapular retraction can help limit extraneous movement of the shoulder girdle and arms, and focus the work in the lumbar spinal region.

2. Stabilize The Torso For Effective Force Transfer

A stabilized torso, which is created by scapular retraction, provides a solid platform from which muscles can exert force or pull. The application of force, via tendinous attachments to the bone, is much more effective when none of the force is transferred away from the intended movement. An upper torso that is not rigid, is in sharp contrast to a stable torso with strongly positioned scapulae and trunk. Quality of movement can be enhanced through stabilization, or compromised without it.

3. Define Range Of Motion For Shoulder Horizontal Flexion

When full scapular adduction is sustained, you realize a "chest crossover" movement using cables, for example, doesn't exist. The movement that occurs when the hands move past the midline (sternum) of the body is provided by scapular protraction, using the pectoralis minor and serratus anterior muscles. These muscles have nothing to do with shoulder movement and the pectoralis major.

4. Protect Small Muscles From Heavy Loads

The small muscles of the chest and shoulder (i.e., subscapularis, pectoralis minor and serratus anterior) should not be loaded with "bench press" weight. The risk of injury is obvious. Though anecdotal, I have heard a number of reports where the exerciser reported protracting her scapulae to drive the arms toward the ceiling when performing a heavy (6 to 12 RM) supine press, and injuring musculature of the "deep" chest.

5. More Efficiently Load The Pectoralis Major

By allowing scapular protraction to occur during pressing movements, the insertion of the pectoralis major can be moved toward its origin without pectoralis major involvement. So in other words, you could largely avoid loading the pectoralis major during pressing movements through at least part of the range-of-motion, which probably is not the goal of a chest press exercise.

Why Not Use Scapular Retraction All Of The Time?

Physical therapists and other experts usually object to the idea of scapular retraction when a trainer or therapist insists on exclusively setting up pushing and pulling exercises with this stabilization step. Training *only* this way, does not train the shoulder joint in the way in which it interacts normally with the humerus and scapula. It is perfectly normal for the glenohumeral joint of the shoulder to dynamically interface and the scapulae to protract, when reaching or pushing movements are performed. For example, try to get something out of a kitchen cabinet, quickly reach for and pick up a child or extend your arm in front of you to catch and absorb the impact of a thrown baseball — without protracting the scapulae. Needless to say, it would feel very awkward and not represent functional movement. It is evident that daily activity and sport requires this type of motion or interaction in the shoulder and upper torso, and should be trained accordingly.

Orthopedic experts (reported in the Pearls Column, Editor: Robert Salis, *Start With Scapular Strength*, Physician and Sportsmedicine, Vol. 26, No. 8, August 1998, pg. 21) identify the scapular muscles as the weak link in relation to arm injuries. Normally, strong scapular muscles serve as the "platform" for arm force. Rounded shoulders, atrophy along the vertebral border of the scapula, hypermobility of the scapula, and scapular trigger points serve as signs of an underdeveloped scapular platform. Shoulder external rotators are probably weak as well. Whether training for fitness, performance or rehabilitation, a balanced exercise protocol calls for a strengthening of the scapulothoracic region (i.e., using retraction and protraction). Also, a balance between the shoulder external rotators and pectoral strength/internal rotation is important. Protraction during pushups (note this usually does not represent a low RM or heavy load) is promoted, rowing movements, arm pulldowns, scapular retraction, shoulder shrugs and a balanced rotator cuff strengthening program are encouraged. The issue is not one of choosing the "right" way, but to instead use a variety of approaches that strengthen and balance this region of the body.

However, when the focus of the training goal is to optimize the strength response, heavy loads will be used. When using around a 6 to 12 RM load in the resistance training room, I generally instruct my clients to "set retraction" for pushing/pressing or pulling movements. When we are working with lighter loads or using sport specific movement drills that replicate "real" life activity and sport, I encourage my clients to "release retraction" to train functional movement patterns of the shoulder joint and scapulae. Also, when thinking about function, consider what partial or neutral scapular retraction represents. This characterizes good posture that should be carried throughout the day, and this awareness should be developed to a point of being "automatic."

Quick Index:

Chapter 11, Discussion of repetition schemes and RMs (repetition maximums)

CHEST EXERCISE CONTROVERSIES

It is possible to talk about pushing or chest exercises for hours. The shoulder joint is a complex structure that supports many varied, and seemingly contradictory movements (i.e., it can flex *and* extend the shoulder, depending on the position of the arm). It is no wonder so much confusion surrounds chest exercise. Let's examine a few of the controversial exercises and theories surrounding this area of the body.

Can You Emphasize Outer And Inner Pecs?

You may have heard it said that working with certain grips or ranges-of-motion will allow you to focus the work on the "outer pecs" or the "inner pecs." If you reference an anatomy textbook, you'll probably decide that working the "outer" or "inner" pectoralis major muscle is a physiological impossibility, since "they" do not exist. People will tell you that a wide grip pressing movement or deep stretch in the same movement targets the "outer pecs." You cannot deny they are "feeling" something near the outer attachment point or insertion of the pecs, but most likely it is joint stress. More succinctly, deep ranges-of-motion and wide grips that place the joint at its outer most limits of tolerable stress can lead to injury and poor muscular development.

If outer or inner pecs existed it would mean that muscular physiology, as currently taught, is inaccurate. A muscle does *not* contract in an all-or-none manner, but a motor unit, of which there are many in each muscle, does contract all-or-none. In other words, once the group of fibers (motor unit) gets the signal to contract, all respond together and fully contract. The pectoralis major muscle spans a wide attachment point along the sternum, and inserts on the upper, inside of the humerus. If, for example, an "outer pec" did exist, that means that some of the sarcomeres (the smallest functional unit of the muscle) that make up muscle fibers and span muscle attachment origin to insertion, would not fire! And, that is impossible.

The claim of "inner pec" isolation often is associated with cable crossover movements. The muscle belly is expanding (just like the biceps brachii does when the elbow is flexed) as the arms are brought toward the midline of the chest, but it is the pectoralis major muscle that is contracting, not the "inner pec." In fact, if you set retraction of the scapulae, there is very little crossover movement available. Many people believe that when the arms cross, that the pectoralis major is more "fully worked." Instead, the "crossover" occurs because of scapular protraction, using the pectoralis minor and serratus anterior muscles. This type of exercise is not wrong, you simply have to know what is, and is not, happening regarding joint actions and muscular involvement. Then, make your joint motion choices accordingly.

Can You Emphasize Upper And Lower Pecs?

While "inner" and "outer pecs" specifically do not exist, it is possible to activate different regions of the pectoralis major muscles. Before I move too far along with this concept, many experts simply believe that a chest exercise is a chest exercise, with little differentiation of muscle activation between flat, incline and decline presses. Often load, or intensity of the effort has more to do with muscle activation than the line of pull of the muscle.

However, without a doubt, incline movements present a situation where the line of pull favors the clavicular fibers of the pectoralis major. Flat or decline presses favor the line of pull of the pectoralis major in these mid to lower fibers. The different lines of pull that exist explain why the pectoralis major can pull the humerus upward (incline press), pull the arm across which represents the strongest action of the pectoralis major and is called "pure" horizontal flexion, or pull the arm down (decline press). No one could argue that these movements are identical and require the same motor unit recruitment patterns and activation for a given load. Common sense and science prove otherwise.

Pectoralis Major Nerve Innervation

Remember, muscles are made up of many motor units (see chapter 5 for a discussion of upper and lower abdominal region emphasis) and those motor units can be more, or less, active depending on muscle line of pull or load — and often are responsible for *different* movements at the joint. Clearly, there is distinction between the action of upper and lower pectoralis major fibers (Kendall, 1993, Muscles: Testing and Function, pg. 276). The clavicular or upper fibers flex and medially rotate the shoulder joint, and horizontally adduct/flex the humerus toward the opposite shoulder. These fibers are innervated by the lateral pectoral nerve C5, 6 and 7. The lower fibers depress the shoulder girdle by virtue of attachment to the humerus, and *obliquely* adduct the humerus toward the opposite iliac crest, which represents a movement distinctly different from the upper fibers. The lower fibers are innervated by the lateral and medial pectoral nerves, C6, 7, 8 and T1. The action of the muscle as a whole, with the origin fixed, is horizontal adduction and medial rotation. Since it is difficult to place resistance in opposition to internal shoulder rotation, the preferred movement to load is pure horizontal flexion. Again, applied anatomy tells the story.

How "Deep" Should A Chest Press Or Flye Be Performed?

It is common, when performing chest exercises to bring the fists to the level of the chest, or to cue "touch the chest" with, for example, a barbell. However, this places the joint in a loaded, horizontally extended/abducted position, which in turn puts the shoulder joint capsule at risk for injury. Cahill (1992) was the first to describe a series of weight trainers who suffered trauma to the distal clavicle. In other words, hyperextension of the shoulder — elbows behind the midline of the body — places excessive stresses on the acromio-clavicular joint during pressing movements, and is likely to contribute to an injury process in this area of the body (Reeves, et al., 1998, Weight Training Injuries, Part 2).

In addition, allowing the elbows to move beyond the body line that divides it into front and back halves decreases the force angle (the line formed from the elbow to shoulder) of the shoulder. As the force angle decreases, the ability of the pectoralis major to produce muscular force continually decreases. When the muscle is extremely stretched at this angle, insufficient actin and myosin overlap occurs. (Actin and myosin are the protein filaments that slide past one another to produce muscular force and movement.) Insufficient overlap leaves the muscle in a position where it is not capable of effectively producing muscle force, which in turn leaves the joint vulnerable to injury. Why? The joint is literally being held together passively by relatively weak shoulder muscles and ligaments, since the pectoralis major is largely incapable of producing significant force. Any exercise that places the elbow behind this mid-body line places the shoulder at a mechanical disadvantage that may contribute to rotator cuff injury or anterior shoulder instability (Reeves et al., 1998, Part 1; Wolfe et al., 1992). The pectoralis major doesn't have a good line of pull until the elbow-shoulder line reaches a point where it is in line with the frontal plane (Chapter 2, movement planes of the body) that divides the body into front and back halves. *See fig. 112*

Regardless of body position — supine, standing or seated — the cue should be that the elbow-shoulder line should not go much deeper than this mid-body position. The range of motion recommended would be similar to performing the pressing movement while positioned on the floor or against a wall. The floor or wall would limit the range of movement of the elbows backward.

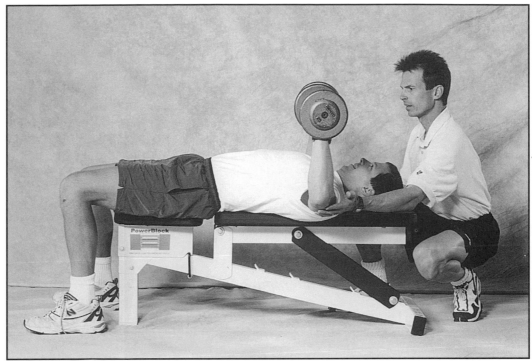

Fig. 112, Recommended depth of pressing movements

Many people shudder at the thought of limiting range like this. The argument claims that the pectoralis major will not be as fully developed. Here's the counter argument. The pectoralis muscle doesn't operate efficiently from an extremely stretched or horizontally extended position. I refer to this point as the "basement" of the movement. When the shoulder is "in the basement," small muscles that are important to shoulder joint integrity are placed at risk of injury, as is the ligamentous joint capsule. Performing chest presses or flyes too deep doesn't allow the pectoralis major muscle to function in an optimal fashion until the upper arm is about in line with the axilla or point where the body would be divided into two equal front and back halves.

If range is limited at the shoulder, as suggested, the fact is that you'll lower your risk of shoulder injury and can probably load the muscle with more resistance. Because the mechanics are "right," you can actually train more aggressively. End result: Better muscular development and reduced risk of shoulder injury. Athletes, body builders and fitness enthusiasts alike, should have no argument with this outcome.

SHOULDER IMPINGEMENT

Shoulder impingement syndrome is common, though not limited, to movements such as the upright row, lateral shoulder raise, pressing movement performed overhead with the weight placed behind the neck, "pec decks," and latissimus pull-downs behind the neck.

What Is Shoulder Impingement?

If a client were asked to describe shoulder impingement they would probably characterize it as a feeling in the shoulder joint that is "painful," "uncomfortable" or "limiting." Impingement is characterized by the physical effect it has on joint tissue and structure, and often by limited movement capability.

Most commonly, the supraspinatus muscle (one of four rotator cuff muscles), which helps hold the head of the humerus in the glenoid fossa of the scapula (this articulation forms the glenohumeral joint of the shoulder), is irritated. Simply put, the muscle is "rubbed," not unlike a rope that is frayed, by bringing it into contact time and time again with a surface that causes it to become shredded, and results in inflammation and sometimes chronic pain. When the shoulder is abducted to about 90-degrees, the greater tubercle which is a bony process or bump — and of which the biceps tendon runs between the greater and lesser tubercles of the humerus — can impact the acromion process of the scapula. The acromion process of the scapula is a roof-like projection of the scapula. The impingement process can be envisioned by cupping or curling one hand with the palm facing the ground. Take the other hand, forming a fist and placing it in the cupped hand. The cupped hand represents the glenoid fossa and roof-like projection of the acromion process. The fist represents the head of the humerus. As the humerus abducts, the greater tubercle (exemplified by the middle knuckle) can rotate and "crash" into the roof-like acromion process. The result is bone impacting on bone, impingement of the supraspinatus and/or irritation of the bursa (fluid filled sacks that reduce tendon friction), and tendinitis of the biceps brachii tendon.

When Does Shoulder Impingement Occur?

Chest exercises that are performed too deep (i.e., dropping the elbows below or behind the frontal plane of the body) contribute to glenohumeral instability through repetitive shoulder capsule trauma. However, when shoulder hyperextension is coupled with external rotation and shoulder abduction at or above 90 degrees, you have some very risky exercises. When performed "incorrectly," a cluster of upper body exercises represent a nightmare from a biomechanical perspective (Reeves et al., 1998; Wolfe et al., 1992; Gross et al., 1993; Neviaser, 1991). It is no wonder that shoulder injuries, discomfort and pain are so common when a close look is taken at the mechanics of the upright row, "pec deck" chest exercise, latissimus dorsi pull-down behind the neck, and press overhead behind the neck.

THE UPRIGHT ROW AND SHOULDER IMPINGEMENT

The upright row has fallen into disfavor among many physical therapists and biomechanists. It's weakness — high-risk to benefit ratio — is related to poor alignment of the wrists, elbows and shoulders, and the likelihood that shoulder impingement syndrome will occur. Specifically, the shoulder is forced to abduct from an inwardly rotated position, and as the elbows "lead" the movement and are drawn toward the chin, inward rotation can become more pronounced. Inward rotation at the shoulder joint, combined with abduction, increases the risk for impingement of the supraspinatus muscle, the greater tubercle impacting the acromion process and bursa irritation. When the shoulder is extremely internally rotated (i.e., therapists refer to this as a "closed-pack" or bone-on-bone position), bone or the thin hyaline cartilage that covers the end plate of bones comes into contact with one another. This can be referenced as "bone-impacting-bone."

Key Point

As a general rule of thumb, any time a joint is at an extreme end range of motion (i.e., extremely internally or externally rotated, hyper-flexed or hyper-extended), the joint is more vulnerable to heavy loads and destabilizing forces that stretch ligaments, strain muscles and inflame bursa.

Fig. 113, Typical performance of the upright row

Fig. 114, Modified upright row performed with dumbbells

The muscles involved in the upright row include the upper trapezius, levator scapulae, mid and posterior deltoids, elbow flexors and supraspinatus. However, the muscles that are typically targeted with this exercise — deltoids, elbow flexors and upper trapezius — are poorly aligned against the force of the weight being lifted. A traditional upright row does not present a favorable or effective line of pull for the targeted muscles.

The upright row is usually executed by standing with upright posture, feet shoulder width apart. A straight-bar is grasped with a closed- or over-grip, with the hands placed together in the center of the bar. At the beginning of the movement the bar rests at arms' length on the upper thigh. The bar is drawn upward toward the chin. *See fig. 113*

Upright Row Modifications

If you choose to perform the upright row exercise, one modification is to move your hands about shoulder width apart, and use dumbbells or a cable so there is less stress to the wrists, elbows and shoulders. Only draw the elbows to a point where the elbow shoulder line is parallel to the ground. *See fig. 114*

The modified figure shows the upright row being performed with the hands moved apart through the use of dumbbells and shoulder abduction is limited. Though this modification is a step in the right direction, risk still may outweigh positive benefits.

Impingement tends to occur at or around 90 degrees of abduction, so by simply limiting range, you might avoid the problem. Some people have suggested externally rotating the shoulder as the humerus reaches 90 degrees of abduction, and though the thinking is solid, there is a weakness. The intelligent aspect of this thinking is exhibited by an apparent knowledge that if the shoulder is externally rotated, the greater tubercle of the humerus rotates to the outside of the shoulder, possibly missing the roof-like structure of the scapula — the acromion process. The weakness in this thinking is that the weight that can be lifted in an upright row movement is not appropriate — it's generally too heavy — for the external rotators of the shoulder to work against in this position. And, the heavy load isn't in a correct position to be placed in opposition to the external rotation movement through the entire range. Bottom line: It's much easier to avoid impingement by simply limiting shoulder abduction or using several exercises to target these muscles more effectively and safely.

The worst cues you can give your client are to "lead" with the elbows and to "draw the weight up to the chin" or higher. These cues heighten misalignment at the wrists, elbows and shoulders, and increase impingement likelihood.

It is simple to effectively target the shoulder muscles, trapezius and elbow flexors with individual exercises that are safer and more effective, when compared to using the upright row. Do you know of any elbow flexor exercises you would perform in an extremely inward rotated position, or a shoulder exercise where you perform shoulder abduction with an extremely inwardly rotated shoulder? In essence, the upright row asks you to do just that! And, if your goal is to work the trapezius muscle, the upright row is only an adequate selection. The fibers of the upper trapezius assist in elevating the scapulae and are further contracted when the scapula rotates upwardly. Therefore, scapular elevation (shrug or drawing the shoulders toward the ears) using a barbell placed behind the body with a wide grip would be a better option. The shrug exercise provides resistance that directly opposes the joint motions without requiring the shoulder to abduct or rotate. Additionally, a dumbbell press overhead can be performed so that it allows full upward rotation of the scapula and can become part of the plan for "replacing" the upright row. Finally, you may also hear an argument that says the pulling movement of the upright row is very common to many athletic activities. While this is true, generally the movement is not loaded with a heavy RM load. Sport specific or occupational training should replicate the movement and forces encountered exactly, or it isn't "specific." Close does not count when it comes to timing and training neuromuscular patterns.

Key Point

It is interesting to note that the end position of the upright row — hands near chin or higher — is the same position physical therapists use as an "impingement test" to assess whether a client is experiencing an impingement syndrome.

In addition to the upright row, three other common exercises or joint motions have the potential to cause shoulder impingement syndrome. The "Pec Deck" motion performed on different machines, a press overhead performed behind the neck, and a latissimus pull down behind the neck, are commonly performed in the gym and have what I call the "threesome malady" in common at the shoulder. At some point in these exercises the shoulder is abducted 90 degrees, externally rotated and hyper-extended beyond the midline of the body. (The midline referenced here is as divided by the frontal plane that runs through the body and divides it into front and back halves.) This combination places the shoulder in a position which makes it vulnerable to injury. The risk increases when challenging loads are added to this disadvantaged position.

THE "PEC DECK" MOVEMENT AND SHOULDER IMPINGEMENT

This type of movement places the pectoralis major muscle at a mechanical disadvantage, which contributes to joint stress in the form of glenohumeral instability that results from repeated bouts of shoulder capsule trauma, and places excessive traction on the acromioclavicular joints (Wolfe et al., 1992; Reeves et al., 1998). Additionally, the neck is usually excessively flexed which loads the cervical spine. *See fig. 115.* An easy fix would be to: 1) have the exerciser perform the exercise with the neck positioned in neutral, 2) adjust

Fig. 115, Typical performance of the "Pec Deck" joint motion

the machine so that the starting position places the elbow-shoulder line even with or in front of the frontal plane, and 3) internally rotate the shoulders back to neutral so that the pectoralis major can perform pure horizontal flexion.

Quick Index:

Chapter 7, Correct performance of chest exercises

THE PRESS OVERHEAD BEHIND THE NECK AND SHOULDER IMPINGEMENT

Extreme shoulder external rotation and abduction that occurs during behind-the-neck "military presses" stress the shoulder capsule and inferior glenohumeral ligament, which can cause anterior

Fig. 116, Typical performance of the press overhead behind the neck

shoulder instability (Esenkaya et al., 2000; Reeves, et al., 1998; Gross, et al., 1993; Neviaser, 1991). Additionally, the neck is usually excessively flexed which loads the cervical spine. *See fig. 116.* A safer way to perform the press overhead is to place the weight in front of the body and to use dumbbells or cables, which don't force external shoulder rotation.

Quick Index:

Chapter 7, Safer execution of the press overhead

THE LATISSIMUS PULL-DOWN BEHIND THE NECK AND SHOULDER IMPINGEMENT

When a bar or other apparatus is pulled behind the head on a latissimus pull-down, the neck must excessively flex (which loads the cervical spine and disks), the shoulders are forced into a position at the extreme of external rotation and the shoulder is hyper-extended. This position puts the shoulder at a mechanical disadvantage that could contribute to rotator cuff injury or anterior shoulder instability. An excessively wide grip does not work the "outer lats," but can increase shear forces across the glenohumeral joint (Reeves et. al, 1998), as well as limiting range-of-motion at the joint. *See fig. 117*

Additionally, the line of pull does not oppose the muscle fibers of the latissimus dorsi, which results in the muscle not being maximally challenged. If the latissimus muscles ran straight up and down from attachment to attachment — which of course, they do not — the line of pull would be correct. But, even if this were the case, the risk of joint stress would still be present. The line of pull of the latissimus dorsi runs at a slight angle, from the sides of the body, up and obliquely forward. From a functional, injury and muscular development perspective, it makes sense to pull the weight from in front of the body, toward the chest.

Fig. 117, Typical performance of a latissimus pull-down behind the neck

Quick Index:

Chapter 7, Safer execution of a latissimus pull-down

Real Life Applications For Shoulder Problems

Supraspinatus tendinitis and subacromial bursitis are problems that frequently challenge physicians. It's interesting to note in one physician's report that treatment protocols often fail because patients sleep with their symptomatic arm abducted and externally rotated (i.e., with their hand behind the head). Sleeping in this position subjects the supraspinatus tendon and subacromial bursa to impingement forces for prolonged periods and may be a major factor in patients' inability to recover (reported in the Pearls Column, Editor: Robert Salis, *The Physician and Sportsmedicine*, Vol. 28, No. 9, September, 2000).

Many adults have embraced the benefits of resistance training, and begin strength training with existing conditions such as chronic rotator cuff/shoulder discomfort. One physician suggests that a practical bit of advice you can offer to clients when training is to have them "keep your hands where you can see them." For example, the hands should be seen, rather than disappearing behind the head, when performing pressing movement overhead and latissimus dorsi pull-downs. During a bench press movement, as the hands approach the chest, they should not disappear from sight. These positions — hands disappearing — are generally at the end range of capsular tolerance and also place the rotator cuff musculature at a mechanical disadvantage, which may increase pain and the tendency for further injury. Or, this type of lifting can be the causative factor of injury onset (reported in the Pearls Column, Editor: Robert Salis, *The Physician and Sportsmedicine*, Vol. 28, No. 6, June, 2000).

KNEE FLEXION CONTROVERSIES

Some would argue there is no such thing as a bad exercise, insisting that correctness is based solely in how the exercise is performed. I disagree, as do many anatomists and biomechanists. This is especially true of knee and shoulder mechanics. Exercises can be performed technically correct — there's no error in how the exercise is being done — and still cause damage to the body.

You often see guidelines for knee extension, squatting, leg press and lower body lunge movements that limit the degree of knee flexion in these exercises based on "proper technique." In other words, guidelines like these are saying degree of flexion by itself is unimportant. For example, depth of a squat might be based on whether or not the back is kept slightly retracted, knees are aligned between the first and fifth toes, neutral spinal posture is maintained and the knees are kept from moving well beyond the toes. I limit depth of squats or degree of knee flexion based on performance characteristics just mentioned, *and* on known orthopedic concerns that surround degree of knee flexion. Both, when considered together, create a better parameter from which to determine appropriate degree of knee flexion.

Joint mechanics research, which looks at the effects movement has on joints, is in direct opposition to the idea that "proper technique" dictates the depth of a squat, lunge or degree of knee extension/flexion. Going back to chapter 4, and the Any Exercise Drill, you must always weigh proper execution with known orthopedic concerns.

As mentioned, I limit the depth of a squat or other lower body exercise that utilizes knee flexion based on proper technique and angle of knee flexion. If the lumbar spine flexes or rounds, or scapular stabilization (retraction) is lost, or the client bends from the waist too much or drives the knees excessively forward of the toes, the exercise is over. If technique is perfect, the client can approach a knee angle of 60 to 90 degrees. *See figs. 118a and 118b*

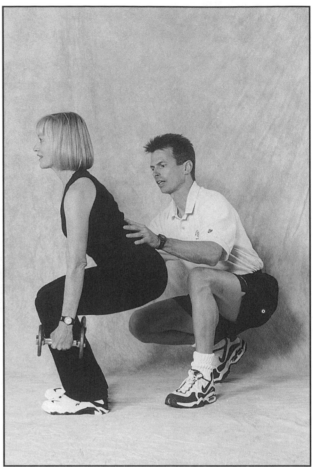

Fig. 118a, Squat at a knee angle of approximately 60 degrees

Fig. 118b, Squat at a knee angle of approximately 90 degrees

For general health and fitness goals, and most athletic training goals, this is adequate to strengthen the targeted muscles and mediate increased risk for injury. The exception to this rule would be, for example, if you were training competitive Olympic or power lifters since their sport demands range of motion where the knee is flexed more than 90 degrees. Additionally, if any other sport specific application is identified, and the risks are understood in relation to what can be expected in relation to improved performance, moving outside these parameters might be defensible. Elite performance sometimes requires taking risks that are inappropriate for most athletes and the general population.

Generally, I encourage my clients to approach 60- to 90-degrees of knee flexion when performing squats, lunges, Smith rack presses, hack squats, seated leg presses, wall squats and seated leg extension. The reasoning begins with what happens to the knee when it is loaded and flexed. The compression force on the back of the knee cap increases, and becomes exponentially greater as the knee moves from 60 toward greater degrees of knee flexion (Reilly and Martens, 1972). Squats can be started with straight legs, as long as the knees are not "locked" or hyperextended, and since shear forces (force that moves across the hinge-like knee joint) are greatest during seated knee extension when the leg is fully extended or straight, a soft knee or slight bend is encouraged, versus attaining a straight leg or hyper-extended ending position.

Why is 60 to 90 degrees of knee flexion a good recommendation for general and athletic populations? You get all kinds of arguments for flexing the knee less or more. The normal range of knee flexion is from zero to 135 degrees. But, when you add heavy load, and couple this with technique error or rotation at the knee, the risk of injury rises greatly.

Anecdotally, major league baseball catchers have many problems with their knees during and post career. It is attributed to the deeply flexed knee stance required in the catching position. In fact, the advent of "knee savers" that limit the degree of knee hyper-flexion in the crouched position are testament to the problem. Yet, crippling arthritis and tendinitis often do not show up on training injury trend surveys, as is true for similar crippling injuries that accumulate over time in the weight training room (Weight Training Injury Trends, The Physician and Sportsmedicine, Vol. 28, No. 7, July, 2000). People simply live with "it" and others follow in the same footsteps, blindly repeating the same mistakes. If tradition — like history — is not challenged, it will be repeated.

Osteoarthritis Of The Knee Joint

The prevalence of patellofemoral or tibiofemoral osteoarthritis in former competitive weight lifters has been reported at 31 percent, versus 14 percent in competitive runners (Kujala et al., 1995; Reeves et al., 1998, Part 2). The same authors found that patellofemoral arthritis was more prevalent in weight lifters (28 percent) than in soccer players, runners and shooters. Sub-optimal technique — related to depth of, for example squats — is likely to be a significant contributing factor for osteoarthritis.

By way of illustration: "...squats performed with heavy loads and in which the thighs descend below parallel to the floor (authors note: about 90 degrees of knee flexion or greater) place significant load on the thinnest part of the femoral articular cartilage. Repetitive shear force likely takes its toll on the cartilage." (Reeves, et al., 1998, Part 2)

Key Point

Armed with existing science, an understanding of joint function and mechanics, and by applying available research that focuses on joint injury, a prudent and responsible decision can be made for individual training and rehabilitation goals.

You've probably heard that the forces on the back side of the knee cap approach several body weights and the resistance being lifted, when the knee is excessively flexed. *Figure K* shows that when the knee joint is loaded and flexed, the compression force on the back of the knee cap *increases* as flexion becomes progressively deeper. High compression forces can speed up the process of wear and tear on the articular cartilage that covers bony surfaces. This process is accelerated if the "tracking" mechanism of the knee cap does not keep the interface between the knee cap and bone properly aligned, and if unnecessary compressive forces are endured by the knee joint. It can be seen that the compression force on the back of the knee cap is equal to a little more than the weight of the body when the knee is flexed to 60-degrees from the fully extended or zero degree position.

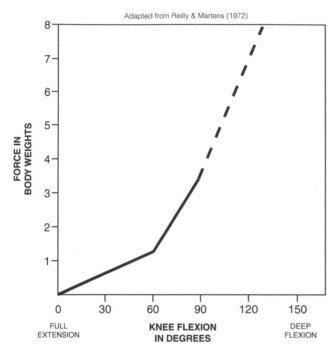

Adapted from Reilly & Martens (1972)

Fig. K, Compressive Force of the Knee Joint When Loaded and Flexed

When the knee is flexed more deeply than 60-degrees the compression force increases at a much faster or exponential rate. At 90-degrees the knee takes on 3 times the compressive force as measured in bodyweights. Needless to say, the more weight being lifted, the more compressive force present at the joint. As the knee is flexed deeper than 90-degrees the rate of increase in compression becomes even more pronounced. Excessive bending of one or both knees over stretches the posterior cruciate ligament within the knee joint, and as mentioned there is an excessive amount of shear load on the knee in this hyperflexed position where the articular cartilage is the thinnest. With excessive bending of the knees, the posterior ligament is placed on full stretch, which can destabilize the joint.

Fine Tuning Squat Technique With The Facts

Is it okay to begin and end a squat, leg press or lunge movement with a straight leg position? When the leg is straightened in this superb closed chain exercise, the forces are distributed via the ankle, knee, hip and spine through the joints, and not across them. Avoid hyperextending or locking the knee, but fully straightening the knee is acceptable. In a deep squat, as the thighs approach parallel to the floor or lower, there is excessive shear load on the knee in a position where the articular cartilage is thinnest and the posterior cruciate ligament begins to be placed on excessive stretch. Descending to this position is done by power lifters who must meet technical specifications during competition, but it must be acknowledged they also place themselves at risk for cartilage and ligament damage (Reeves et al., 1998, Part 1). Most people who train with resistance should avoid deep squats and extremes of hyper-flexion and hyper-extension of the knee, and should maintain lumbar spinal stability throughout squat lifts or when performing similar leg press movements.

Key Point

Even with perfect execution of the squat movement — or any exercise that uses deep knee flexion movement — the risk of injury to the knee does not decrease.

Fine Tuning Knee Extension Technique With The Facts

What is the optimal angle for the knee at the start point of seated knee extension? Should a seated leg extension exercise be finished with a fully extended or straight knee (zero degrees of knee flexion), or should this exercise be ended with a slightly flexed (10 to 20 degrees) finish position? Knee extension exercise is an example of open chain exercise, which isolates the quadriceps in this case. This type of movement involves load distal (away from) to the axis of the joint. Unlike the squat, loads are placed at the ankle that result in force being exerted across the hinge-like joint. An every day analogy would liken this to hanging excessive weight on the top of an open door. Eventually, the force would cause the door hinges (the knee) to interface poorly. The door would creak and grind (i.e., knee crepitation and cartilage damage), and likely not operate tightly and smoothly (i.e., joint laxity due to ligament damage). When the knee angle is greater than 90-degrees at the starting point, the forces exerted across the joint are greater than when the starting knee angle is 90-degrees or less. *See figs. 119a and 119b*

"During knee extension, potentially damaging tibiofemoral shear forces are greater during the last 5- to 10-degrees of extension (as the leg nears a straight leg position), and if the person "hyperextends" or locks the knee joint (Reeves et al., 1998, Part 1)." "In addition, at the extremes of knee flexion (greater than 60 degrees), increased patellar compression is potentially harmful (Reeves et al., 1998, Part 1; Beynnon et al., 1995; Palmitier et al., 1991)."

The remedy, of course, is to avoid "hyperextension" of the knee and consider performing the exercise 5- to 10-degrees shy of straight or full extension, since the potential for tibiofemoral shear forces are greater at this end range-of-motion. *See fig. 119c.* Avoid extremes of knee flexion, as discussed throughout this "knee flexion section" and in "fine tuning squat technique." These suggestions especially hold greater importance as resistance is increased.

Would I ever say it is "wrong" to flex the knee deeper than 90 degrees? No. Am I, or any researcher, certain it will cause injury? No. Would I say that for most people, depth limitations and avoiding a straight leg position when performing a seated leg extension are prudent ideas? Yes.

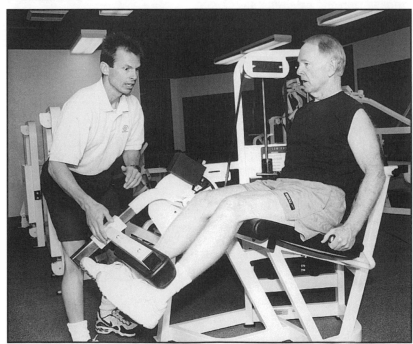

Fig. 119a, Performing seated leg extension starting at 90-degrees of knee flexion

Fig. 119b, Performing seated leg extension moving to 60-degrees of knee flexion

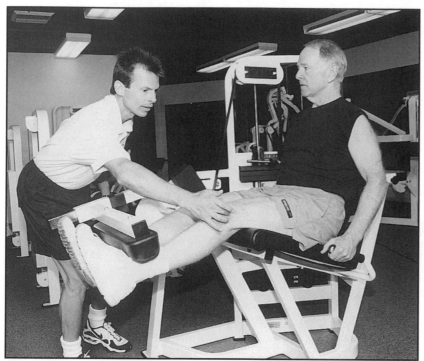

Fig. 119c, Performing seated leg extension ending at 10- to 20-degrees of knee flexion

TRUNK FLEXION CONTROVERSIES

Various positions of the trunk can present more, or less risk of spinal injury. During trunk or spinal flexion there is a compression of the discs in the front or anterior side of the spine, while simultaneously occurring on the other side of the spine is a tensile pull, or stretching, of the discs. Intradiscal pressures double at about 40 degrees of trunk/spinal flexion. As the trunk continues to flex, supportive ligaments are stretched, particularly at the end range of motion.

Quick Index:

Chapter 5, Understanding neutral spinal posture and for a more in-depth discussion of trunk flexion and extension mechanics

Unsupported Spinal Flexion

Refer to chapter 4 and the section titled, *"Illustrating The Drill," which uses* the "unsupported bent-over row" exercise as the example.

Fixed Leg Trunk Flexion (Full Sit-Up)

Does a "full sit-up" guarantee immediate and irreparable spinal damage? Of course not. The controversy that surrounds the fixed leg, full sit-up revolves around lower-back strain that occurs with incorrect performance. Poor execution is more likely to occur with fast speeds, and feet fixed on an incline. A preexisting imbalance between tight hip flexors and weak abdominal muscles also increases the likelihood of poor sit-up performance.

The hip flexors (iliacus and psoas) attach to the lower spine and pelvis (typically the origin and more stable attachment point), and insert on the femur (less stable attachment point). Classic hip flexion draws the leg forward by pulling the insertion toward its origin and is common to running, cycling and kicking activities. When the "feet are fixed" or the thigh is held stable, these same muscles reverse the pull of the insertion toward the origin. In other words, the origin is pulled toward the insertion, causing compression and sheer force on the spinal discs, and resulting in a movement where the trunk moves toward or "flexes on" the femur.

In instances where full trunk flexion is desirable, proper technique is the key to safety and effectiveness. To lower the risk of creating back strain or soft tissue damage, the spine should be fully flexed prior to the "full sit-up." After flexing or curling the spine the hip flexors can take over, as the torso moves to the upright, full sit-up end position. If complete trunk flexion is used, the ribs are drawn toward the pelvis. Once full flexion of the spine is attained, the client engages the hip flexors and begins to slowly lift the trunk toward a completely upright position. As the client reaches a position where the torso is perpendicular to the floor, the motion is stopped since the resistance provide by gravity diminishes. Reverse the process and return to start position.

Another way to teach a full sit-up is to instruct the client to maintain neutral posture or slight trunk flexion through the range of motion. Maintaining neutral lumbar posture requires the abdominals to work very hard as stabilizers to counter the pull of the hip flexors as the trunk is moved forward toward the femur and back. If the abdominals are not strong enough to keep the spine fully flexed or neutral, the pull of the hip flexors cause the lower back to arch.

Generally, I would recommend *not* allowing the feet to be fixed or "held" in any manner when performing a full sit-up. When the feet are fixed, a powerful leverage advantage is created and the use of the hip flexors can over power the stabilizing strength of the abdominals, especially when the exerciser tires. Keeping the feet unanchored, the client can flex the trunk, or set neutral posture, and perform the movement in a controlled manner.

With increasing force and ballistic movement — typically seen when this exercise is done on an incline board with the feet fixed — neutral posture will be difficult to maintain and it is hard to justify the safety of this type of movement. Performed in this manner, the full sit-up potentially introduces unacceptable compression and shear forces that are exerted on the spine due to the hip flexor attachments off the front of the pelvis and sides of the spine. Done "perfectly," even avoiding an arched back, these forces still exist.

Quick Index:

"Leg Raise" or "Leg Lift"

Telling someone, without an explanation, that a leg raise is a hip flexor exercise and not an abdominal exercise may cause you to lose some credibility. Though the primary movers of this exercise are the hip flexors (iliopsoas and rectus femoris), it really can be characterized as a trunk exercise because of the challenge the abdominals receive to maintain proper spinal alignment. When the legs are raised by the hip flexors, the abdominals receive more challenge countering the pull of the hip flexors and maintaining a neutral lumbar posture, than the hip flexors receive challenge as the primary movers.

You may be wondering where a variety of other active hip flexor exercises fall within this discussion. Varied names include 1) pike-up, jack-knife or V-up, 2) "runners" where the legs alternate in and out with the feet elevated slightly off the ground from a supine position, 3) double leg accordion or bicycling knee-in and knee-out movement from a seated position on a bench, 4) leg and knee pull-ins from a variety of apparatus, 5) dip stand leg raise or knee tucks, and 6) "windshield wipers" performed with a straight or bent leg side-to-side movement. All use the hip flexors as the prime mover, with the abdominals resisting the pull of the hips flexors. Longer lever (straight legs) variations are more challenging to the abdominals when compared to short lever (knee is flexed) variations, and generally introduce a higher level of risk.

Key Point

Leg lifts, while involving the hip flexors as the prime movers, may represent one of the best ways to challenge the abdominal muscles in their role as spinal stabilizers — as long as the exercise is performed within the exerciser's capabilities.

It should be noted that physical therapists sometimes use a supine straight leg "lowering" test (Kendall, pg. 154) to assess strength in the lower abdominal region. Adequate strength is defined as the ability of the rectus abdominis and external oblique muscles to resist the pull of the hip flexors, which try to pull the pelvis into an anterior pelvic tilt (arched back). The test is graded by the client's ability to keep the low back flat while slowly lowering the legs from a vertical position toward the floor. The angle between the extended legs and the floor is noted at the moment the pelvis starts to tilt anteriorly and the low back arches. This assessment could also be performed by instructing the participant to attempt to maintain a neutral lumbar posture throughout the movement. Of course, testing does not require numerous repetitions and is usually supervised by highly trained individuals.

Should trunk flexion or ab curls be substituted for leg raises? Do leg raises challenge the abs since all of the movement is at the hip? The risk is hip flexor traction or stretch on the lumbar spine, and the question that needs to be answered is, "Is the person performing the movement able to maintain spinal neutral?" Let's come full circle with the analysis. Is it for everyone? No. Does it work the abs? Yes. Is it a poor exercise choice? Maybe and maybe not, depending on which client or patient is performing it and their specific goals.

Quick Index:

DEAD LIFT CONTROVERSIES

The straight-leg dead lift is often labeled contraindicated, but when performed with the proper load, limited range of motion and neutral spinal alignment, it can be performed safely and can serve as a functional exercise if taught with a "hip hinge." Don't get this exercise confused with the "Good Morning" exercise (*See figs. 120a and 120b*). Another name for this high-risk exercise is "good morning to your orthopedic surgeon." All joking aside, placing resistance behind your neck creates an unacceptable shear, destabilizing force across the spine (See unsupported bent over row analysis in chapter 4).

The "dead lift" I refer to is really nothing more than standing hip extension (see chapter 8, lower body exercises), performed using dumbbells or a barbell. This exercise targets the gluteus maximus and hamstrings during the lowering portion using eccentric force produc-

Fig. 120b, The "Good Morning" exercise ending position

Fig. 120a, The "Good Morning" exercise" starting position

tion, and the same muscles contract concentrically to return the torso to the start position. This standing hip extension exercise strongly challenges the low back muscles as stabilizers. The depth of the exercise is dependent on hamstring flexibility and the ability of the back musculature to stabilize lumbar neutral. Generally, I also limit the degree of hip flexion to about 30 degrees from vertical, as the potential for spinal shear forces (forces that move across the spine rather than down through it) increase beyond this. A good "ball park" cue is that the hands should hang no lower than the knees, though the real marker you're gauging is not where the hands fall, but the degree of hip flexion. Spinal position should not change from a stabilized, neutral starting position. The client should "hinge" into and out of the movement from the hip, and avoid locking the knees or forcing an extreme stretch of the hamstrings. Though the "dead lift" can be a very functional exercise, it is a complex skill and difficult to learn.

Can A Straight-Leg Dead Lift Be Performed Safely?
I've skirted the issue of straight-leg dead lifts by offering the previous modification. When taking the weight from the floor — versus a safety rack — the legs must have adequate hamstring flexibility or the back usually rounds as a compensatory action for the hip flexion that cannot take place. This places the spine in a loaded and flexed position, and can easily strain the lower-back muscles.

As the trunk flexes forward from the hip to this low position, the force angles of the erector spinae, which help keep the spine properly positioned, are not aligned to exert force as efficiently, when compared to a more upright (i.e., about 30 degrees of hip flexion from vertical) position. The biggest contributors to performing this exercise unsafely are an inability to maintain neutral spinal posture throughout the motion, allowing the back to flex, inadequate hamstring flexibility and forcing the stretch toward the floor. In addition, if the amount of weight is improperly chosen or progressed, this can lead to injury.

SUMMARY

Put every exercise to the test of the "Any Exercise Drill" and take into account the individual you're working with. Science should lead your decisions, though common sense and experience sometimes leads us to a conclusion that a "textbook" approach is not always appropriate.

Though stated in the introduction to this book, the following information bears repeating. When an exercise is criticized or praised, it is important to explain "why" from a mechanical/biomechanical, kinesiological and anatomical standpoint. Additionally, this rationale must be appropriately aligned with the training goal(s) and individual being trained. Then, it is important to supply solutions in the form of exercise alternatives or modifications if called for.

On the other hand, many people who teach or participate in strength training justify using, or continuing to use, an exercise that has come under criticism because the exercise in question "hasn't yet caused injury" or simply base its use on the fact the exercise has "been used forever, by everybody." Both positions represent very weak arguments and are not in the best interest of someone you are training.

To bring my point home, consider the following logic. Many people have stated, for example, "I wouldn't use this exercise if I had bad knees or a bad back." So, what they are saying is that they'll keep using the exercise until they do indeed have bad knees or until they injure their back, at which point they might consider a modification or jettisoning the exercise. Sounds ludicrous, but rationale that reflects this type of thinking abounds. It would seem that if an exercise is not a great idea for people with injured knees, backs or shoulders, then there exists a high probability that the exercise being questioned is probably not a great exercise for people with apparently healthy knees, backs and shoulders.

Key Point

If the science is there to support the assertion that the exercise falls short of safe biomechanical standards, a more prudent and receptive approach might be to acknowledge the underlying weaknesses and potential problems of a given exercise and take corrective action.

To follow is an important dilemma to consider when placing resistive exercise controversy in proper perspective. When deciding whether or not you will perform an exercise in a specific manner, do you demand proof that unequivocally shows the exercise to be unsafe? Let's say no research exists to prove the exercise's absolute guilt or innocence, which is more often than not the case. Does that imply it is safe to use and that you can conclude that "research" — or the lack of its existence — proves it is safe to use? Many guidelines are based on this premise alone. Or, when anatomical evidence, available research and common sense says the exercise imposes increased risk, do you turn the tables and choose not to use the exercise or modify the exercise toward safer ground, until research has proven the technique safe?

> ## Key Point
>
> Many times I am asked to document research that proves why the exercise is labeled high- or unacceptable-risk for certain populations. It's a fair request and I build the best argument I can, like I've done throughout this book. But then, I reciprocate the request made of me by challenging my audience with, "Where is the research that documents its safety." Black and white research may never exist for either case, but the evidence you have at hand still requires that you make a decision and reach a verdict!

REFERENCES AND SUGGESTED READING

American College of Sports Medicine (ACSM); (1998). **ACSM Resource Manual for Guidelines for Exercise Testing and Prescription,** 3rd edition. Baltimore, MD: Williams and Wilkins

American College of Sports Medicine (ACSM); (1995). **ACSM Guidelines For Exercise Testing and Prescription**, 5th edition. Philadelphia, PA: Williams and Wilkins.

American College of Sports Medicine (ACSM); (1997). **Exercise Management for Persons With Chronic Diseases and Disabilities.** L. Durstine (Ed.). Champaign IL: Human Kinetics

American Council on Exercise (ACE); (1999). **Clinical Exercise Specialist Manual: ACE's Source for Training Special Populations.** R. Cotton and R. Andersen (EDS.). San Diego, CA: ACE.

American Council on Exercise (ACE); (1998). **Exercise for Older Adults: ACE's Guide for Fitness Professionals.** R. Cotton (Ed.). Champaign IL: Human Kinetics

Beynnon, B.D., Fleming, B.C., Johnson, R.J., et al (1995). **Anterior cruciate ligament strain behavior during rehabilitation exercises in vivo.** American Journal of Sports Medicine; 23 (1): 24-34.

Beynnon, B.D., Johnson, R.J., Fleming, B.C., et al (1997). **The strain behavior of the anterior cruciate ligament during squatting and active flexion-extension: a comparison of an open and a closed kinetic chain exercise.** American Journal of Sports Medicine; 25 (6): 823-829.

Bouchard C., Shepard R.J., and Stephens, T. (1993). **Physical Activity, Fitness, and health Consensus Statement.** Champaign, IL: Human Kinetics.

Cahill, B.R. (1982). **Osteolysis of the distal part of the clavicle in male athletes**. Journal of Bone Joint Surgery (Am); 67 (7): 1053-1058.

Charette, S.L., et al (1991). **Muscle Hypertrophy Response to Resistance Training in Older Women.** Palo Alto, CA: American Physiological Society.

Esenkaya, I., Tuygun, H., Turkmen, M.I., (2000). **Bilateral Anterior Shoulder Dislocation in a Weight Lifter.** The Physician and Sportsmedicine: Vol. 28, No. 3, March, pps: 93-100.

Feigenbaum, M.S., and Pollock, M.L., (1997). **Strength Training: Rationale for Current Guidelines for Adult Fitness Programs.** Physician and Sports medicine 25:44-64.

Fiatrone, M.A. et al (1990). **High-intensity strength training in nonagenarians.** Journal of the American Medical Association, 263, 3029-3034.

Frontera, W.R. et al (1988). **Strength Conditioning in Older Men: Skeletal Muscle Hypertrophy and Improved Function.** Palo Alto, CA: American Physiological Society.

Gross, M.L., Brenner, S.L., Esformes, I., et al., (1993). **Anterior shoulder instability in weight lifters.** American Journal of Sports Medicine; 21 (4): 599-603.

Howley E., and Franks B. (1997). **Health and Fitness Instructors Handbook** (3rd. ed.). Champaign, IL: Human Kinetics.

Jones, Chester et al., (2000). **Weight Training Injury Trends: A 20-year survey.** The Physician and Sportsmedicine, Vol. 28, No. 7, July, pps. 61-72.

Kujala, U.M., Kettunen, J., Paananen, H. (1995). **Knee osteoarthritis in former runners, soccer players, weight lifters, and shooters.** Arthritis Rheum; 38 (4): 539-546.

Mazzeo, R.S., Cavanagh, P., and Evans, W. J., et al (1998). **ACSM Position Stand on Exercise and Physical Activity for Older Adults.** Medicine and Science in Sports and Exercise, 30 (6): 992-1008

McArdle, W., Katch, F. and Katch, V. (1997). **Exercise Physiology Energy, Nutrition and Human Performance** (3rd ed.). Philadelphia, PA: Lean and Febiger.

Neviaser, T.J., (1991). **Weight lifting: risks and injuries to the shoulder.** Clinical Sports Medicine; 10 (3): 615-621.

Palmitier, R.A., An K.N., Scott, S.G., et al (1991). **Kinetic chain exercise in knee rehabilitation.** Sports Medicine; 11 (6): 402-413.

Pollock, M. L., and G. A. Gaesser et al., (1998). **The recommended quantity and quality of exercise for developing and maintaining cardiorespiratory fitness, and flexibility in healthy adults.** Medicine and Science in Sports and Exercise 30 (6): pps. 975-991.

Post, William R. (1998). Patellofemoral Pain, **Physician and SportsMedicine**, Volume 26, No. 1, pp. 68-78, January.

Reeves, Ronald K., Edward R. Laskowski, and Jay Smith (1998). Weight Training Injuries— Part I: Diagnosing and Managing Acute Conditions. **The Physician and SportsMedicine**, Volume 26, No. 2, pp. 67-83, February.

Reeves, Ronald K., Edward R. Laskowski, and Jay Smith (1998). Weight Training Injuries— Part II: Diagnosing and Managing Chronic Conditions. **The Physician and SportsMedicine**, Volume 26, No. 3, pp. 54-63, March.

Reilly, D., and Martens, M. (1972). **Experimental analysis of quadriceps muscle force and patellofemoral joint reaction force for various activities.** Acta Orthopedic Scandinavia, 43: 16-37.

Salis, Robert E., Editor (2000). Pearls—Stay In A Safe Rotator Cuff Range. **The Physician and Sportsmedicine**. Vol. 28, No. 6, June, pg. 23.

Steinkamp, L.A., Dillingham, M.F., Markel, M.D., et al (1993). **Biomechanical considerations in patellofemoral joint rehabilitation.** American Journal of Sports Medicine; 21 (3): 438-444

US Department of Health and Human Services (1996). **Physical Activity and Health: A report of the surgeon general.** Atlanta, DHHS, Centers for Disease Control and Prevention, National Center for Chronic Disease Prevention and Promotion.

VanNorman, K. (1995). **Exercise Programming for Older Adults.** Champaign, IL: Human Kinetics.

Westcott, W.S., and Baechle, T. R., (1998). **Strength Training Past 50.** Champaign, IL: Human Kinetics

Westcott, Wayne (1996). **Building Strength and Stamina.** Champaign, IL: Human Kinetics

Westcott, W.S., (1995). **Strength Fitness: Physiological Principles and Training Techniques** (4th edition). Dubuque, Iowa: William C. Brown.

Wolfe S.W., Wickiewicz, T.L., Cavanaugh, J.T., (1992). **Ruptures of the pectoralis major muscle: An anatomic and clinical analysis.** American Journal of Sports Medicine; 20 (5): 587-593.

Resistance Training Program Design

10

A MODEL FOR RESISTANCE TRAINING PROGRAM DESIGN

*A*t some point, if your goal is effective and time efficient resistance training, you will have to "put it all together" with regard to resistance training program design. The information in this chapter, as well as in chapters 11-13, will help you to design resistance training programs that are time-efficient and goal oriented. In addition, you will be able to reconcile and choose between a myriad of rep, set and load options, as well as be able to sort out much of the seemingly contradictory information that abounds in the area of strength training program design.

RESISTANCE TRAINING SYSTEMS

Training systems can be defined as *any* combination of sets, repetitions and loads. Every imaginable kind of training system exists. At least 27 different systems, such as super set, compound, cheat and pyramid to name a few, have been analyzed by Fleck and Kraemer (1997), and this is not an exhaustive list.

Training systems are often thought of as easy-to-follow recipes, but it is sometimes difficult to identify which one will be most helpful in attaining resistance training goals because there are so many training systems to choose from. There are literally hundreds of strength programs you can follow. How do all of these programs differ from one another? How can you discern their safety, effectiveness, and potential to deliver results in a time efficient manner? Careful evaluation is important for optimal resistance training program design.

Understanding How "Systems" Originate

Different strength programs are lumped under a term called, "systems." As mentioned, a system represents any combination of reps, number of sets and resistance you or your client work against. Most training systems are based on solid science, and effectively accomplish an intended training goal. However, it's important make sure the goals of that system are in line with your goals or the goals of your client. While a "recipe" or system may be effective for one client, that same system may be ineffective or even harmful to another client.

Occasionally a system's driving force is hype that is intended to sell products or services. These are the systems to beware of, although fortunately most of them don't stick around for long. Remember that anyone can name a system and popularize a new approach to strength training. The danger is that it could quite possibly hurt or frustrate someone who follows it. I've had trainers ask me about systems with names such as "The 100-Rep System" and "Pump Until You Puke." You get the point. These types of systems have nothing to do with sensible training.

Key Point

Most systems or combinations of reps, sets and loads will produce results, sometimes in spite of their design, simply because the person is working against a load to which they are not accustomed!

Do not make the mistake of blindly adopting a program simply because it was used, for example, by a successful athlete. Do not jump on the bandwagon because "everyone is doing it." Make sure the training system you choose will meet your client's needs and current situation.

STEPS FOR DESIGNING RESISTANCE TRAINING PROGRAMMING

Information about your client's goals and current conditioning level are critical to the success of a program. Use the following process to ensure that you are addressing them:

Step 1: Analyze Your Client's Needs

In other words, what are your client's goals? Common goals include muscular hypertrophy, weight loss, increasing maximal lifts, increased performance in a particular sport, decreased body fat, feeling stronger, personal physical independence and increased self-esteem.

Step 2: Match The Client's Goals To The Right System

All systems fit into the Resistance Training Specificity Chart (found in Chapter 11), which you can use to match your client's goals to appropriate work loads. The *goal repetition range*, or number of reps, is determined by a variety of factors that include: a) your client's current fitness level specific to resistance training, b) current exercise history, and c) stated resistance-training goals — for example, whether the client wants to emphasize muscular endurance, strength and/or hypertrophy.

Step 3: Identify The Appropriate Overload

Choose a safe starting resistance. For most people, this amount of resistance allows completion of at least 12-20 repetitions. This intensity level, of 12 reps or greater, equates to less than 70% of a one repetition maximum (or one RM). Research indicates that a 10 RM lift loosely equates to about 75% of a person's maximum lifting capacity for any given lift. A 6 to 10 RM intensity seems necessary to *optimize* muscular strength and hypertrophy gains, but it should be reached in a progressive manner.

Quick Index:

Chapter 11, How to determine a safe amount of resistance to lift, and determining the right mix of reps, sets and loads

VARY YOUR RESISTANCE PROGRAM WITH CROSS TRAINING

Cross training is associated with changing from one activity or component of fitness to another. You can "change-up" your program by varying activities *within* a component of fitness. For example, cross train with running, swimming and cycling for cardiovascular fitness, rather than performing the same activity day after day. You can also create change *between* all of the major components of fitness. For example, vary the activities within one balanced workout, which includes cardiovascular, strength training and stretching.

Cross Training Within The Strength Component

If you simply need variety, try cross training *without* initially changing the intensity. An easy first step is to change the sequence of exercises that you are already doing to create variety and a new overload. Because of this change, it is theorized that the fatigue pattern of the involved motor units will be changed, causing them to adapt to the new stimulus (Fleck and Kraemer, 1997; Plowman and Smith, 1997).

Another step would involve replacing exercises in your client's foundation routine, with new ones. Look at the joint actions and muscle groups being utilized and choose the replacement exercises accordingly. Take care to replace each exercise with one that targets the same muscle group(s) to preserve balance.

For example, a bench press can be "replaced" by push-ups, dumbbell presses, or incline and decline presses, dumbbell or elastic resistance chest flyes because all these movements use shoulder horizontal adduction/flexion. Movements that replicate shoulder extension, such as dumbbell or elastic resistance pullovers, one arm "low" rows, or straight-arm pullbacks with dumbbells or elastic resistance can replace machine pullover movements.

Any changes in movement patterns (new exercises or slight body position changes), even if you are targeting the same muscle group(s) and utilizing similar joint actions, will require a different motor-unit recruitment pattern (Fleck and Kraemer, 1997). This recruitment of muscle fibers (motor units) in a different order can act as a stimulus to create further strength gains. Cross training *within* the muscular strength and endurance component can positively affect compliance, motivation and interest, as well as stimulate the body toward additional strength gains.

Quick Index:

Chapters 11-12, Information you can use to initiate or further strength gains

PERIODIZATION: HOW TO PLAN YOUR CLIENT'S STRENGTH WORKOUTS

While there is quite a bit of information in reference to periodization training developed for elite athletes, these programs are very technical, highly specific, focus on "peaking" for athletic performance, and are often confusing since there is no one, standard approach. Very few formulas explain how to incorporate a periodized program into fitness routines for the average person in a simple way. Fortunately, when existing models of periodized programs for athletes are carefully studied, it's possible to identify common characteristics that you can use to bridge seemingly ambiguous and complex training principles into fitness results.

Planned Results

Periodization is probably most simply defined as "planned results." By manipulating volume of work and intensity of effort, and by strategically placing rest, maintenance and recovery phases in the overall periodization plan, you can transfer the concepts of periodization to fitness goals such as weight management, improvements in cardiorespiratory fitness and increased muscular strength.

A periodized approach has the potential to:
1. Promote optimal response to the training stimulus or work effort.
2. Decrease the potential for overuse injuries.
3. Keep a client fresh and progressing toward training goals.
4. Optimize personal efforts.
5. Enhance compliance.

Periodization Principles

Periodization is a method used to organize training. A periodized program cycles volume (reps, sets) and intensity (load or weight lifted) over specific time periods.

Key Point

Periodization attempts to provide for adequate recovery while simultaneously optimizing results and preventing detraining or overtraining.

The most obvious difference between elite athletes and most fitness participants is that the need to "peak" for performance is minimal or nonexistent for the latter. For the average client, training phases translate to 1) preparation or buildup, 2) goal attainment, and 3) restoration/recovery. For most active people who have achieved a desirable level of fitness, the goals may be variety of activity, solidifying current fitness levels and establishing commitment to exercise on a regular basis.

A well-planned periodized program looks at the short-term, mid-term and long-term needs of each individual. Such a planning process considers:
1. Daily workouts or *microcycles*
2. An agenda that accounts for about 4- to 6-weeks of training or mesocycles
3. An overall annual scheme that may incorporate several months of planning or macrocycles

The essence of periodization is represented by:
1. Training with variety of activity
2. Training with varied and progressive intensities
3. Training with 4- to 6-week mesocycles of progressive overload — always followed by several workouts of active recovery

PERIODIZATION MODEL FOR HEALTH AND FITNESS

For the average person, periodization should mean varying workouts over set time periods to optimize performance and fitness gains. Follow these steps to plan a progressive, goal-oriented training program that achieves superb results.

Step 1: Set the Goal(s)
- Muscular hypertrophy, strength or endurance
- Other

Step 2: Determine How to Achieve the Goal(s)
- Assess time availability
- Match training to goals
- Identify types of equipment available
- Choose equipment and exercises that accomplish the training goal

Step 3: Identify Training Phases
- Develop a 7-day short-term plan (microcycle)
- Develop a 4- to 6-week training plan (mesocycle)
- Develop a yearly organizational training plan (macrocycle), or at least 3 to 4 months of mesocycles
- Plan a general preparation phase of 4- to 6-weeks (one mesocycle), which may repeat several times

Step 4: Create an Exercise Plan
- Manipulate frequency, intensity and duration for specific strength results
- Control results by proper intensity of effort (load) and adequate recovery (restoration)

Step 5: Plan Volume and Intensity
- Vary volume and overload on a cyclic basis
- Plan to increase or decrease volume and intensity

- Use lower intensities and less duration during restoration (active rest)
- Start the new mesocycle after active recovery at a slightly lower intensity than the previous cycle

Step 6: Allow For The Restoration/Recovery Process
- Generally, do not increase progressive overload for more than 4 to 6 continuous weeks
- Follow any sustained, progressive overload of about 4- to 6-weeks with several days of active recovery activities at a lower intensity
- After active recovery, the new mesocycle should start at a slightly lower intensity than where the previous cycle ended
- The key to optimal results is *not* steady, relentless increases in intensity over long periods of time

Step 7: Regularly Evaluate The Periodization Planning Process
- Monitor results and progress
- Use fitness assessment if appropriate
- Recognize goal achievement
- Maintain an ongoing observation/evaluation of the program progression
- Observe compliance and enthusiasm toward the program

TRACKING A PERIODIZED PROGRAM

There are several ways you can track periodized programs for your clients. One idea is to label manila folders with each mesocycle and keep the client's weekly workout sheets or cards (microcycles) in the file. Place the manila folders that represent mesocycles into a hanging folder that represents the yearly macrocycle. You can organize the same system on your computer by creating a file for each mesocycle and placing documents for daily/weekly workouts in it. Also, consider using software that can assist you in efficiently handling this record-keeping and planning task.

It is obvious that periodization and program organization are not inherently complex. However, planning does require some forethought and time investment. On the other hand, it is well worth that investment, since periodization makes you and the client accountable for results.

Key Point

Because the periodization process involves management, planning and organization, it is "results oriented," and that creates a win-win situation for client and trainer.

WHEN SHOULD A STRENGTH PROGRAM BE CHANGED?

The first question to ask when considering a change in a resistance-training program is, "Why?" Is it you, the trainer, who needs a change? Or is it the client?

A program that has hit a plateau in terms of resistance (intensity), or number of reps and sets that can be completed, may or may not be a problem. If the client is pleased with her body image and strength, such a program can be termed "maintenance." Maintenance can be a positive state of training, meaning the client's fitness is at an "optimal" or acceptable level.

Valid reasons for changing a resistance-training program include client boredom, lack of motivation, lack of results, desire for change in muscle strength, hypertrophy or muscle endurance, or a need to change the training environment (type of equipment being used, location etc.). Planned change and variety encourages optimal training. It helps alleviate injury and unproductive training.

Key Point

Maintenance of fitness should not be considered regression, and in fact, represents the ultimate goal of maintaining desired health and fitness levels for the rest of a client's life!

Quick Index:

Chapter 11, Using the right combination of reps, sets and loads
Chapter 12, How to use variety and intensity to keep strength results coming

PERIODIZATION REFERENCES:

Bompa, Tudor (1999). **Periodization: Training for Sports.** Human Kinetics: Champaign, IL.

Bompa, Tudor (1996). **Periodization of Strength.** Toronto, Canada: Veritas Publishing, Inc.

Fleck, Steven and Kraemer, William (1996). **Periodization Breakthrough!** Advanced Research Press: Ronkonkoma, NY.

11

RESISTANCE TRAINING GUIDELINES

At some point, if your goal is effective and time efficient resistance training, you will have to "put it all together" with regard to resistance training program design. The information in this chapter, as well as in chapters 12-13, will help you to design resistance training programs that are time-efficient and goal oriented. In addition, you will be able to reconcile and choose between a myriad of rep, set and load options, as well as be able to sort out much of the seemingly contradictory information that abounds in the area of strength training program design.

CONTINUUM OF TRAINING PROGRAMS

There is a wide continuum of training programs that range from what I call the "far left" of cardiorespiratory training to the "far right" of maximal muscular strength and power. There is a *huge* gap in terms of similarity that exists between cardiovascular fitness and muscular endurance. *See fig. L*

Fig. L Training Program Continuum			
Cardiovascular Fitness	Muscle Endurance	Muscle Strength	Maximal Muscle Power

Cardiorespiratory fitness gains result in a physiologic adaptation that is very different from those adaptations seen in the muscular strength and endurance component. Precisely, to produce strength training improvements, specific thresholds must be crossed that result in training responses, whereby:
1. The nervous system is able to recruit muscle fiber more effectively,
2. Amino acids are assimilated to build muscles and
3. Anabolic hormonal surges "bathe" stimulated fibers, which plays a role in muscle hypertrophy.

Cardiorespiratory adaptations are well documented (Brooks, 1997; McArdle et al., 1996; Wilmore and Costill, 1994; Plowman and Smith, 1997), but these metabolic adaptations that occur in response to large muscle, rhythmic activity that promotes a simultaneous increase in heart rate and large return of blood volume to the heart, cannot be characterized as the same type of responses that are seen as a result of appropriate strength training exercise.

Do High Repetition Overloads Work?

Muscle endurance is defined as the ability to sustain repeated contractions without undue fatigue over a longer time period (for example about 12-25 reps or higher). As your client becomes stronger her muscles simultaneously become more endurant and she can perform more reps at a given resistance.

High rep exercise starts to *resemble* the overload definition for cardiorespiratory conditioning (i.e., continuous, rhythmic movement). However, *do not* interpret this statement to imply that significant cardiorespiratory conditioning takes place with high-repetition resistance training schemes. Actually, the load generally does not engage enough muscle mass to generate significant cardiorespiratory training effect (i.e., when performing a biceps curl or lateral shoulder raise) and the light resistance does not promote significant strength gains.

For increases in strength, you have to present a load to your client's musculature to which it is unaccustomed, on a regular and progressive basis. This type of intensity is necessary to stimulate the "cellular machinery" for muscle growth, hormonal surges that are anabolic in nature, or to stimulate motor learning for synchronous and additional motor unit recruitment. For the beginning to conditioned exerciser, that means 6 to 20 repetitions to muscular fatigue. The number works for older adults, young adults, athletes, women and men since it does not define an absolute weight that must be "lifted." Instead, the amount of resistance the client works against reflects the current strength level of the individual and requires a resistance that causes the client to fatigue within a specific time or repetition framework.

High-repetition schemes are usually quite ineffective in promoting any kind of health and fitness gains. They do not produce significant gains in muscular strength and endurance over an extended period of time and have little to no effect on cardiorespiratory conditioning, especially when small muscle masses are involved in the exercise. Repetitions that are redundant in their numbers are *not* harmless. They can lead to overuse injuries, not to mention lack of results, frustration and high-exercise dropout rates.

The "Hurt" Scale

It's important to understand the difference between 1 to 10 scales that represent "Physiological Effectiveness" and "Hurt." Generally, high rep overloads rate a 10 on a 1 to 10 *Hurt Scale*. In terms of a *Physiological Effectiveness Scale* — increased strength or cardiorespiratory endurance — they rate low. You may have painted a ceiling before, and on a 1 to 10 *Hurt Scale*, you would give it a numerical rating of at least 10 and maybe place it off the scale. In terms of producing strength or cardiovascular gain, on the *Physiological Effectiveness* 10-point scale, painting a ceiling rates a zero. Yet, why do many people believe that doing countless reps is effective? In two words, because "it hurts." But, "hurt" is not a good indicator of training effectiveness.

Strength training is best accomplished by doing a set of repetitions in an approximate range of time that is between 30 to 90 seconds. If your clients are doing a lot more reps than 6 to 20, or are not fatiguing in this time period, they may feel some "hurt," but "they're still only painting the ceiling."

Key Point

No one would ever characterize painting a ceiling as strength training, even though it is certainly uncomfortable keeping your arms raised overhead for extended periods of time. But, you have to wonder why some individuals believe performing a mind-numbing number of reps represents strength. Remember to tell your clients, if they're doing endless reps, they're painting a ceiling—not strength training!

When Is An Exercise A Strength Exercise?

Is a lunge or squat a strength, or cardiovascular exercise? The answer is dependent on one factor — the amount of resistance. If you can perform "walking lunges" around a track for longer than 90-seconds, it's not going to cause a significant strength training adaptation. On the other hand, load up a stationary lunge or squat with enough resistance to fatigue between 6 to 20 reps, and you'll get strength results.

Key Point

The overload and activities that are required to stimulate change in these components of fitness are very distinct. *Optimal* cardiorespiratory, and muscular strength and endurance conditioning cannot be developed simultaneously.

INTENSITY "RULES" IN RESISTANCE TRAINING

The neuro-physiological principle of motor-unit recruitment order ensures that slow-twitch (ST) motor units are predominantly recruited to perform low-intensity, long-duration activities. FT motor units (especially FT IIb) are primarily recruited when high-intensity (anaerobic) activity is performed. FT motor units are held in reserve until the ST motor units can no longer perform the particular muscular contraction. This order of recruitment, based on firing thresholds of the ST and FT motor units, reflects a ramp-like recruitment effect. The bottom of the pile (ST) fires or is used first. *See fig. M*

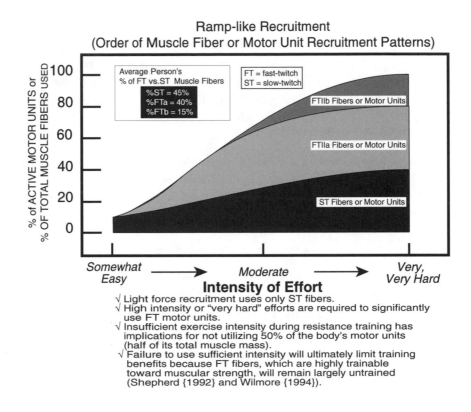

Fig. M, Ramp-like Recruitment

In order to recruit FT fibers and attain an *optimal* training effect, the exercise must be of an intense nature. Loads that are 70 percent or greater of one RM will most likely activate this type of motor unit. This equates to fatiguing the musculature in about 12 reps or less.

Key Point

Exercise resistance—intensity—is the key factor in determining resistance training result. Generally, exercise does not *significantly* contribute to strength gains unless 15 or fewer repetitions are performed to failure.

Correct or sufficient intensity has huge implications for involving greater amounts of muscle mass, which can influence increases in resting metabolic rate and gains in strength through both hypertrophy and nervous system adaptations. Light loads involve only slow-twitch fibers, whereas heavy loads will involve *all* 3 fiber types. If light to moderate muscular force is used, only about 50 percent of your muscle mass will be challenged.

This discussion leads to several important points that need to be highlighted regarding fast-twitch (FT) and slow-twitch (ST) motor units:
1. Both ST and FT fibers or, motor units, can hypertrophy.
2. "Selective" or "preferential" hypertrophy is not limited to FT fibers, but based on FT fibers' physical and biochemical (metabolic) characteristics, they are likely to be more of a major contributing factor to gains in strength and hypertrophy. This point is evident when, for example, individuals do not train intensely enough to elicit significant response from FT motor units and consequently see less than optimal strength training results.

Results depend on proper intensity. If, in the repetition schemes suggested (6 to 20 reps), you can bring the muscle near fatigue, exceptional results will occur for most people. You must present the exercising muscle with sufficient challenge or intensity to cause muscular fatigue. The key is *not* how much absolute weight or resistance is used. More important are the questions, "Is the overload relative to my current strength levels? Can I fatigue the muscle in the suggested repetition/time framework?"

What Is The Right Load?

An absolute weight that is lifted may reflect a light loading for one person, whereas for another it may represent a heavy or even maximal loading. For example, if a client can only do 5 push-ups, that number to failure represents a heavy 5 RM load, whereas if another client can "crank out" 50, that represents a light load. The light load contributes little to strength gains, while the heavy load, might be inappropriate. Intensity is relative to — and dependent on — your client's current strength fitness level.

REPS, SETS AND LOADS

"How much resistance should I use to optimize training result?" A lot of people ask this question. It's the right idea, but the wrong question! It is not how much weight your client lifts that is the key, but the number of repetitions she performs. Just the number of reps? Well yes, sort of! You need to have your client work within a specific framework or number of reps, and work her muscle until it's tired or fatigued.

What Does Muscular Failure Or Fatigue Represent?

The terms muscle failure, muscle fatigue, maximal volitional muscular fatigue and maximal voluntary muscle action (MVMA) — all represent the idea of reaching momentary concentric muscle failure. Simply, in a specified rep range, the client cannot perform another repetition without breaking form, or otherwise being assisted. At some point during training, it is important to incorporate MVMAs. Be certain that you do *not* identify this point as a 1 RM (repetition maximum), or the most amount of weight your client can lift once. An RM set to failure can be represented by, for example, a 6 RM, 8 RM, 10 RM, 11 RM, 15 RM or 20 RM set to failure or MVMA.

Should every client be encouraged to reach "failure?" Yes. At some point in the program, *optimal* gains in strength are produced by using MVMAs (Fleck and Kraemer, 1997, pg. 20). Is an MVMA too heavy for a deconditioned or frail, older adult? Probably not. Remember, the reference to "failure" is not in relation to an absolute amount of weight. Instead, a load must be identified that allows the client to attain failure in a specific repetition/time frame. The load could represent one pound, or hundreds of pounds, depending on the strength fitness level of the client.

Key Point

Endless reps using low resistance produce little strength gain, increase the risk of overuse injury and discourage clients who have invested adequate training time — but do not see the desired training result.

Starting Weight

If your client is just starting a strength program it's important *not* to test her ability to lift the most amount of weight she can for a given lift. This is called a 1 RM or one repetition maximum test. If the client is just beginning a strength program don't put her in a high-risk, maximal-performance situation. This situation totally ignores the progressive adaptation principle and the concept of prudent progression. Err on the side of using too little weight, rather than too much, to determine starting points. For example, if your client is doing more reps than you've set for her repetition parameters, it is easy to bring the number of reps down by increasing resistance. An appropriate resistance that fatigues the muscle within the stated repetition goal range determines the starting load.

Number Of Repetitions

Most of your clients know that "rep" is gym slang for "repetition." As you know, your client completes a strength exercise rep when she returns to the start position. Most of the clients you train should be doing around 6 to 20 reps to "fatigue," from a health and fitness perspective.

If your client is new to strength training she might be thinking, "What's this fatigue or failure stuff?" Make sure you explain to the client how muscular fatigue is characterized. Once again, muscular fatigue, failure, exhaustion or MVMA refers to a point — somewhere between about 6 to 20 reps — where your client can't do another repetition with good form.

Should every client work to fatigue? I know this is a "threatening" word, but as mentioned earlier, the answer is yes... everyone. If you're client is just starting, or out-of-shape, the number of reps to fatigue that she should complete should fall between 15 to 20, but it's better to initially shoot for 20. This number will give your client's muscles, tendons and ligaments a chance to get in shape and prevent her from doing too much, too soon. Once she's been training 4 to 6 weeks at 15 to 20 reps you may want to aim for 12 to 15 reps to see continued and significant changes in strength and muscle size. To maximize your client's strength and muscle size gains, drop down to 6 to 12. This means you'll have to increase the "weight" your client is lifting if you want her to move into this lower repetition framework. After your client has trained consistently for about 6-months, you can probably begin to periodize her program to utilize this entire rep range of 6 to 20. Strength benefits occur at the low-, mid- and high-end of this repetition range. Don't make the mistake of progressing your client to the low-end of the range and having her do all of her strength training there, forever! This ignores the concept of periodization.

Number of Reps	Outcome	Intensity	Progression
15 to 20	Muscle endurance, strength, tone and health benefits	Enough resistance to cause muscle fatigue between 15 to 20 reps	First 4 to 6 weeks of training whether the client is just starting or out-of-shape, regardless of age
12 to 15	Muscle endurance, strength, size and health benefits	Enough resistance to cause muscle fatigue between 12 to 15 reps	After 4 to 6 weeks of training at 15 to 20 reps, if you want to continue to significantly progress your strength program
8 to 12 or 6 to 10	Maximum muscle strength and size (hypertrophy), and health benefits	Enough resistance to cause muscle fatigue between 8 to 12 or 6 to 10 reps	After 4 to 6 weeks of training at 12 to 15 reps to fatigue to maximize strength and muscle size

Table 1 *What You Need To Know About Reps and Intensity*

Muscular strength and endurance conditioning is anaerobic work that should last only about 30 to 90 seconds and causes the targeted muscles to fatigue or fail within this time frame. (Two-minutes is about the outside parameter.) Generally, 6 to 20 repetitions (about 4-7 seconds per rep), performed in a controlled manner, will fit into this time parameter and produce significant strength gains. *See table 1*

Let's go back to the question of, "How much weight?" Remember, wrong question! Pick enough resistance to fatigue your client's muscles in one of these four repetition frameworks. Regardless of whether the goal is 15 to 20, 12 to 15, 8 to 12 or 6 to 10 reps, you'll find clients of differing strength levels will have to work with *different* amounts of weight or resistance to optimize their personal training results. Consider, for example, two clients performing an arm curl (i.e., elbow flexion) side-by-side. While, for example, both may fatigue at 15 reps, one is using a 25-pound weight, the other is using an 8-pound weight. Nevertheless, both will see significant gains in strength and are working at the effort that is productive for them.

Number Of Sets

A set is a number of reps. Every group of reps (for example 6-10, 8-12, 12-15 or 15-20) to fatigue represents a set. Don't go for conventional wisdom, which says your client *has* to do 2 or 3 sets, unless she's been doing strength training for awhile, is looking for more results and the client is willing to invest more time.

Recent guidelines (ACSM, 1990, 1995, 1997, 1998) suggest that a basic program can maintain both muscular strength and endurance, as well as balanced strength between agonist and antagonist muscles. The program's effectiveness is based on performing 6-20 repetitions, at least 2 times a week, for each major muscle group of the body (8-10 exercises). Remember to begin with 15-20, and progress to 12-15, 8-12 and 6-10 reps to fatigue. Here's an important key. At least one set to failure should be performed for each exercise.

Studies (reported in Brooks, 1997; Westcott, 1996) have shown that there is little difference between training with 1, 2, or 3 sets if you're untrained. (Newer research indicates that even those who are seasoned veterans may experience this same effect.) Any additional increase in muscle gain or strength is minimal for each set performed after the first. Untrained participants will see about 75 percent of the gains they'll ever get by doing *one* set of exercise to fatigue, for each exercise they perform. Would the person get more result if they did more? Yes, but it's a case of diminishing returns.

Key Point

Similar strength benefits can come from single-set training, when compared to multi-set training, especially in the initial stages of a resistance training program.

When does a client require multi-set training? Eventually, (i.e., after about 3-6 months) your client might have to commit more time if she wants to take the next step in strength fitness. But initially, one set of exercise will get her strong, give her excellent results and minimize the time she has to spend lifting! For general fitness, it has been recommended that healthy adults should complete at least a minimum of one set, of at least one exercise for all of the major muscles groups (ACSM, 1990). This general recommendation is for adults who desire good fitness gains with minimal time requirements, and is a good starting point for most inactive people. This is in contrast to athletes, where research has shown that multiple sets result in greater strength gains than single-set programs (Fleck and Kraemer, 1997). Also, one set programs, performed at the intensity at which the athlete last trained, is excellent to use as a short-term in-season, or off-season, training method. It is not recommended as a long-term program for competitive athletes who desire to *optimize* strength and performance gains. Remember to match the training goal and experience level of the client with the right program design.

OTHER IMPORTANT RESISTANCE TRAINING VARIABLES

Though strength training results rely heavily on proper intensity, as tied to the number of repetitions performed to fatigue, a collection of other important variables contribute and include:

Available Time Commitment

Can clients *optimize* strength training result training two days per week? No. But, two 20- to 30-minute strength workouts per week can give them an excellent return on this minimal time investment. It is not necessary to spend hours "lifting weights" to see superb results. Align the training goal and expected outcome with available time commitment.

Muscle Activation

Physiologists view strength and size gains from the standpoint of whether or not the training process can optimize muscle activation. Muscle activation must occur if the client wants to get stronger or gain size. Muscle is "activated" or recruited by using proper intensity, variety and a periodized program. Of the three, intensity is the most important but can represent a double-edged sword. The analogy works like this: One edge can cut you, while the other can work to produce excellent training results. For example, a person can labor against resistance using terrible technique, and still get result if the load is sufficient. This represents the one side of the intensity-sword that can cut. In other words, training adaptations can occur with poor technique. Often times, obtaining results justifies the method, whether or not it is less than optimal.

The other side of the intensity-sword represents the important aspect that training intensity, does in fact, hold the key to strength results. Yet, when proper intensity is coupled with good technique, you can take advantage of the intensity-factor, without one side of the intensity-sword having a negative impact on training.

Key Point

You can use perfect form and technique, focus and concentrate — but if the load is not sufficient to cross thresholds in the body that signal the body's musculature and nervous system to adapt and become better at producing force — little to no strength training adaptation will take place.

Correct Mechanics

Intensity "rules" for certain, but the ideal combination would be to combine proper lifting mechanics and intensity to optimize training result. This combination, along with understanding joint mechanics, and how they do or do not contribute to injury, enhances compliance toward the program, as well as decreasing the risk for injury.

Frequency Of Strength Workouts

Your client needs to strength train a minimum of two times per week, with at least a day of rest between strength workouts. That's really all the client needs if she's just starting a strength program. Again, research confirms that training two times per week (with one set to fatigue, per exercise) will give a deconditioned person about 75 percent of the gains they would see when compared to training 3 times per week (reported in Brooks, 1997; Westcott, 1996). However, after about 3 to 6 months of progressive strength training your client will probably have to work out about 3 to 4 times per week to *optimize* strength gains. On the other hand, it's easy to maintain strength gains with only a couple of workouts per week, if intensity of the workout is maintained on a regular basis (reported in Brooks, 1997).

Conflicting study results confuse the issue of the optimum number of times to train per week. Based on several studies, a tentative conclusion can be reached. Generally, more frequent training sessions result in greater increases in strength. To *maximize* strength, it seems the research supports training 3-times per week in novice subjects over an initial, short term training period (Fleck and Kraemer, 1997). When interpreting these conclusions, carefully weigh the words "optimal" and "maximize." Even though an approach may be believed to optimize training, generally it is a case of diminishing returns. Training twice per week, one set of each exercise to failure, gets the client "a whole lot" from a health and fitness perspective. What this means is that often the time spent does not justify the training gain for clients interested simply in health and fitness returns, especially when you identify that the number one reason people quit or don't begin training is "not enough time." Once again, match the training approach with the goals, expected outcome and available time that can be committed toward exercise.

Number Of Exercises

At a minimum, choose 8 to 10 exercises that target all of the major muscle groups in your client's body. This leads to equal development in all of the opposing muscles. If your client only does arm curls and chest presses, this poorly balanced approach will impact her posture, and not serve her from a functional exercise standpoint. Choose more exercises if you wish, but using only about 10 exercises doesn't take much time and gets the job done.

Workout Length

If you follow science backed recommendations of about 6 to 20 reps performed to fatigue, one to two sets of exercise for each major muscle group in the body, and your client lifts twice a week, only a 20- to 30-minute time investment for each strength workout is required. This is something any client can fit in and doesn't necessarily require more training sessions.

More advanced strength training programs require more time. A "minimalist" approach has been presented here because every trainer should know that clients don't have to do a lot, to get fantastic strength results! That's good news for runners, triathletes or busy moms and dads who would like to strength train, but didn't think they had time.

Exercise Order

Generally, it is a sound idea to perform exercise for "big muscle groups" first, followed by "smaller" ones. For example, work your client's hips and buttocks before you isolate muscles like the front and back of the thighs, calves and "shins." Go for the chest and back before you "fry" your client's shoulders and arms. This makes sense because if muscles are pre-fatigued and can't contribute to a movement they become the "weak-link" in an exercise using several joint motions. If you fatigue your client's quadriceps before she performs a squat or lunge, it's likely her buttocks muscles won't get a great challenge because the quads will tire and give out well before her glutes do. Also, there remains a safety issue when performing complex multi-joint exercises with pre-fatigued muscles. As an example, I usually wouldn't have my client try a heavy squat lift after fatiguing her quadriceps using an isolation exercise.

Prioritization

After your client has trained for several months, it's important to train differently even if your approach is counter to the logic presented in the previous point that discussed exercise order. Always training the same way will limit results and can lead to injury and burn-out. I use what I call the "prioritization" or "priority system." In other words, I train first what I am emphasizing that day. For example, if I prioritize isolation exercises of small muscle groups, I might avoid complex or compound movements that use those same muscles.

When you have your client do a total body workout, the muscle group you start with is not important. Most of my clients do a total body workout when they strength train because they don't have the time to perform split routines (emphasize different body parts over several days) over 4 or 5 days. You can begin with your client's lower body, followed by upper body exercise, and then switch to the abs or back. In fact, hip-hopping around to different body parts is a great idea because it keeps your client working out while the body part she just worked gets a chance to recover. This is called "active rest" and keeps your client from wasting precious time until she feels ready to lift again.

Rest Between Sets

If you want to finish your client's strength workout in 20- to 30-minutes you can minimize rest down-time, as mentioned, by changing from upper body, to lower body and then to ab and back work. The order in which you do this is *not* critical—simply switching from one

body part to another unrelated part is what's important. If you "hop-scotch" all over the body as you target muscles, you save time. This is important because most of your clients have a finite amount of time set aside for working out, so this method lets you maximize the amount of time *actually* spent working out. Again, this concept represents "active rest."

Generally, 30-seconds to 2-minutes is recommended for recovery from an exercise your client just completed to fatigue, if your goal is to allow a full-recovery before you target that particular area of the body again. Your choice of recovery duration will depend heavily on program goals and fitness level.

Key Point

Any time recovery periods are reduced, relative intensity will be increased. Recovery periods should be intentional, versus random, and should be planned with forethought to match expected training outcome and current level of fitness.

Table 2 summarizes the previous discussion regarding reps, sets and rest between sets, as well as the strength result that can be expected. Use it to clarify your training direction and planning.

Resistance or Relative Loading	Result or Expected Outcome	% of 1 RM	Repetition Range	# of Sets	Rest Between Sets
Light	Muscular Endurance	50-70	15-20 & 12-15	1-3	20-60 seconds
Moderate	Hypertrophy (increased muscle size) and strength	70-85	8-12 & 6-10	1-6+	60-120 seconds
Heavy	Maximum Strength and Power	85-100	1-6	1-5+	2-5 minutes

Table 2: Resistance Training Specificity Chart

Note: Generally, assume a heavier load as soon as the client is able to complete the required number of reps listed in the *Specificity Chart.*

Note that an intensity of 12 reps or greater equates to less than 70 percent of a one repetition maximum (one RM). While this load is reasonable to create strength gains, it is not so intense that it would put a deconditioned exerciser at risk for injury. Research indicates that a 10 RM lift roughly equates to about 75 percent of a client's maximum lifting capacity for any given lift. A 6 to10 RM intensity seems necessary to *optimize* muscular strength and hypertrophy gains, but it's important to progress to these higher percentages of a 1 RM in a progressive manner. Consider that many of your clients will not choose a goal that is reflective of *optimizing* strength gains. Be certain to match their goals, interests and desire with where you take them! A recommended 6 to 20 RM repetition range correlates loosely with working out at between 85 percent (6 RM) to 50 percent (20 RM) of a client's maximum or 1 RM lifting capacity.

Time Between Strength Workouts

A day between strength workouts is about right when you're targeting all of the major muscles. If you use split routines, give the muscles groups at least a day of recovery before targeting the same muscle group again. Adequate recovery is essential to avoid injury, and to give the body time to assimilate the benefits of the previous strength training session. Though your client may enjoy challenging workouts, the muscles need that recovery to grow stronger.

Recovery between workouts is based on the intensity of the workout and your client's individual "recovery ability." Generally, about 48 hours is appropriate between workouts that are intense, or of an overload to which the body is not accustomed. Adequate recovery is essential to avoid overtraining and strength plateaus, and for progressive improvements in muscular strength and endurance.

Increasing Resistance Or Load

When your client can easily complete more than 6 to 10, 8 to 12, 12 to 15 or 15 to 20 repetitions (depending on her current rep range), it's time to up the ante! Add enough weight so that your client can drop back into the rep framework she's working in, but don't add so much she can't complete the minimum number of reps (i.e., 6, 8, 12 or 15). Depending on how you progress or periodize a client's program, it may be appropriate to move the client into an entirely different rep framework. The move can be in any direction. *Progressively* increasing how hard your client works will keep her mind stimulated, body guessing, muscles pumping and the results coming, but don't forget to allow for recovery and to challenge the whole repetition continuum.

Speed Of Movement

For the average person, gains in strength are best accomplished by moving the weight slowly (about 4 to 7 seconds per repetition), through a full range of motion and accomplishing fast-twitch muscle fiber recruitment by using an appropriately intense overload. Following are 7 reasons to control speed of movement (Westcott, 1991):
1. Consistent application of force
2. More total muscle tension produced
3. More total muscle force produced
4. More muscle fiber activation (both ST and FT)
5. Greater muscle-power potential through high-intensity force development using controlled speed of movement and appropriately intense overload
6. Less tissue trauma
7. Greater momentum increases injury potential and reduces training effect on target muscle groups
Note: Exceptions to the above may be appropriate in sport-specific applications and when the risks are understood.

Movement Control

Movement speeds can be categorized as slow, moderate and fast, but the issue is control and weighing risk against benefit. For a given or accommodating load, controlled movement speeds activate more muscle, or scientifically put, more muscle force is produced at slower movement speeds when compared to faster movement speeds (Westcott, *Strength*

Fitness, pg. 91, 1991). It would not only appear that slow strength training is more effective than fast strength training for muscle development (Clarke and Manning, 1985), but that it is also safer.

With regard to lifting speed, never say "fast." Instead, think "control!" Your client is lifting in control if she could stop the exercise "on a dime," if asked. I tell my clients that if they leave skid-marks or roll into the intersection, they're lifting too fast. Another good guide is to spend 3 to 4 seconds lifting a weight in a steady controlled motion, followed by 3 to 4 seconds lowering the weight, with the same degree of smoothness and control. I encourage about a seven-second repetition, but control is the issue, not the particular count you use. For example, whether you lift in a concentric/eccentric manner that represents, for example, a 2-2, 2-4, 4-2, 3-4, 4-3, 5-2 or 2-5 up/down count, these counting configurations simply represent another programming element of variation. I'm not too keen on keeping an exact accounting of seconds per repetition, but if I asked a client to stop the movement at any point during a given strength exercise, and she could, this would tell me she's lifting at the correct speed, which is defined as "controlled."

Breathe Correctly

First and foremost, your client should breathe regularly during strength training. If you want to take it a step further, try to have your client coordinate breathing out when she begins a strength exercise. For example, let's say she's performing a supine chest press, using dumbbells. Her goal is to push her arms away from her chest. As your client begins to push her arms away, it is natural for her to hold her breath for a moment. But, she shouldn't maintain the held breath. Your client should let her breath escape just after, or as she begins the press. Generally, your client should breathe in as she returns the weight toward her body. If in doubt, simply instruct your client to breathe, breathe, breathe!

Your client shouldn't think she only gets "one breath out, and one in." Common sense should tell you that it's okay for your client to take small sipping breaths more often if she's lifting with control, which can result in a repetition that takes 4 to 7 seconds to complete. My clients tell me that lifting in control requires them to work hard on both phases of their lift!

If your client holds her breath during the entire lift this can cause blood pressure to rise higher than it should and put unnecessary stress on your client's heart and vascular system. Breathing correctly can help your client avoid nausea, dizziness and the possibility of fainting. At a minimum, just have your client remember to breathe regularly throughout each repetition.

Lifting Technique And Safety

This heading represents the focus of this book. But, a few points need to be made from an application perspective. The most important focus of early workouts is *not* to create muscle failure, though this can occur and is an important goal. The most important aspect of early sessions is to work on correct exercise technique. The emphasis on good form gives your client's muscles a chance to adapt progressively to the demands she's placing on them, create a "motor memory" of correctness and lets her learn how to perform exercises correctly before she works against heavier resistance.

When your clients work against resistance they should:
• Keep their concentration and focus.
• Lift weight that they can control.

- Lower the load or start again with less weight if the weight is hard to balance or control because, for example, it is too heavy or they've reached a point of fatigue.
- Remove dumbbells or other load carefully from storage areas and replace them with precision and control. (Many injuries during strength training come from carelessly picking up or returning weights to storage racks or the floor.)
- Learn how to move in and out of an exercise safely, independent of equipment being used.

SPOTTING RESISTANCE TRAINING EXERCISES

A spotter's "job" is to assist with the proper and safe execution of an exercise, only as needed. Superb spotting allows your clients to work harder and makes resistive training exercise a safer activity. Being inattentive in a small group, personal training or clinical rehabilitation setting is inexcusable, and is a leading cause of serious "weight room" injuries.

For the sake of explanation, I pose this question. "What represents an effective verbal exercise cue?" Answer: "One that works." So it is with spotting techniques. Do you spot a barbell bench press with both hands placed in an overgrip, or do you alternate grips using one over- and one undergrip? Choose the one that works, you're comfortable with and that keeps the client safe.

Key Point

Opinions on correct spotting techniques are numerous. But, a "good" spotting technique is one that facilitates correct movement, helps a client to better understand or "feel" an exercise, and keeps the client — as well as the spotter — from being injured.

CHECKLIST FOR SPOTTING SAFELY AND EFFECTIVELY

1) Before the exercise begins, be certain that the equipment is adjusted to fit the client properly, or bars are evenly and appropriately loaded and that the client has stabilized her start position.
2) The spotter should place her body in proper neutral spinal alignment, and generally, keep her hands as close as possible to the bar, equipment or person without hindering equipment or client movement.
3) Generally, the spotter should maintain neutral spinal posture and flexed knees and hips.
4) Use "hands-on" spotting technique as is appropriate to the exercise and with permission of your client. Hands on spotting is an excellent way to facilitate movement sequencing and coordination, and to keep the trainer and client "involved" in the session (Touch Training for Strength, Rothenberg and Rothenberg, 1995).
5) Know when and how to guide the movement in its intended path of motion.
6) Know when and how much lifting assistance should be used to help a client complete a repetition.
7) Communicate verbally with the client regarding intended number of repetitions to be completed, and about the general performance requirements of the exercise.
8) Only assume all of the resistance, or responsibility for the completion of the lift back to a start or safe-position, when the person being spotted has lost control and risks certain injury without intervention.
9) Avoid having to assume the "last resort" spot by properly instructing and progressing the client.

10) Both client and trainer should know their limits.

Trainer's Safety During Spotting

During exercise performance, not only should a spotter be concerned with overseeing correct and safe exercise execution on the client's behalf, fitness professionals need to be concerned about their own health, especially as related to low back and shoulder injuries. Spotting with poor technique can result in debilitating injury, and usually occurs as a result of poor technique used over time, as in contrast to a catastrophic, one-time incident.

Besides using correct body mechanics and maintaining proper spinal alignment during lifts, it is important to communicate to the client what her role is in creating a safe relationship during spotted resistance training exercises. It's important to avoid a "crisis" scenario or a required, "heroic" save. Set a mutual goal that identifies, for example, the number of repetitions that are intended to be completed. During the exercise, the client should indicate when she needs assistance if the trainer has not anticipated the need. As a spotter, you need to "stay with the movement," by closely following the movement path of the bar, machine and/or client's body. Do you spot the bar, equipment or client's body? Answer: Spot where assistance or stabilization is required.

The client must "never give up on the exercise." In other words, she should never stop exerting effort or assume the trainer is capable of "taking over the movement." I remember telling a client, "I cannot curl your bench press weight!" Needless to say, that helped to keep his attention during the entire exercise.

Key Point

"It's not over until it's over!" Neither the spotter nor exerciser should ever quit on the movement until a safe resting position is attained, or the load is safely "racked."

Quick Index:

Chapters 6-8, See photos of trunk, upper and lower body exercises, and general body positioning and placement of hands for effective spotting

THE ART OF SPOTTING

How a trainer spots is largely dependent on the strength and skill level of the client. I do not spot every client the same. Spotting a maximal lift with an experienced lifter is very different than spotting a beginner who is performing a supine dumbbell press. To say, for example, that you should *always* spot a pressing movement using dumbbells, at the wrist, is not correct. For example, an experienced lifter who is "forcing reps" during a supine dumbbell press exercise, may only need a light spot under the elbows to assist the movement. Keep open to what is *appropriate* for each given training situation. The yellow caution flag should begin to wave in your brain if "black" and "white," "always" or "never" statements are used with regard to spotting techniques, or for that matter, any exercise technique.

The use of a spotter is important for certain exercises that require balance or are complex, or if heavy loads are being used. For example, failure to raise from a squatting position or press out of a barbell bench press can result in serious injury. Spotters should facilitate the movement and not take over. If the trainer assists the movement or helps to lift the weight, interference and effect should be minimal. Spotters should be aware of individual client conditioning and experience levels. Hands-on spotting technique that is nonverbal — along with verbal instruction and demonstration — can enhance exercise performance and safety.

12

HIGH-INTENSITY STRENGTH TRAINING TECHNIQUES

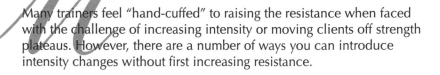

Many trainers feel "hand-cuffed" to raising the resistance when faced with the challenge of increasing intensity or moving clients off strength plateaus. However, there are a number of ways you can introduce intensity changes without first increasing resistance.

CHANGING VARIABLES FOR STRENGTH GAINS

Varying your client's routine will help her move past strength training plateaus and keep the program interesting. Plateaus and overtraining often result from the indefinite use of one training program approach. The following ideas can help minimize the possibilities of a situation where your client's training is going nowhere.

1. Repetition Variation

Vary the number of reps either up or down. Both methods will stimulate an adaptation. Any kind of variety will help break plateaus and stimulate the body to adapt. Both higher-rep schemes (12 to 20), as well as lower-rep sets (6 to 12) contribute to muscle hypertrophy and strength development. Rest and/or lighter weights are often warranted because many clients do not allow for the recovery/building process. Train your client in a manner that he or she does not regularly train!

2. Set Variation

Increase the number of sets for the targeted muscle group. One set training "will get you a lot," but won't *optimize* the training response.

3. Sequence Variation

Sequence so there is very little recovery between sets targeting the same muscle group. This will allow for a different motor-unit recruitment pattern to occur, and thus new stimulation.

4. Intensity Variation

Utilize high-intensity training techniques and systems. Training examples include tri-setting, pyramiding, compound training (often called super setting), breakdown (breaking down the weight being lifted, not the muscle which you stimulate to build), super slow (10-15 seconds per repetition) and forced reps or assisted training. (See the section on *High Intensity Training Techniques*, later in this chapter.)

5. Program Variation

Periodize training using some or all of these techniques. A periodized program cycles volume (sets and reps) and intensity (load or resistance) over specific time periods. This type of organization encourages a process that maximizes adaptation and progression specific to program goals and intensities.

Quick Index:

Chapter 10, For a periodization model and useful references

THE HIGH-INTENSITY TRAINING EDGE

If your client has been training at an advanced level, high-intensity training may be the edge she needs to move off strength plateaus. At some point in an advanced training program, one of your clients will be looking for more results within the same time schedule. If so, it's important to consider high-intensity strength training. High-volume work (working out more times per week and longer each workout) is not realistic in most personal schedules that require a balance between family, work, community and church commitments, health and fitness pursuits, and recreation. While high-volume work is somewhat effective with elite body builders and other professional athletes, it can lead to overuse injury and burnout in many other people. However, even when the time and motivation are present to perform high-volume workouts, many experts still argue that quality reigns over quantity, when applied to training results. Many competitive lifters are experimenting with decreasing volume of overload and increasing intensity of effort.

Without a doubt, high-intensity strength training is fierce, concentrated and requires focus! However, for those clients who are prepared and motivated to move their stalled strength training program to the next level, this chapter may present exactly what they need to jump-start their strength gains.

When a client complains about "lack of result," she is experiencing a training plateau. Plateaus occur when a client's rate-of-gain or improvement, as related to her training, slows down. This can result from the indefinite use of one training program approach or simply because the client has been a dedicated strength trainer for a long time and her body needs new stimulation.

High intensity strength training provides a way to train harder, without increasing client workout times. In other words, she can increase intensity without doing longer workouts, but the client will have to work harder to get the results. High-intensity training techniques require greater muscular effort and place more intense physical demands on your client's muscles. These techniques push your client to a greater degree of fatigue.

Key Point

High intensity strength training provides a way to train harder, without increasing client workout times, and can move a stalled strength training program forward.

How High Intensity Training Works

In theory, this type of training recruits muscle fibers (motor units) that are not normally challenged because the workout protocol doesn't allow the fatigued motor units a chance to recover and be used again in the exercise the client is currently performing. Manipulating the amount of resistance the client works against, eliminating recovery upon reaching momentary muscle fatigue, performing more reps while fatigued, and controlling how fast the weight is moved (speed of movement) are commonly employed methods to move strength training into the "high-intensity" realm.

Who Should Train With High Intensity Techniques?

If you have a client who is highly motivated and has a strong strength base, you might want to consider using one of the high intensity strength training techniques that are discussed next. Make sure your client's goals are in line with what these approaches offer. They require a good strength conditioning base and high degree of physical effort, and are associated with physical discomfort (your client is really pushing it here!).

High intensity training requires more recovery, so make sure you mix hard workouts with easy ones, or days off, for muscle tissue recovery and building time. Remember that approximately 50 percent of the building equation is rest. Don't use these approaches more than once or twice per week, and keep these tough workouts to around 30 to 45 minutes and about 10 exercises. Generally, perform one to two sets per exercise.

After doing high-intensity strength training, take at least one day off before strength training again. After that 48-hours of recovery, follow this type of workout with a strength workout that is of moderate or light intensity.

HIGH-INTENSITY TRAINING TECHNIQUES

High intensity training allows clients to overcome fitness plateaus, without significantly increasing exercise duration, by increasing intensity. Following are several of the most highly used and effective high-intensity training techniques, many of which require a workout partner/trainer to assist. It's essential to have a spotter for safety reasons when using high intensity strength training techniques, which is not a problem when you're with a client, but if she trains on her own and uses high-intensity techniques, encourage her to team up with a capable partner. Also, make sure your client is interested in trying these techniques, and is physically and mentally capable, before you begin.

Key Point

High-intensity training techniques require a high degree of physical effort and are associated with physical discomfort.

If your client is fit and highly motivated, consider using one of the following techniques:

1. Breakdown Training
Breakdown training usually begins with a normal set of training (i.e., 10 to 12 reps to fatigue after a warm-up). Upon reaching momentary muscle failure, each repetition is performed with less weight than the one preceding it. Reduce the weight enough (usually about 5 to 15 percent) so that your client can do 2 to 4 additional repetitions (more repetitions is okay if she can maintain good form).

2. Pyramid Training
Pyramid training is a variation of breakdown training, or vice-versa. Upon reaching momentary muscle failure, each exercise is performed with slightly less or more weight than the one preceding it. The result is the option of an "up" pyramid (weight increases) or a "down" pyramid (weight decreases). Let's say your client's goal is to start with a weight she can lift 10 to 12 times (10 to 12 RM). After fatiguing at 10 to 12 RM, the trainer could reduce about 5 to 15 percent of the poundage (down pyramid) and encourage the client to "force" out more reps. Each time your client reaches a point where she can not complete anymore reps, "strip-off" additional weight and force more reps, and continue in this manner. If you reversed the process, you'd create an up pyramid, which is extremely difficult. In this situation, increasing the weight by as little as 5% is often sufficient and you find that it is not too long before the client can not do even one repetition.

3. Assisted Training Or "Forced Reps"
Simply, the trainer assists the client in completing a number of reps she could not have completed on her own. Begin the client with a set of repetitions to fatigue (i.e., 10 to 12 RM). When she reaches fatigue, yet still having maintained good technique, the trainer assists her in completing an additional number of reps she could not have completed on her own. Typically, the trainer/spotter lifts 5 to 15 percent of the weight load to assist the client in completing 2 to 4 more reps with good form.

4. Negative Training

Negative or eccentric training allows for about 30 percent more force production than occurs during concentric contraction. Typically, negative training is accomplished by 1) adding manual resistance on the lowering phase of any lift, 2) adjusting the weight lifted and lowered when using a selectorized plate machine (lighter when lifting and change to heavier weight when lowering), or 3) assisting your client through a concentric phase with an amount of weight she could not lift on her own, and then allowing her to lower the weight during the eccentric phase without assistance.

Negative training is often used with a highly trained individual who has plateaued. Though caution should be used with any of these techniques, delayed-onset muscle soreness is highly associated with this type of training. Therefore, this type of training should not be used with deconditioned clients.

5. Super Slow Training

Super slow training or slow training is often described as tedious, tortuous, excruciating and productive! Slow training takes the emphasis away from number of reps and weight being lifted, and focuses on increasing the time of each repetition. Slower movement speed reduces any contribution from momentum in assisting with completion of the range-of-motion. This results in more tension on the muscle and total force development (meaning more muscle is used or activated).

Super slow training is often referred to as 10 - 15 second training, though any number of seconds can be assigned to each lifting phase. A popular version is comprised of a 5-second concentric lifting phase, followed by a 10-second eccentric, lowering phase for each repetition. You can also reverse the emphasis. Aim for failure in about 4 to 6 reps. There is no "miracle" number of seconds that will produce the "best" results. Record your results and experiment.

Super slow training repetitions can last from a 15 to 60 seconds. However, if increases in strength and hypertrophy are your goal, keep the repetition length at about 15 seconds or less. As duration of the repetition is increased the amount of weight that can be lifted decreases, and each point of the range-of-motion receives less than an optimal strength stimulus. For example, if the weight is light enough to perform a 60-second rep, though the effort will be perceived as very difficult, the resistance is not heavy enough to stimulate significant strength gains. Discomfort is not always an indicator of physiological effectiveness. Compare an effort like this to painting a ceiling. Painting a ceiling is very uncomfortable on the upper body muscles involved, but in no way would any professional ever consider it effective and progressive strength training.

Quick Index:

Chapter 11, Discussion of discomfort versus physiological effectiveness

6. Super Set And Compound Training

Super set training usually refers to working opposing muscle groups (paired agonist and antagonist muscles) in succession (i.e., biceps/triceps or chest/back). This is a common approach to training, but allows for the muscle group(s) to at least partially recover while the opposing muscle group(s) is working.

Another type of super setting, correctly referred to as compound training, consists of working the same muscle group back to back — two sets of consecutive exercise targets the same muscle group, but not necessarily with the same exercise. Compound training involves performing a set to fatigue, immediately followed by, or with little rest, another set of exercise that targets the same muscle group.

Super set and compound training seem to work especially well in producing muscular hypertrophy when using a rep scheme of 6 to 10 repetitions to fatigue.

QUALITY OVER QUANTITY

High intensity strength training gives you a potential win-win situation. Use high-intensity training to maximize your client's training result within a limited time schedule, but don't go overboard. Just as with volume training, science tells us that "more intensity is not always better," even if your client has the where-with-all and desire! For optimal muscular development, variety and quality of training is the name of the game.

Key Point

It seems that the best stimulus for increased gains in strength is to make the muscle work harder, not longer.

13

THE KEYS TO OBTAINING OPTIMAL RESISTANCE TRAINING RESULTS

*I*t's no secret — genetics, consistency, progression, intensity, correct exercise biomechanics, cross-training within the component of strength training, periodization and record keeping define, or contribute to, the outer boundaries of strength training improvement. Of these listed, genetics — the "cards" you were dealt at birth — probably plays the biggest role. However, regardless of genetic standing, every individual, independent of gender, can improve greatly from any starting point. This chapter summarizes the points discussed in detail in the previous chapters.

MAKE THE MOST OF THE TRAINING APPROACH

It is imperative to determine the goal of the individual or program before training is ever started. Understanding how reps, sets and intensity affect training outcome will always help trainers sort out the seemingly contradictory statements regarding resistance training reps, sets and loads and what they can, or can not provide. Additionally, correct "lifting" technique limits the occurrence of joint mechanics that can contribute to injury, arthritis, pain and discomfort. Proper execution of resistance training exercises enhances the participating musculature's line-of-pull, which in turn enhances the load placed on the muscle and training result.

It is likely that no two people will respond in the same manner to a given training program. Make sure you keep accurate lifting records which include reps, sets, resistance, order of exercise and periodization planning, so that you can determine the combinations that best stimulate your client's mind and body.

TEN POINT CHECKLIST FOR EFFECTIVE STRENGTH TRAINING

Following these 10-steps will not only lower the participant's risk of injury, but will increase the efficiency of the exercise being performed, as well as client compliance, all of which will payoff in better training results.

1. Focus On Exercise Execution

Each resistance training exercise is unique in its relation to correct performance. Visualize and understand the correct motion to be performed and stay connected mentally. Simply "going through the motions" will not optimize personal enjoyment, results or compliance. Resistance training can be approached as a mindless task composed of pushing, pulling and effort, or it can be thought of as a "choreographed dance" that must be done with absolute precision and concentration.

2. Understand The Goal To Be Accomplished

Believe that the training being undertaken is intentional, rather than haphazard. If the goal is hypertrophy, the training must reflect that goal. The training program for a person who simply wishes to attain a goal of physical independence, will be different from the person whose goal is maximal strength and hypertrophy. In other words, define and understand the goals to be accomplished, and how they will be attained.

3. Position The Body Correctly

Utilize the concepts of neutral spinal posture, correct body alignment and internal stabilization, versus a machine or trainer being responsible for stabilizing and maintaining posture of the client throughout the entire set of repetitions. Additionally, position the body so that it minimizes any known orthopedic risks associated with unsafe joint mechanics, poor body alignment, or poor angles of muscle pull.

4. Place Resistance In Direct Opposition To The Exercise Motion

The exercise motion being performed must be directly (or as closely as possible) opposed by the type of resistance being used if strength development is to be highly effective. Body positions must be adapted to the strength training equipment that is being used, but correct mechanics must not be compromised.

5. Use Sufficient Intensity Or Load

In resistance training, one key principle stands out: "Intensity rules!" You *can* get strength results with poor technique — though this is not recommended — but you *cannot* get significant strength gains with resistance that is too light!

6. Determine Functional Range Of Motion To Be Loaded Or Resisted

Functional range of motion (FROM) is considered to be the appropriate range-of-motion that should be used and loaded when the unique anatomical individuality of each client or patient is considered. FROM is determined by having the client perform the exercise unresisted, which establishes the active range-of-motion (AROM) available for that movement. Subsequently, this defines the client's current exercise AROM and the ROM that should be loaded.

7. Stabilize Before And During An Excercise

Maintaining a proper set-up or start position through a resistance training exercise is crucial to safe, efficient and effective exercise. Stabilization, or the start position, must be held through the entire set of repetitions. Only movement that is necessary to perform the exercise should occur. Generally, strength exercises that are properly executed in terms of maintaining stabilizing force through a series of reps are deemed "quiet," "pure" or "clean." No extraneous movement or form breaks are noted, nor does momentum or "cheat" contribute to the completion of any repetition. Stabilization, referred to as "internal" stabilization, is best accomplished by the body's musculature, versus relying on positioning in a machine or using the skeletal system (i.e., locking out on a joint, like that which occurs when hyperextending the knee or elbow joint).

8. Control Speed Of Movement

From a health perspective, controlled speed of movement contributes to safer exercise and enhanced muscle activation when proper loads are utilized. Participants should focus on controlling the exercise motion and keeping tension on the muscles throughout each repetition. Generally, repetitions should last from 4 to 7 seconds, and if asked, the participant should be able to stop the motion on command.

9. Breathe During The Strength Exercise

Breathing should be done with intent, purpose and be timed to what feels like a natural coordination with the exercise movement. Though a partial Valsalva maneuver, or temporary breath holding, occurs naturally when lifting heavier loads, generally it is prudent to breathe out during concentric contractions, to breathe in during eccentric contractions, and to continue to breathe during an isometric, stabilizing or functional-type of muscular force. It is dangerous to extend breath holding for prolonged periods of time since exponential increases in heart rate and blood pressure can occur and unnecessarily put the heart and vascular system at risk for heart attack, stroke and other vascular-related incidents. In addition, fainting or dizziness can occur as a result of sustained breath holding which needless to say, also puts the individual at risk for a resistance training-related injury.

10. Evaluate Risk Versus Effectiveness

The potential benefit of a resistance training exercise must be weighed against any known orthopedic risk or concern. For example, many strength exercises can produce significant gains in strength when the proper resistance is used while simultaneously causing joint damage, other soft tissue injury or otherwise injuring the body. If this is the case, choosing different (and safer) exercises that achieve the same goal, would change this risk/effectiveness ratio positively.

Key Point

The mastery and implementation of a comprehensive approach to effective strength training can help any client or patient to expertly perform resistance training exercise, as well as see outstanding strength related benefits that go far beyond only getting stronger!

Client records, client feedback, exercise adherence, training result, appropriate testing, and body fat and circumference measurements will help determine any resistance training program's effectiveness. Resistance training program design is a process that demands constant evaluation, manipulation and change! All health and fitness professions represent, to some degree, interpretive art forms that should be based on accurate science. Yet, it is how we interpret all of the information presented to us — and then design the program — that sets us apart.

Quick Index:

BIBLIOGRAPHY, REFERENCES AND SUGGESTED READING

Aaberg, Everett (1996). **Biomechanically Correct.** Lubbock, TX: Parks Printing.

Atha, J. (1981). Strengthening muscle. **Exercise and Sport Sciences Review**; 9:1-73.

American College of Sports Medicine—ACSM (1998). The recommended quantity and quality of exercise for developing and maintaining cardiorespiratory and muscular fitness, and flexibility in healthy adults. Position stand. **Medicine and Science in Sports and Exercise**, Vol. 30, pps. 975-91

American College of Sports Medicine (ACSM). (1998). **ACSM Resource Manual for Guidelines for Exercise Testing and Prescription,** 3rd edition. Baltimore, MD: Williams and Wilkins

American College of Sports Medicine (ACSM). (1997). **Exercise Management for Persons With Chronic Diseases and Disabilities.** L. Durstine (Ed.). Champaign IL: Human Kinetics

American College of Sports Medicine (ACSM). (1995). **ACSM Guidelines For Exercise Testing and Prescription**, 5th edition. Philadelphia, PA: Williams and Wilkins.

American College of Sports Medicine (ACSM) Position Stand (1990). The Recommended Quantity and Quality of Exercise for Developing and Maintaining Cardiorespiratory and Muscular Fitness in Healthy Adults. **Medicine and Science in Sports and Exercise,** Volume 22, No. 2, April, pp. 265-274.

American Council on Exercise (ACE) (1996). **Personal Trainer Manual.** Published by ACE, San Diego, CA.

Baechle, Tom, and Groves, Barney (1992). **Weight Training - Steps To Success**. Human Kinetics Publishers, Champaign, IL.

Basmajian, John and DeLuca, Carlo (1979). **Muscles Alive - Their Functions Revealed By Electromyography**. 4th edition, Williams and Wilkins, Baltimore, MD.

Beynnon, B.D., Fleming, B.C., Johnson, R.J., et al (1995). **Anterior cruciate ligament strain behavior during rehabilitation exercises in vivo.** American Journal of Sports Medicine; 23 (1): 24-34.

Beynnon, B.D., Johnson, R.J., Fleming, B.C., et al (1997). **The strain behavior of the anterior cruciate ligament during squatting and active flexion-extension: a comparison of an open and a closed kinetic chain exercise.** American Journal of Sports Medicine; 25 (6): 823-829.

Bompa, Tudor (1999). **Periodization: Training for Sports.** Human Kinetics: Champaign, IL.

Bompa, Tudor (1996). **Periodization of Strength.** Veritas Publishing, Inc.: Toronto, Canada

Bompa, T. (1983). **Theory and methodology of training.** Dubuque, IL: Kendall-Hunt.

Bouchard C., Shepard R.J., and Stephens, T. (1993). **Physical Activity, Fitness, and health Consensus Statement.** Champaign, IL: Human Kinetics.

Brooks, Douglas (2001). **The Complete Book of Personal Training.** Human Kinetics Publishers, Champaign, IL.

Brooks, Douglas (1999). **Your Personal Trainer: The expert training companion for total fitness.** Human Kinetics Publishers, Champaign, IL.

Brooks, Douglas (1997). **Program Design: Bridging Theory Into Application**. Moves International Publishing, Mammoth Lakes, CA (760) 934-0312 and Human Kinetics

Brooks, Douglas and Copeland, Candice (1997). **Total Stretch On The Ball— Stability Ball Training Guide For Fitness Professionals.** Moves International Publishing, Mammoth Lakes, CA (760) 934-0312.

Brooks, Douglas et al., (1995). **Total Strength On The Ball— Stability Ball Basic Training Guide For Fitness Professionals.** Moves International Publishing, Mammoth Lakes, CA (760) 934-0312.

Brooks, Douglas (1995). **Planning Your Strength Program**. IDEA Today: San Diego, CA, September.

Brooks, Douglas (1995). **Shaping the Shoulder**. IDEA Today: San Diego, CA, October.

Brooks, Douglas (1995). **Training the Upper Back**. IDEA Today: San Diego, CA, November/December.

Brooks, Douglas (1996). **Sculpting the Chest**. IDEA Today: San Diego, CA, January.

Brooks, Douglas (1996). **Strengthening the Upper Arms**. IDEA Today: San Diego, CA, March.

Brooks, Douglas (1997). **Targeting the Buttocks**. IDEA Today: San Diego, CA, March.

Brooks, Douglas (1997). **Targeting the Inner and Outer Thigh.** IDEA Today: San Diego, CA, April.

Brooks, Douglas (1997). **Targeting the Hips**. IDEA Today: San Diego, CA, May.

Brooks, Douglas (1997). **Targeting the Upper Leg**. IDEA Today: San Diego, CA, June.

Brooks, Douglas (1997). **Targeting the Lower Leg**. IDEA Today: San Diego, CA, September.

Brooks, Douglas and Copeland-Brooks, Candice (1993). **Uncovering the Myths of Abdominal Exercise**, IDEA Today, April, pp. 42-49.

Bruner, R., et al. (1992). **Soviet training and recovery methods.** Pleasant Hill, CA: Sport Focus Publishing.

Cahill, B.R. (1982). **Osteolysis of the distal part of the clavicle in male athletes.** Journal of Bone Joint Surgery (Am); 67 (7): 1053-1058.

Cailliet, R. (1988). **Low Back Pain Syndrome.** 4th edition, F.A. Davis Company, Philadelphia, PA.

Charette, S.L., et al (1991). **Muscle Hypertrophy Response to Resistance Training in Older Women.** Palo Alto, CA: American Physiological Society.

Clark, D.H., and Manning, J.M. (1985). **Properties of isokinetic fatigue at various movement speeds in adult males.** Research Quarterly for exercise and Sport, 56: 221-226.

Esenkaya, I., Tuygun, H., Turkmen, M.I., (2000). **Bilateral Anterior Shoulder Dislocation in a Weight Lifter.** The Physician and Sportsmedicine: Vol. 28, No. 3, March, pps: 93-100.

Feigenbaum, M.S., and Pollock, M.L., (1997). **Strength Training: Rationale for Current Guidelines for Adult Fitness Programs.** Physician and Sports medicine 25:44-64.

Fiatrone, M.A. et al (1990). **High-intensity strength training in nonagenarians.** Journal of the American Medical Association, 263, 3029-3034.

Fisher, Garth and Jensen, Clayne (1990). **Scientific Basis of Athletic Conditioning.** 3rd edition, Lea & Febiger, Philadelphia, PA.

Fleck, Steven and Kraemer, William (1996). **Periodization Breakthrough!** Advanced Research Press: Ronkonkoma, NY.

Fleck, Steven and Kraemer, William (1997). **Designing Resistance Training Programs.** Human Kinetics Publishers Champaign, IL.

Francis, Peter, et al. (1994). **The effectiveness of elastic resistance in strength overload.** Pilot study, San Diego State University.

Freedson, Patty (2000). **Strength Training for Women.** IDEA Personal Trainer, July-August.

Frontera, W.R. et al (1988). **Strength Conditioning in Older Men: Skeletal Muscle Hypertrophy and Improved Function.** Palo Alto, CA: American Physiological Society.

Gross, M.L., Brenner, S.L., Esformes, I., et al., (1993). **Anterior shoulder instability in weight lifters.** American Journal of Sports Medicine; 21 (4): 599-603.

Howley E., and Franks B. (1997). **Health and Fitness Instructors Handbook** (3rd. ed.). Champaign, IL: Human Kinetics.

Jones, Chester et al., (2000). **Weight Training Injury Trends: A 20-year survey.** The Physician and Sportsmedicine, Vol. 28, No. 7, July, pps. 61-72.

Kendall, Florence, et al., (1993). **Muscles - Testing and Function.** 4th edition, Williams and Wilkins, Baltimore, MD.

Komi, P.V., editor (1992). **Strength and Power in Sport**. Distributed by Human Kinetics Publishers, Champaign, IL.

Kraemer, William, and Fleck, Steven (1993). **Strength Training For Young Athletes**. Human Kinetics Publishers, Champaign, IL.

Kujala, U.M., Kettunen, J., Paananen, H. (1995). **Knee osteoarthritis in former runners, soccer players, weight lifters, and shooters.** Arthritis Rheum; 38 (4): 539-546.

Mazzeo, R.S., Cavanagh, P., and Evans, W. J., et al (1998). **ACSM Position Stand on Exercise and Physical Activity for Older Adults.** Medicine and Science in Sports and Exercise, 30 (6): 992-1008

McArdle, William et al., (1996). **Exercise Physiology - Energy, Nutrition, and Human Performance.** 4th edition, Lea & Febiger, Philadelphia, PA.

Metveyev, L. (1981). **Fundamental of sports training.** Moscow: Progress Publishers.

Neviaser, T.J., (1991). **Weight lifting: risks and injuries to the shoulder.** Clinical Sports Medicine; 10 (3): 615-621.

Ozolin, N. (1971). **The athlete's training system for competition.** Moscow: Fizkultura i Sport Publication.

Palmitier, R.A., An K.N., Scott, S.G., et al (1991). **Kinetic chain exercise in knee rehabilitation.** Sports Medicine; 11 (6): 402-413.

Plowman, Sharon and Smith, Denise (1997). **Exercise Physiology for Health, Fitness and Performance.** Needham Heights, MA: Allyn and Bacon

Plowman, Sharon (1992). Physical Activity, Physical Fitness, and Low Back Pain. **Exercise and Sport Sciences Reviews,** Volume 20, pp. 221-242.

Pollock, M. L., and G. A. Gaesser et al., (1998). **The recommended quantity and quality of exercise for developing and maintaining cardiorespiratory fitness, and flexibility in healthy adults.** Medicine and Science in Sports and Exercise 30 (6): pps. 975-991.

Post, William R. (1998). Patellofemoral Pain, **Physician and SportsMedicine**, Volume 26, No. 1, pp. 68-78, January.

Reeves, Ronald K., Edward R. Laskowski, and Jay Smith (1998). Weight Training Injuries— Part I: Diagnosing and Managing Acute Conditions. **The Physician and SportsMedicine**, Volume 26, No. 2, pp. 67-83, February.

Reeves, Ronald K., Edward R. Laskowski, and Jay Smith (1998). Weight Training Injuries— Part II: Diagnosing and Managing Chronic Conditions. **The Physician and SportsMedicine**, Volume 26, No. 3, pp. 54-63, March.

Rothenberg, B., and Rothenberg, O. (1995). **Touch Training for Strength.** Human Kinetics: Champaign, IL.

Salis, Robert E., Editor (2000). Pearls—Stay In A Safe Rotator Cuff Range. **The Physician and Sportsmedicine**. Vol. 28, No. 6, June, pg. 23.

Steinkamp, L.A., Dillingham, M.F., Markel, M.D., et al (1993). **Biomechanical considerations in patellofemoral joint rehabilitation.** American Journal of Sports Medicine; 21 (3): 438-444

Thompson, Clem (1989). **Manual of Structural Kinesiology**. 11th edition, Times Mirror/Mosby, St. Louis, MO.

Townsend, Hal, et al. (1991). Electromyographic analysis of the glenohumeral muscles during a baseball rehabilitation program. **The American Journal of Sports Medicine**, Vol. 19, No. 3.

Vorobyev, A. (1978). **A textbook on weight lifting.** Budapest: International Weightlifting Federation.

Westcott, W.S., and Baechle, T. R., (1998). **Strength Training Past 50.** Champaign, IL: Human Kinetics

Westcott, Wayne (1996). **Building Strength and Stamina**. Champaign, IL: Human Kinetics

Westcott, W.S., (1995). **Strength Fitness: Physiological Principles and Training Techniques** (4th edition). Dubuque, Iowa: William C. Brown.

Westcott, Wayne (1991). **Strength Fitness**. 3rd edition, Wm. C. Brown Publishers, Dubuque, IA.

Wilmore, Jack, and Costill, David (1994). **Physiology Of Sport And Exercise**. Human Kinetics Publishers, Champaign, IL.

Wilmore, Jack, and Costill, David (1988). **Training for Sport and Activity: The Physiological Basis of the Conditioning Process.** 3rd edition, William Brown Publishers, Dubuque, IA.

Wilmore, Jack (1991). Resistance Training For Health: A Renewed Interest. **Sports Medicine Digest**, June, pg. 6.

Wolfe S.W., Wickiewicz, T.L., Cavanaugh, J.T., (1992). **Ruptures of the pectoralis major muscle: An anatomic and clinical analysis.** American Journal of Sports Medicine; 20 (5): 587-593.

Yessis, M. (1987). **The secret of soviet sports fitness and training.** Published: Arbor House.

Recommended Video Resources:
1. **Strength: Upper Body**—Advanced Upper Body Strength Training Analysis & Application for the Fitness Professional. (Length: 1.5 hours) Moves International, with Douglas Brooks.
2. **Strength: Lower Body**—Advanced Lower Body Strength Training Analysis & Application for the Fitness Professional. (Length: 1.5 hours) Moves International, with Douglas Brooks.
3. **Strength: Abs & Back**—Advanced Trunk Strength Training Analysis & Application for the Fitness Professional. (Length: 1.5 hours) Moves International, with Douglas Brooks.

ABOUT THE AUTHOR

Douglas Brooks, MS, with his wife, Candice Copeland Brooks

Douglas Brooks, MS, has successfully bridged his academic background, program design and communication skills to become one of the country's premier personal trainers. While his career has expanded as an author and lecturer, video and television educator, Douglas remains a "trainer's trainer" because he practices what he teaches. He writes articles and lectures to trainers internationally on exercise science, strength training and personal training. Douglas also incorporates his experience as a marathon runner, triathlete and skier. He lives near the top of a mountain in Mammoth Lakes, California with his wife and two sons, and cross-trains with all the toys according to the season.